Tom McMullen reserves all rights to be identified as the author of this work. No copy or extract in any format may be reproduced without prior permission of the author.

Other books by the author:

A Cheyenne Trilogy - Between the Rivers (2015, Amazon)

Only the Earth Shall Last: The Second Cheyenne Trilogy

(2019, Amazon)

Under an Iron Sky:

The Third Cheyenne Trilogy

By

Tom McMullen

Preface

Like most of America's original people, the Cheyenne hunted and fought across, what must have seemed to them, a limitless land. They were restless, roaming nomads who depended on the earth's resources to survive. Though relatively late in embracing the advancing Plains Indian horse culture of the late Seventeenth and early Eighteenth Centuries, they mastered it quickly and made a distinct and formidable impact on other tribes as well as advancing Europeans.

As before, this book is about an independent kindred band of the *Suhtai* Cheyenne; it has fictional characters set against a real cultural background. Some of the tribal structures and ceremonies are fictional though they are taken from the mould of reality. The events that provide a chronological and historical framework are mainly true and well documented.

Though this is the third book in the series – the story will not end here. The 'Fading Trails' section at the end of the book hints at this…

I take full responsibility for any mistakes or cultural shortcoming encountered in the story.

Tom McMullen
Cumbria, England
November   2023

BOOK ONE

'Responsibility looms over all leaders – it is like riding under an iron sky; sometimes the sky will fall and crush you.'

(Bad Elk, chief of the Suhtai Cheyenne)

Chapter One

See the Dark held his left eye in his hand and poured water on it. Water was in short supply out here so he carefully dribbled the liquid from the neck of a skin pouch.

The young warrior sighed ruefully as he looked at it in his palm. It wasn't his true eye of course – that had been lost many summers ago when he was young – just a polished black stone globe with the engraving of an antelope on it.

The stone fitted well into his eye socket but, occasionally, seeds, grit and flies found their way under his eyelid and distracted him. The eye needed to be taken out and cleaned.

He rubbed a soft deerskin patch over the shiny black ball, greased it from a pouch of buffalo fat and slid it back into place. The weight of the stone eye seemed to give him balance in his head and, with the engraving pointing outwards, made him feel better. Now he was ready for his task.

Kicking his heels into his pony's flanks, he rode to the crest of a shallow hill and stopped to get a better look at the two wagons.

Both wagons showed promise - neither had the tall, white canvas roofs that usually meant that that people were inside. No, these had canvas coverings but only up to the height of their wooden walls and both looked to be full of cargo. Even better, each wagon only had one driver – no armed escort sitting alongside – so, less guns to worry about.

He swung off the skyline, confident that he hadn't been seen by the men on the wagons; they would need the eyes of an eagle to be able to see through the thick dust cloud that rose up behind them. He would get closer and see if there was anything else of interest and then report back.

Riding in a wide loop, using a dried creek bed as cover, he cantered ahead of the slower wagon teams and halted, hidden by a high cutbank. This time though, his choice of scouting place was poor…

Now he was so close to the passing wagons that their dust made him sneeze. But he was lucky - the shouting of the drivers, the gunfire crack of whips and the braying of their labouring animals drowned it out. His pony snickered in annoyance as the cloud of fine earth rose around them. Dark covered his good eye with his hand – dust could blind him if he didn't take care.

On the creaking wooden seat of the lead wagon, Miguel Armijo was happy. Fort Union was still a long way off, but their heavily-laden Conestoga wagons were making good time along this easy stretch of almost flat prairie along the Cimarron Cut-Off. If he and his brother Ernesto kept going at this pace, they could save nine, maybe ten, days rather than taking the steeper Mountain Route to the fort near Santa Fe. With luck, their cargo would make them quick and easy money once they got it to the soldiers.

A family of jackrabbits bounded out of the way and ran further back into the shelter of the spiky, dry grass, as the iron-rimmed wheels rumbled past. Miguel flicked the long reins and called out encouragement to his lead mules:

"*Ir más rápido, muchachas! Rapido!*"

He stood up, still holding the reins, and looked back to see how Ernesto was doing - swaying as the rumbling wagons crunched over the flats. It was too dusty though; he couldn't see a thing – his older brother wouldn't be happy eating trail dirt.

Miguel pulled his neckerchief back over his face and grinned to himself; Ernesto was more cautious. He wasn't so keen to use this part of the Santa Fe Trail. Back in Leavenworth, he had argued that the Cimarron trail was a gamble – too little water and too many Indians – Kiowa and Comanche still held sway here.

But Miguel, persuasive as ever, had convinced him that it would be worth it just to get the jump on the rest on the rest of the wagon train as it crawled through the high country. The brothers could charge high prices for the early delivery of that whisky and tobacco crammed into their Conestogas; but that market would slump once the bulk of the other wagons turned up. All they had to do was keep moving.

As the wagons passed, Dark's pony stiffened its neck against the bridle as its rider reined it back behind a rocky outcrop; the animal whinnied in complaint - the strange scent of the mules and the odd cries of the humans had disturbed it.

The young warrior's horse, its rump swaying, shoved its way alongside another pony already in place; saddles and stirrups clicked and creaked as the two animals jostled each other. The rider of the second horse put his moccasin on the rump of Dark's pony and pushed it away.

"What about the back trail? Did you see anything?" asked the other rider

"Nothing – no pony soldiers, no other wagons. Those two wagons are alone – they would be easy prizes."

Dark squinted across at the blurred images of the sun-flayed skin and black eyes of his companion as they swam back into watery focus.

"Hah," snorted Viajero; "If we attack them, we'll need prizes that are *worth* fighting for. Not like the last one…"

Despite his good eye smarting with dust, Dark grinned as Viajero mangled the beauty of the Cheyenne language with his own Apache version of it. The warrior had been with Dark's people for almost ten winters now and still found it tricky to converse properly.

"…Little brother, it's been a long and worthless summer. If we're not careful, we'll go home as paupers. We've nothing to show for it – no ponies, guns, scalps or even brave deeds that *you* can boast of. Our women will never let us forget it…"

Dark laughed – Viajero always left the bragging at the village campfires to him and the Cheyenne women were very loud in criticisms of warriors who weren't successful. Without captured goods or trophies, they were in for a rough time. Worse, their food and water were running low – neither warrior wanted to end the raid early but failure could force it.

The young Cheyenne blew a frustrated breath. They had stopped a lone wagon some days ago - the first they had seen after watching the white man's trail for a long time. There were no soldiers as escort, so stopping the heavy wheeled freight carrier had been easy – the Mexican driver and his shotgun-carrying guard were scared and obedient.

The Apache had spoken some Spanish to the men who told him that they were just carrying building materials for the white soldier fort – Fort Union, they said, was an important place these days as the war between the *gringos* in the east spread west. The men hoped to get home to Santa Fe earlier by using this shorter trail.

See the Dark had clambered on the wagon, slashing at the canvas coverings to discover that the men had spoken the truth – only white men's tools, clay bricks and planks of timber lay in neat lines in the dusty wagon bed. He had thrown the coverings onto the trail and howled in angry disappointment.

The young Cheyenne had wanted to kill the men, take their scalps and burn the wagon as some sort of compensation for their wasted time but Viajero was more cautious – this was Kiowa and Comanche country and it may be considered disrespectful to deny those people their war prizes if they wanted them. So, after filling their water skins and taking the men's food, gun and ammunition, they had let the driver and his companion go on their way.

It had been a bitter moment, leaving Dark in a seething temper – wise counselling rarely sat well with him. Viajero had recognised the familiar signs of petulance borne out of impatience and stayed out of the young man's way.

Still, the Apache *did* have a plan for the two wagons that had just passed:

"We'll sneak close to their camp tonight, wait for the morning star and see what is in each wagon. If there are good prizes, we'll attack."

See the Dark nodded in miserable agreement; the Traveller – his Cheyenne name for Viajero - could always be relied upon for sound judgement.

Dark was confident in himself as a warrior – his courage and experience now tested in battles against the Pawnee, Comanche and Utes – but he was always frustrated by his own inability to come up with a good plan when they needed one. Fighting was much easier than thinking. His father had told him that natural wisdom came with getting older and Dark looked forward to it; having a blank mind at the wrong moment was annoying. He shook his head to dismiss his mood and looked round.

The Traveller had dismounted and was offering his pony some water in a cupped hand; the animal slurped at it greedily. See the Dark did the same, using the water they had taken from the earlier wagon. He glanced across at his war brother; Viajero still dressed in the style of his White Mountain tribal band, fought in the same way and spoke to his own god. Living amongst the Cheyenne hadn't made him one of them. If the Apache brought wisdom, it was a benefit and Dark was glad of it.

Despite his low mood, the young Cheyenne had given one thing some thought:

"Did you see the guns that both those drivers had?" he said.

"Hard to see for the dust, but they looked the same as the one that we took from the other Mexican wagon – the gun that fire bullets that scatter," replied Viajero, hefting the long-barrelled shotgun so he could look at it.

"No, I don't think so…" said Dark "… the barrels on that scatter-gun are side-by-side – the ones that I've just seen have one barrel on top of the other."

Viajero was about to interrupt but See the Dark hadn't finished:

"They also had a loop of iron under the stock – this scattergun doesn't have that."

Viajero remounted and mused on the information. The young Suhtai, impetuous as he may be, was sometimes good at details that could be useful:

"Good, we'll take their guns from them tomorrow and see if they are better than ours."

See the Dark smiled with pleasure at being taken seriously and swung into the saddle. He drew his rifle from its rawhide sheath and cradled it across his saddle cantle, stroking the smooth woodwork.

"Those Mexican guns will need to be much better than this one…" he said, "…it would be hard to give this one up."

The Traveller nodded; their own guns were very powerful and could shoot over long distances. The power that these rifles brought to them and their small village – in the hunt or in war - would be hard to replace; though the linen or paper wrapped cartridges that they fired were now in short supply. *They* would need to be conserved – perhaps those Mexican wagons carried some?

Now, with the prospect of action and trophies, Viajero noticed that the Cheyenne's mood had lightened and nudged his pony forward with his heels.

Both riders swung out onto the wagon road then crossed to a wild pig run that ran parallel to it– the warriors could hear the *javelinas* somewhere close; the small and speedy animals grunted and squeaked, unseen among the low branches of the chaparral. One would be good for supper but trailing the Mexican wagons came first. A coyote, on the trail of the little pigs, fell in behind them.

"Those pigs would make a good meal," said Dark.

The Traveller just grunted and said:

"I prefer dog."

Dark nodded – the Apache spoke the truth. Viajero had told stories of creeping up on white or Mexican farmsteads in his own country and noting if they had a guard dog. Most did, so he always killed the dog first then slaughtered the inhabitants before running off the stock. But he always remembered to pick up the dog's carcass for a good supper on the way back to his *wickiup* near the Gila River. He ate it, he joked, 'bark and all.'

Apache and Cheyenne settled their ponies into an easy walk to the north of the trail, following the wagons. Their attention was distracted as the coyote dived into the chaparral behind them to catch his prey – small, sharp bodies exploded out into the open squealing and zig-zagging across the track. The coyote caught an inexperienced piglet and trotted off with it still writhing in his jaws. See the Dark nodded; signs were good – if a coyote could profit from today, so could they.

The two warriors kept a carefully measured distance behind the straining and bawling mules – close enough to catch up at a gallop if needed or, at worst, far enough away to escape if anything went wrong. The two men rode side by side where the trail allowed.

The Apache was in a conversational mood; this in itself was rare as the Traveller didn't usually talk much. Perhaps he had something on his mind or, with the prospect of action now delayed until dawn, maybe he was just bored:

"I saw my spirit creature today – when I was waiting in the *arroyo* for you…it ran across the ground in front of my pony."

Dark nodded, pleased that the Apache got comfort from such a trifle:

"Is that a good omen for us?" he asked, knowing that the Traveller always felt better when he'd seen the little creature.

"Yes, the horned lizard is a good sign. I like them – they can live on little and survive in hard country, just like we people of the N'De."

Dark knew the Apache always gave this homily when mentioning the lizard; it was his way of boasting. The Cheyenne swung his pony past a rock on the path and caught up to the Traveller:

"I'm not sure you could go back and live with your own people any more – you've grown fat on buffalo instead of eating snakes; you live in a skin tipi rather than a brushwood shelter and you get to eat the occasional dog. You, my friend, have too comfortable a life."

There was always a balance to Dark's teasing – he knew full well that the Apache had been a dark and terrible shadow of death and destruction down in his own land – his very hardness and lack of any sentimentality probably came from his sparse and dangerous life. Viajero could take teasing either way – he was unpredictable.

"At least *I* have a spirit sign that *Usen,* the Life Bringer of the N'De, uses to show me which trail to take – unlike you, a godless youth," said the Apache with what passed for a smile.

Dark sighed with relief that the banter had been taken well and spurred his pony to catch up with Viajero, both dropping back slightly as the tail end of the last wagon came into view through the dust.

The wagons disappeared round a bend in the trail, obscured by a large outcrop of red mesa rock. The mules were quieter now, just grunts and whipcracks marking their passage.

Both warriors watched as a covey of sage hen scuttled out from under a clump of greasewood, squawking loudly; this was followed by two turkey vultures flapping noisily into the air. The men cautiously reined in their ponies - it took a lot to disturb vultures. It was then they heard the yelling…

---- o o o ----

Etsay, the Kiowa leader of the small war band, smiled in satisfaction. His warriors from the Black Leggings soldier society had stopped the two wagons easily. The young braves whooped with pleasure as, painted, armed and eager for glory, they had surged out of a shallow depression in the ground that kept them hidden from those on the trail. They had daylight to spare and would not kill the Mexicans quickly, though they hadn't yet disarmed them of their shotguns.

Wisely, Etsay took no chances and yelled to his horsemen to keep a safe distance from the guns, dividing his small group of warriors between each wagon. The young men shrieked to encourage each other to do brave deeds. Kiowa ponies raced round the wagons, encircling them in dust; the yelling got louder.

His Black Leggings boys had done well – the plunder they would take from the wagons would be well received back in their village and the twenty mules from the wagon teams would always be welcome trade animals in anyone's pasture. Out of the eight warriors only he was armed with a gun – a sawn-off trade musket crammed with powder and a large lead bullet – painted eagle feathers and two scalps hung from it. Still, he reasoned, when they killed the Mexicans that would be two more guns to make them stronger and more deadly. Now it was time to advance…

Viajero and See the Dark arrived on the rimrock ledge above the wagon trail after a short, hard gallop up the escarpment, chasing the source of the noise. They leaped from their saddles, Dark with rifle in hand, and crawled quickly to the overhang as the Kiowa, still yelling their war songs, closed in on the halted wagons. The Apache motioned Dark to be silent and not to join in on the attack – this was now Kiowa business. The shadows of the two disturbed turkey vultures swooped across the clearing as they lofted on the air currents and waited their turn.

Etsay was puzzled as his young men rode towards the wagons – normally these mule drivers tried to run off or beg for their lives. But these two stood up on their seats, guns in hand and didn't seem to be afraid. The Mexicans were actually speaking to each other though the Kiowa couldn't understand Spanish…

The conversation between the brothers was short and urgent as Miguel Armijo called out to his brother:

"Now, *hermano!*"

It was the signal that Ernesto had been waiting for – a pre-arranged action that they had practised back at Leavenworth. Both men dropped into the deep footwells of their wagons and opened fire. It was then that Etsay realised that the Mexicans were not carrying shotguns.

A furious burst of rapid gunfire spat out of the wagon footwells as the mules jerked the wagons forward in panic, straining against the wooden block brakes.

Three Kiowas died instantly in the saddle, tumbling from their horses into the dust. Warriors at each wagon, though shocked by the unexpected heavy fire, shot arrows at the half-hidden Mexicans but, as Miguel had foreseen, the extra planking they had nailed across the high arching frame of the wagon seat acted like a small fort and the arrows thudded harmlessly into the woodwork.

Etsay was angry and charged right up to one of the wagon seats and fired his old gun at point blank range. Though heavily loaded with powder, the bullet just careened off the double plank and hit his horse. The pony went down with a broken shoulder, screaming with pain; mules bawled even louder and tried to buck the traces holding them to the wagon shaft. The war yells of the remaining Kiowas were now tinged with the same panic.

Two of the Black Leggings saw Etsay go down and spurred their ponies towards him to help. Pinned under his injured pony, their chief waved them away but it was too late – the Mexican in the wagon just above him, stood up and calmly fired four bullets at them. Both his warriors fell; one, his foot still in the stirrups, was dragged away by his terrified horse.

The Kiowa war leader crawled out from under his squirming, screaming pony. Now he had to set the example for his remaining companions – shocked as he looked around, he realised that only himself and two others were left. Out of sight of the Mexicans he drew an arrow from his quiver, took his war bow from round his shoulder and walked out into the open, his long Black Leggings war sash trailing on the ground behind him.

Up on the rimrock, Viajero and See the Dark were impressed with the courageous action of the Kiowas but they were more impressed by the Mexican guns. Neither of them had seen either of the drivers stop to reload their rifles – how could that be? Back home, some warriors had repeating rifles but they only fired five or six bullets each and still needed reloading with powder and ball. The guns used today had fired many more than that. Their plan for sneaking into the Mexican camp that night and just looting the wagons had been abandoned – they would need a better way of getting hold of and understanding the deadly new guns.

Down in the shallow valley, the Mexican rifles had fallen silent as Etsay rallied the remnants of his war party, standing in a defiant line off to the side of the wagons. There were no horses to escape on and their Black Leggings rituals weighed heavily on them.

Viajero and See the Dark looked on as the Kiowa soldiers all did the same thing – they pinned their war sashes to the ground with an arrow and sang their death songs. No-one could release them now – they were here as war brothers to confront death.

See the Dark nodded in sympathy. He had never sung his death song yet but he admired the courage of those who did.

Etsay led his men in a version of the Sitting Bear dance, though his leg was numb from being trapped under his pony. He called on them to remember their Kiowa blood. One of the survivors was his own brother, he smiled at the younger man who grimaced in pain from a leg wound. He sang his prayers to his own God as they all turned to face the enemy in true Kiowa fashion.

Then there was a silence as Miguel and Ernesto watched the three Indians:

"How many cartridges have you got left?" shouted Ernesto

"Four in the magazine and one in the chamber – and you?"

"Three and one ready in the breech."

Etsay was still praying when the Mexicans shot them down.

---- 0 0 0 ----

Chapter Two

Worm wasn't his real name, just one that the Crow had given him when he'd been dragged into their village over six summers ago. He didn't speak their language then and tried to tell them his true name using hand sign, but they beat him to his knees and ignored it. The Crow name contained just enough of an insult to remind him that he was a lowly captive and could never be trusted.

He drove his animals out of the Crow camp and along to the creek to drink. Two brindled dogs ran behind the small herd, nipping at the ankles of the slow-moving mules. Sullen Crow women looked up at him from their fleshing frames; girls and old men shooed children out of his way. Worm just ignored them.

He looked around him with distaste. Some of the people in the village wore white men's clothes from the trading posts - the colour and brightness of the cloth contrasting with the worn and tattered skins of the tipis, blackened by smoke from countless cook fires and soiled from many tribal moves. The camp had an air of neglect. Though he kept his young face immobile, Worm sneered inwardly – his grandfather's stories had proved to be right. These people were not the true hunters and warriors of the great grasslands - just despicable outsiders who only dared to hunt buffalo when others let them.

But now, even going about a menial task like watering the stock, he wasn't allowed to ride a horse in case he escaped; instead, he had been forced to ride a sway-backed mule that shuffled out onto the trail and rattled his teeth with its odd gait. And, to make sure he didn't leave the mule and just run away, he had an escort:

"Don't wander off," ordered Red Horse pompously, "Stay where I can see you…"

Worm looked across at the smirking youth, sitting aloof on a well-groomed pinto pony, and gritted his teeth. The Crow boy was only a couple of summers older than him but his job was to stay by Worm's side if he left the encampment. Menial task or not, Red Horse had been instructed by his father to keep an eye on the young slave.

Red Horse reined his pony to one side to let the small herd get to the trail as the dust rose:

"Those Pawnee were glad to see you go; they traded you to us for some tobacco and a rusty musket – you Medicine Arrow people aren't worth much," he shouted as Worm passed. The boy sat on his mule, concentrating on keeping the stock in check and stayed silent.

But, unseen by his tormentor, Worm smiled. He had come through all the beatings of the Crow without ever becoming one of *them*, his hated enemies.

Other boy captives that came to the *Absaroka* village had seemed too troublesome - they had been killed immediately. He often wondered why the Pawnee – his original captors - hadn't killed *him* first when he had been ripped, kicking and yelling, from his own family during a raid on his village. Or even why they hadn't tortured and killed him once he'd been dragged to their camp up on the Loup River. Perhaps he wasn't yet old enough to be much danger to them but had been judged useful as a slave. But he'd only lasted a few months as their prisoner.

Just after arriving in the Pawnee camp, a hard winter hit and many of their people starved to death. The medicine man, covering his own lack of visions to predict such savage weather, blamed the boy as bad medicine and so he'd been traded quickly to the Crow.

But today, of all days, Worm was happy. Red Horse may have been his keeper but he was stupid and unobservant. The Crow boy hadn't noticed that on every other occasion, Worm had ridden the mule bareback. Today, he sat on a blanket with the front rim curled over in front of him; hidden inside the fabric were a few concealed scraps of food stuffed inside a piece of buffalo gut. But the food wasn't to fend off hunger while watering the stock, he needed it as part of his plan – for, today Worm would escape.

He had no weapons to kill Red Horse though he had briefly toyed with the idea of using a rock from the creek to smash his head in. But, knowing his luck, there would be none of the right size and weight. No, he would need to time his theft of one of the ponies just right - probably when Red Horse had dismounted to drink – then switch his blanket onto a swift horse, scatter the rest of the stock and head south.

Worm knew that his plan was simple but it was also weak. Red Horse always carried his bow, arrows and hatchet with him – even when dismounted. If something delayed him galloping off, Red Horse was probably skilled enough to put an arrow into him…. but, with a youth's casual disregard for detailed planning, Worm just shrugged his shoulders. There was little else he could do. He had prayed the night before to *Maheo*, the One God and so he would leave that part of his escape to the Life Giver who rules the destinies of all men. He smiled again and settled into his riding.

The drinking place for the animals was some way downstream from the Crow camp, far enough away from where the women washed clothes and drew water; the close stands of cottonwoods around this part of the creek gave shade from the heat of the day and the ponies enjoyed it. Some twenty horses and a few mules grunted and jostled each other to get to the cool water. Sunlight dappled their coats – all were in good condition from the lush summer grazing.

Worm rode around them and tapped the skittish ones with a knotted rope or pushed them with the sole of his moccasin and soon there was an orderly line of stock drinking along the shallow sand banks. When the herd had settled, the boy reined his mule towards the stream to get its share as Red Horse trotted up behind him.

"My father says that you are not fit to eat our food and if I get the chance to shoot you, I should do it…"

Worm thought on the Crow words for some time – it was not his own language and he had to work out the meaning. He had planned to ignore the taunts of Red Horse today – to keep him calm and less watchful. But he was not a patient youngster and his limited *Absaroka* words came tumbling out:

"Then shoot me or are you too afraid?" Worm snarled. He knew Red Horse was not well liked in the Crow camp – even the women who made him collect firewood with them talked openly about it - the boy was unsuitable as a warrior. He was deemed too selfish and that would endanger others. So, the words of Worm, a mere foreign slave, stung.

Red Horse replied by spurring his pony up alongside him and quirted the boy in the face, knocking him from his mule.

"You Medicine Arrow cowards should stay in the dirt where you belong," he shouted down at the motionless youth.

Worm stayed still and traced the line of the bloody laceration to his cheek; it was yet another marker of his humiliation.

Revenge burned alongside the pain of his wound but his reckoning with Red Horse would have to wait. He looked anxiously at the mule, now drinking from the creek, the blanket still intact on its back. If the Crow boy found the food, Worm knew he'd be finished. He decided to keep calm and move into a position where he could quickly grab one of the ponies when Red Horse dismounted.

Worm got up and walked upstream of the stock to the water's edge, keeping watch on what the Crow youth was doing out of the corner of his eye. He hissed through his teeth in frustration as Red Horse stayed in the saddle.

Squatting down on his haunches, he scooped some water into his mouth and slathered some on the streaming line of blood; rivulets ran down his chin and washed off some of the dust.

A breeze blew as the wind changed direction and, as if responding to a silent signal, all the heads of the drinking animals jerked upwards at the same time. Something different, and possibly dangerous, was close by, upwind.

Worm was just in the act of swallowing some water when the arrow hit him.

The boy yelled in pain and jerked upright; the horses and mules, spooked by the new scent and the sudden noise, backed away from the water's edge in alarm and began to mill around in panic, whinnying and braying. Shocked, Worm crawled into some chokecherry bushes grimacing as the iron arrowpoint, deeply embedded in the fat part of his leg, ground against his thigh bone. Another arrow thudded into the ground beside him. Red Horse had obviously decided to kill him!

He changed his mind when several shots rang out and a slim body crashed into the bushes almost on top of him; it was Red Horse – the boy had been wounded but was still alive. They were under attack. The Crow youth was about to yell when Worm clamped his hand over his mouth:

"Silence! They'll find us."

Then came the yelling of the enemy as they crashed out of a thicket close by – wild exultant shrieks of power and triumph – as they rounded up all of the stock and, with more laughter and shouting, drove it off.

Worm held tightly to Red Horse's mouth. Some of the unseen riders drove their mounts through nearby bushes but they were only after the scattered animals. None of them seemed to be hunting for the youths or to collect their scalps. The ground trembled as hooves thudded past them – the flat cracks of pistol shots cut through the din.

There was something odd about the yelling though and Worm, releasing his handhold on Red Horse's face, peeped out of his hiding place. He couldn't see much in the swirling dust of the departing raiders but then he heard it again – just a faint ululation in the cacophony of sound; an oddness of tone on his own small battlefield.

Worm seethed in frustration; his one chance of escape had gone. Now he was wounded and afoot – all the stock had been driven off, including his mule. At least, the incriminating food scraps beneath the saddle blanket had also gone so there would be no awkward questions later.

He looked down as Red Horse groaned in pain beside him; the youth had been shot through the right side of his skinny chest – the bullet had come out through his shoulder blade, a puckering of bloody flesh showing the exit wound. It probably wasn't fatal – though Worm wished it had been. Then he spotted the spare arrow embedded in the dust close by. It was an opportunity too good to miss…

Worm leaned across Red Horse's shoulder to draw the arrow out of the dirt as the arrogant Crow boy continued to give him instructions:

"Get to the village and bring my …"

Worm always thought that it was a shame that Red Horse's final words in this life were so ordinary as he rammed the arrow into the youth's chest and split his heart. Blood welled out of the wound and onto the edge of his hands as he held the shaft in the Crow's heaving chest.

Red Horse arched his body in pain and flailed his arms in the dust but it was no use. Worm pushed harder on the arrow, feeling it sever sinew and tissue, remembering all the insults and beatings at his rival's hands and held it there until the young Crow's final rattling of breath allowed him to relax. Red Horse lay splayed on the ground, twitching slightly as his spirit left him. He looked for all the world like he had been killed by the enemy raiders; Worm smiled – the day hadn't been a complete failure after all.

The striped markings on the arrows gave the identity of the attackers and Worm smiled again – perhaps *Maheo*, the Life Giver, had a sense of humour? He had been wounded by his own people! If it hadn't been for the pain, he would have laughed. Then he heard the drumming of hooves as riders from the Crow village, alerted by the shooting, arrived in a flurry of dust and anger.

Leaving Red Horse's body, Worm crawled to the creek and washed the dust from his face and the bloodstains from his hands. He caught his reflection in the water. There, barely visible these days as he'd slowly matured from boyhood, was his birthmark – a small, red serpentine scar on his right cheek that had given him his child's name among his own people. He looked back over his shoulder as the noises got louder.

There were anguished shrieks as the Crow riders arrived and searched the riverbank for their stock and missing son. Red Horse's father had found him first and wailed uncontrollably, throwing dust over himself. Another warrior walked over to Worm, nocked an arrow onto his bowstring and pointed it at him threateningly:

"Those arrows belong to the Cheyenne; they are your people – you probably organised the raid and brought them here!"

The wounded boy looked at him steadily and said:

"If that is true, why did they shoot me and then leave me here?"

The Crow, stuck for an answer, grunted in disbelief and walked off to console Red Horse's father.

No-one came to Worm's aid and the old hate welled up in him – his life was just something to be thrown away as the Crow judged. He looked down at the creek edge as a small wave lapped over his handprints and swept them away. It gave him an idea.

In an act of defiance, he rolled onto his belly, scooped up a handful of sand and for the last time spoke his Crow name into the pile of earth on his palm and rubbed it on the ground. Another lapping wave took it away. It was gone now.

Now, though he hadn't done it for many years, he spoke his real name:

"I am Little Snake of the *Suhtai* Cheyenne."

No more was he Worm, a captive of the despised Crow, he was a man – and with his killing of Red Horse, now a warrior - of the Medicine Arrow People. He decided never again to submit to his slavery without making the Crow pay.

He'd decided one other thing too - he would never reveal to the Crow what he had seen and heard during the raid. He was sorely tempted, just to see the look on their stupid faces but they would probably never believe him anyway – as Little Snake could scarcely believe it himself. But he was sure now - the piping ululations and the odd way that he had seen the raiders sit in their saddles — the Cheyenne raiders had all been women.

---- 0 0 0 ----

Little Snake had been left to walk – as best he could with an arrow stuck deep in his leg – back to the Crow camp. It had taken a while as the blood loss had weakened him. The Crow didn't even bother to check to see that he hadn't run away.

The young Cheyenne's mind was now clear. His arrow wound and the death of Red Horse had brought clarity of his purpose on this earth – he needed to get back to his own people and quickly. And he would kill anyone who got in his way.

One withered old woman had taken pity on him and bathed his wound while he lay under a skin shelter tied to a tree. She was hard to understand as she mumbled and had no teeth but her advice was the same that Little Snake had heard when he was a boy – don't pull the arrow out, push it through. So, he did.

Little Snake broke off the bigger part of the arrow shaft with the goosequill feathers that stood aloft from his thigh, then pushed hard with a flat stone at the rest embedded in his leg. The pain was almost unbearable but he wouldn't let any passing Crow see him weep or hear him yell.

The arrow was hard to push through the remainder of his flesh and it scraped on a bone as he did it but eventually, he had a bloody iron arrowpoint and broken shaft in his hand. He threw the arrowhead away into a sage bush and he was about to do the same with the quilled shaft when, on a whim, he changed his mind and kept it.

Blood poured out of the open wound but the old crone plugged it with moss and spider webs; she gave him some soup and told him to hide and rest up – the village would be taking Red Horse's body to his funeral scaffold soon and he shouldn't be seen.

Little Snake thanked her but she shrugged and said:

"You are not the only slave in this camp – I was taken from my Nez Perce family as a girl and married off to a Crow war leader. He died many moons past."

"Was he killed in battle?" asked Little Snake.

"No, I poisoned him," said the old woman with a gaping, toothless grin.

Little Snake nodded in satisfaction – he may have found an ally.

---- **0 0 0** ----

Chapter Three

Yellow Bear knew the woman was there but chose to ignore her. He had seen her shadow flit across the ground as she sat down behind him.

He sat cross-legged in front of the framed buffalo skin and dipped a sharpened stick into the paint gourds at his side. The hide had been peeled and scraped and washed in the waters of a special creek that turned dressed skins white; it was bound by sinews to a square frame of cottonwood boughs. On the skin were Yellow Bear's drawings that marked the significant things that had happened to his People as the seasons on the great grasslands rolled through their cycle. He would sometimes hang it outside his tipi so fathers could bring their children and explain the history of their kin.

Today, he had nothing new to add but the hide had been rolled and unrolled so many times that some of the past years' painted symbols were starting to crack and peel off; it was time to repair them. He straightened the frame and set to work.

He traced the events with his finger as they stretched out in a spiral from one small, central image; this image was of Yellow Bear himself - showing how he had discarded his weapons as a warrior some years ago to follow his calling as the tribe's spirit diviner. He knew his shaman powers had sometimes waned or been found wanting but, in the main, his reading of his dreams and natural signs kept his small band of Cheyenne out of extreme danger or hunger.

The skinny medicine man leaned forward and applied a line of black paint to some rectangular shapes and sat back to look at the result:

"What are those?"

The question startled him slightly even though he knew the woman was there – he had not expected to have to engage anyone in conversation. Though his work today was not spiritual or needed his permission to view it, Yellow Bear blew through his teeth to hide his irritation. These younger women seemed to enjoy flouting tribal traditions. He remained silent and continued to work on the shapes; the woman cleared her throat and spat on the ground:

"Those shapes – what are they?" the woman almost barked the words. She had a strange accent – a harsh interpretation of his beloved Cheyenne tongue.

Yellow Bear shuffled round to look at her, his body masking the painted spiral of events. He recognised her of course – his band of *Suhtai* Cheyenne was only small; everyone knew their neighbours. Though he had never really troubled himself to remember women's names, he did remember that this particular young woman had been taken as a captive from the *Hunkpapa* Lakota in the long-ago times when the Cheyenne had fought the Sioux; it explained her odd way of speaking his language.

Hiding his impatience at such abrupt questioning, the medicine man moved to one side of the painted skin, pointed with his stick and answered steadily and clearly:

"Those straight-line shapes represent our funeral scaffolds after the Pawnee raid on our village almost seven winters ago – we lost a lot of warriors and almost starved…"

The woman nodded her head impatiently:

"I remember. Didn't the People blame you for losing their children?"

Yellow Bear blinked back the unexpected tears at the painful reminder; this young woman had little sense of tact but she was right. His job during the attack had been to get the children to safety and he had failed – a great many had been slung across Pawnee war saddles and taken off into captivity. He had been a scapegoat for Cheyenne disgrace for a while afterwards.

The woman saw the spirit diviner's head droop and noted the watery film in his eyes. She decided to change her approach:

"But you had great visions before our revenge raid on the Pawnee villages that gave us success – is that marked on there?"

Yellow Bear nodded but still couldn't speak – the reminder of his failure cut deep; he stretched out his stick and pointed to a series of red hoofprints and an outline of dead, scalp locked Pawnee warriors:

"It was a good raid," admitted Yellow Bear. The woman nodded:

"It was the birth of our own soldier society…" the woman said, "…I assume you have drawn the other war deeds of the Forked Lightning Women on there? What about our raid on the Comanche in the Texas country?"

Yellow Bear looked coldly at her. Her soldier society flew in the face of all Cheyenne traditions. Like all the Forked Lightning Women, the young Hunkpapa girl wore men's leggings under her split deerskin skirt and carried a pistol in a Mexican leather holster on her waist – a war prize when they had attacked *Comanchero* traders almost five summers back. Their deeds against the Comanche were well known now – the original young women warriors being the envy of the upcoming generation of Suhtai girls - some wanted to emulate them, instead of being wives or child-bearers. He snarled at her impertinence:

"No." It was a flat rejection of her sense of entitlement; the woman looked angry now.

"On that raid, you women were led by two male warriors - See the Dark and the Traveller…" he pointed to the two images on the hide. The woman craned her head forward – a circle with a red hole as an empty eye socket represented the one-eyed warrior, See the Dark, and another circle, wearing a blue bandana over his hair, was the boy's Apache companion.

"...The plan to take weapons from the Comanche traders was theirs, not yours."

The woman jumped up and stood feet apart as she pointed rudely at the medicine man:

"The men acted as decoys! We women were the ones who brought the guns out! One of our warriors died doing it." Her voice had raised to a screech. "We are tired of not being fully recognised as fighting Cheyenne!"

The medicine man looked steadily at her. She was right in her argument of course - the Comanche guns that they had brought into camp had greatly strengthened their small band; they had even shared some of them with other male warriors. But refuting sacred traditions of motherhood and stability that Cheyenne women had followed from the times of his grandfather's grandfather did not sit well with the spirit diviner. Yellow Bear stood up, flushed with anger, and picked up the cottonwood frame; he would go back to his *tipi* to cool off.

A group of women carrying deerskins they had washed in the river, walked into the clearing but, noting the tense atmosphere, walked on giggling nervously. A huge flock of passenger pigeons passed overhead, darkening the sky.

"No! Please wait…" the young woman had darted forwards; aware she had used the wrong tone with the medicine man. She stood contritely with her hands clasped in front of her and head slightly bowed. Even with her neck bent, she was still a hand taller than Yellow Bear.

"I am called Willow – I apologise for my outburst. Our warriors seek your help."

Yellow Bear nodded sagely, trying to make it look as though he had actually remembered her name. He was pleased at the *Hunkpapa* girl's change of tone – he smiled slightly.

"How can I be of service?"

He was surprised when the girl took his sleeve and led him through the circle of lodges. Bad Elk, the Suhtai chief, saw him with the woman warrior and raised his chin in a questioning gesture. Yellow Bear just shrugged and followed her.

Willow took him down to the edge of the horse herd. There, roped against a tree, kept apart from the rest of the grazing animals, stood a badly spavined mule with a saddle blanket over its sagging spine.

Around the mule were the rest of the Forked Lightning Women – Yellow Bear panicked slightly but was relieved to remember the name of at least one of them - White Rain Woman, their leader.

He strode forward and spoke to her:

"Sister, what help can I be? None of my potions can help this ugly creature much…" he joked, pointing to the mule.

White Rain Woman smiled politely but took off the saddle blanket and pointed to a yellow smudge of paint at the base of the mule's neck. The spirit diviner walked cautiously to the mule, its quivering hide twitching under an attack by biting flies, and peered at it.

"The mule came with the stock we raided from the Crow, three days ago."

He nodded but said nothing – the raid hadn't been approved by Bad Elk and had certainly gone unblessed by Yellow Bear. The women had given no thought to any possible reprisals. The medicine man sighed regretfully.

He moved the mule out into the sunlight and looked again at the paint mark. It was worn and smudged, hard to read.

"We just want to be sure that we haven't brought a Crow bad spirit mule into camp," said White Rain, pointing to the paint smudge.

"We'd heard that yellow is a bad spirit colour," said Willow, though she didn't say from whom she had heard it.

Yellow Bear had no idea what a bad spirit mule might be or even if it came with any special markings. He shook his head in disbelief; these young women had too much time on their hands. A little more time at their own weddings and less on the war trail trying to copy the men might improve them. But he kept his own counsel and said:

"The colour is not important, especially as it is part of my own given name…" he glared at the smirking women, "…This is just a hand print; a left hand – small; perhaps from a youth."

He knew he was telling them something that they could work out for themselves. One of the women warriors rolled her eyes upward; he ignored the bored looks:

"But…" he continued as he inspected the mark closer; the women suddenly regained interest and leaned in.

"…the handprint has these marks on the first finger…" he pointed out two faded, downward black slashes across the yellow stub. The women had been too concerned with bad spirits and colours; they had missed the important message of the daubed paint.

"But then that's…," said White Rain. Yellow Bear smiled politely but with satisfaction - knowing that she hadn't spotted the tell-tale marks.

"Yes, it is the Cut Finger or Striped Arrow hand sign of our own People..." Yellow Bear said it slowly and carefully; he was, after all, talking to women.

"...that Crow camp you raided many have had a Cheyenne in it."

---- 0 0 0 ----

Chapter Four

Miguel and Ernesto Armijo had been thwarted by their mules. After the Indian attack, getting to Fort Union at speed seemed to be the best plan but the animals had been spooked by the gunfire and resented being pushed onwards. To the best of the brothers' knowledge, mules couldn't communicate – but somehow both teams stopped at the same time in the middle of the trail, still surrounded by dead Indians. No amount of cajoling or cracking of whips could move them.

Both men dismounted from their seats, heaved at their lead animals, imploring them by name and dedication of saints to move out of this charnel house. The mules just dug in their heels as if to demonstrate the futility of human effort.

After a short discussion, the Armijos just shrugged - mules were mules - and tapped into the water barrels on the side of each of the Conestogas. Filling wooden pails with the precious liquid, the brothers went down each side of their teams and allowed every mule a good swallow of water before they took them out of harness for the night. There was no grazing here but the men dragged a bundle of grass forage from one wagon and fed their animals.

Setting up night camp was a routine but after the ambush, they took extra care – someone would come looking for the dead warriors eventually and may want to seek revenge. They tied all the mules to two headropes and hobbled the outside pairs to prevent them from being run off in the event of an attack.

As the night shadows lengthened, the brothers dragged the dead bodies of the Indians into a shallow pile, some way from the camp. It wouldn't be long before wolves came to investigate – they were welcome to the dead flesh – but they didn't want the mules spooked again.

Both men sweated with the effort and sat down under a stubby tree. They lit no fires but ate jerky and sipped warm, slimy water from a tin cup.

Miguel yawned and took out a battered cheroot from his work shirt – it reeked of his own sweat but at least he was alive to enjoy it:

"These Henry rifles were a good investment, eh *hermano*?" he said, blowing the smoke up and out against the starry sky and patted the cold metalwork of his gun on the ground next to him.

Ernesto just grunted. He was four years older than his brother and had baulked at paying the high prices for the rifles back at Leavenworth – he'd complained loudly that he could buy a good horse for much less money. Miguel had persisted though – and Ernesto was pleased he had. They still had their scalps, mules and wagons. The firepower of the Henrys had made the difference even though they had been outnumbered. The boy had been right - though, of course, it wouldn't do to tell him that; praise would make him insufferable.

He was about to reply with a sarcastic remark when a heavy metallic click right next to his ear broke the stillness.

---- o o o ----

Viajero and See the Dark had been surprised at the Mexicans' choice of campsite; spending the night amongst enemy dead was not something either of them would have done. It showed a certain courage, as the spirits of the dead would be wandering the camp and there was no telling what they might do.

The warriors had led their ponies back down the shallow escarpment and hobbled their ponies some way from the campsite which was now in darkness. They were downwind of the tethered mules with enough rocks and scrub to approach on foot. Patchy cloud hid the moon though it occasionally lit up the small pile of Kiowa dead.

For once, it had been See the Dark who had been against killing the Mexicans outright and taking their rifles; for him, scalps and plunder normally went together but this was different. Viajero had been surprised when his younger war companion mentioned it as they had planned their attack. He had smiled in the darkness and patted Dark on the shoulder:

"Good thinking, little brother. They'll need to tell us how to use those rifles."

Dark had taken the praise shyly but, ever the opportunist for humour, had said he hoped Viajero's Spanish was up to the task.

"Just hope it is – I'd hate to rely on you with your bow and arrows if we get into trouble," growled the Apache.

Dark snorted in mock outrage; his skills with a bow had been poor from childhood and Viajero, as well as others in the tribe, constantly joshed him about his failings. Sometimes he could hit a target that he'd aimed at, but it wasn't reliable. Carrying a rifle that he could aim just using his remaining eye, evened up his chances in battle.

The young Cheyenne had waited until Viajero had carried out his spiritual preparations for the coming attack; Dark had none himself, other than a cursory prayer to *Maheo*, the Cheyenne Creator. His main preparation before battle rested on his inclination to just hope for the best.

He stood next to his pony and patted its flank as the Apache spat into the coloured powder he always carried and applied his own battle paint – he couldn't see him clearly but he knew that two stripes – one yellow and one red – would be drawn across the bridge of his nose and both cheeks. It was a simple design but one that always focused the Apache's mind onto the actions to come. The older warrior had a high reputation as a killer of many people – men, women and children – and, to most, those face stripes would have been the last thing they saw in this life.

Dark heard the saddle pouch on Viajero's pony open and close; the painting was done. The Apache uttered a short, murmured prayer to *Usen* in his own tongue. Now it was time.

They approached the camp cautiously; the Mexicans would be jumpy after their tangle with the Kiowa and a sentry would probably be posted. They sniffed the cigar smoke in the air and crawled the last few paces to avoid being silhouetted against the starlight. The pinpoint of light that the cheroot made in the pitch blackness guided them to their prey.

The Mexicans were still talking in low tones and the two warriors followed the sounds; both men were sitting together and chatting – there was no sign that the warriors' stealthy approach had been seen or heard. A shaft of moonlight showed the Mexicans sitting with their backs to a dead mesquite stump, one rifle was on the ground next to its owner and the other man had the gun cradled across the top of his thighs. Conversation dropped off as sleep beckoned.

Viajero rose up from his belly, crept up to one man and cocked the hammer of his own gun right next to the ear of the Mexican. The metallic click was loud in the still night air.

Miguel Armijo started at the unexpected sound, his stomach lurching with fear as his bowels loosened. He scrabbled at the Henry rifle on the ground next to him but only found the rough buckskin of an Apache moccasin standing on it. Viajero sharply jabbed the muzzle of his gun into the Mexican's head to remind him how close death was.

Ernesto was not treated to such a lenient approach; See the Dark had merely waited until he was close enough then smacked his man across the side of his head with his rifle butt. He snatched the new rifle out of the Mexican's lap before he toppled to one side.

Both Mexicans were dragged to the Conestogas and tied to the wheels; the fatter one took more effort to haul through the dust. Dark walked back and collected their hobbled ponies and brought them to the campsite; the mules, sensing something different were uneasy and began to bray as shafts of dawn light broke across the spine of the far mountains.

The older Mexican was still groggy from his blow to the head; his speech was slurred, so Viajero held up one of the new rifles and spoke to the younger one:

"Dog! I want to know how this gun works, *comprender*?"

Miguel looked at the warpainted Apache and quailed. He nodded dumbly – every Mexican knew that Apaches hated them and considered them less than human. Even if he told them all he knew about the Henry rifles, only torture and death lay ahead for him and his brother. A sudden surge of rash courage, knowing the end of his life was close, made him stare blankly back into the dark-skinned face with the coloured stripes. Miguel shook his head. This was a mistake.

Viajero put his rifle down and took out a small knife with a double-edged blade; he held it horizontally in front of the Mexican's face, twirling the point on his fingertip. See the Dark saw the change of mood and walked over; he liked to watch the Traveller at work.

Miguel's brain raced as he braced himself for the knife-thrust, muscles bunched up, teeth snarling in a face contorted with fear.

However, instead of killing him, the Apache leant over to Ernesto, sliced the knife edge into his brother's head skin, made a circular cut along the hairline and scalped him.

The Apache smiled grimly as the Mexican, groggy until then, sat up and screeched in pain and terror. Enemies crying out in pain gave power to warriors like him. It was a sound that went with being a warrior of the N'de. He would never weary of it.

Viajero tugged at the remaining strands of skin and hair and threw the bloody hank into Miguel's face and picked up the Henry again.

"Now dog – the rifle, *por favor?*"

---- o o o ----

The four riders crested a small hill overlooking the Arkansas River; Lobo, the leader, reined in his pony and the small war party watched in silence. They had been attracted by the dust cloud and wondered if they might profit from it; sometimes whites or Mexicans would drive horses and cattle to the river to drink – they made easy pickings. It looked and sounded like madness below – the dust was thick and Lobo couldn't tell if the riders were white, though they weren't wearing hats. Whoever they were, they hadn't spotted him and his warriors.

Viajero was sweating heavily - driving the mules back to the Cheyenne camp was embarrassing; there was no glory in looting animals that had once pulled the wagons of white men but See the Dark insisted that they try. Though their new rifles were much prized, they only had two of them - the tobacco, along with the spare boxes of ammunition, now in a makeshift pack across the back of one of the stubborn creatures, seemed poor reward for so long a raid. Mules were a sort of wealth, but not as precious as horses. According to Viajero, riding a mule was only slightly better than walking and it didn't taste as good as dog.

The Apache was unhappy; he had hated the two mules that he and Dark had taken down to Texas on their raid against the Comancheros. They had been contrary, loud and given to stopping whenever they liked; he'd wanted to kill them. Now, with the remainder of the wagon teams in a small herd in front of them, they drove the complaining and awkward animals in a welter of dust and whipping chaparral.

Their ponies were tired with the unusual work of racing backwards and forwards to control the small *remuda* and breathing in their dust; their hides were ripped by thorns and low hung branches. Their riders had similar stripes.

Suddenly, the mules split into two groups - both moving round a clump of trees ahead. Then, for no reason that Viajero could see, all the mules stopped and watched the treeline, fear starting to turn them around and bump into their neighbours. Both groups became milling clumps of mule flesh and their bawling got louder.

See the Dark emerged from the remuda's trail dust shielding his right eye from the grit and took in the scene, puzzled as to why the mules had stopped. The explanation came in a crashing of breaking branches and a welter of whirling leaves from the treeline – a rangy longhorn bull, with his harem behind him, angrily confronted mules and warriors:

"It's just a cow," said Dark with relief, still spitting out dust and blinking his eye to clear it.

Viajero was not so sure:

"No, it's pawing the ground like the buffalo do – it's going to charge. Shoot it!"

Apache and Cheyenne both clawed at the new rifles in their hands. Readying the weapons for action had seemed a simple thing when the frightened Mexican had shown them; now, as they fumbled with cocking levers and finding the target in the settling dust, they realised that one short lesson may not have been enough.

The bull charged the nearest group of mules, driving one of its horns deep into the flank of the closest; the mule screamed, kicked out backwards and tore itself free, lacerating the wound even more. Blood streamed down to its fetlocks as it crumpled to its knees. The bull whipped its head round to seek another victim but the rest of the mules were disappearing fast into the distance, heading to the river to drink – only the ponies and the plunging pack mule of the warriors were left.

Lobo watched closely but joined in the laughter of his companions; the two riders below weren't white and they weren't good with animals. They watched as the bull pawed the ground and charged them.

Viajero was first to shoot, firing twice. It was hard to say if he hit the bull as it continued to gallop towards him, clods of earth flying from its sharp hooves. There were three more shots from Dark and the animal, seeming to pause in mid stride, bellowed loudly and crashed onto its knees, ploughing a dark notch in the sand. Its head thrust forwards, then fell to one side, blood streaming from its nostrils. The harem of cows bawled in fear and fled to join the mules at the riverbank. The Apache nodded his thanks to Dark.

Like all warriors, Lobo and his riders were curious as to how the rifles used by the two mule-herders fired so quickly; they advanced slowly and, because of the new guns, respectfully – using hand sign to indicate their peaceful intent. They shouted to ensure that the riflemen knew they were approaching through the dust.

See the Dark turned in the saddle and saw the approaching riders:

"Brother – we have visitors!"

Viajero had heard them too and swung his rifle up into the aim again; they may not turn out to be enemies but he never took any chances.

Lobo and his warriors stopped short in the bush when they saw the gun pointed at them: he signed 'peace' again and called out who they were:

"*Na-ishan-dina!*". He used their own term for themselves as Kiowa-Apache.

Suddenly, See the Dark laughed – his own mother, Badlands Walking Woman, had been one of their people! She had often spoken in their tongue to him when he was younger and still said she was of the *Na-ishan-dina* when she quarrelled with her husband. Unbeknown to Smoke on the Moon, she had secretly taught Dark some words of her own Kiowa-Apache language, saying it may be useful one day. Dark smiled – his mother, like all mothers, was always right…

Dark waved the riders to come forward, though the Traveller glared at him and kept his rifle in the aim. The young Cheyenne then gave his own sign of the Cut Finger or Medicine Arrow. Lobo nodded and grinned - the Cheyenne were known to them. His warriors, though still unsettled by the presence of an aimed rifle, hung their weapons around their backs. None had a gun.

Lobo looked at Viajero's face and headdress – or as much as he could see behind the muzzle of the rifle barrel – and thought he might be a man of the N'De people; his own mother had been Mescalero Apache and the rifleman looked similar. He tried his limited vocabulary.

Viajero lowered his rifle, surprised to hear a mangling of the Mescalero tongue come from a Kiowa-Apache. His own woman, Bright Antelope, was of the Mescalero people and they each had to get used to the other's language when they had first met.

The short stranger then resorted to hand sign:

"Friend. Peace. We help gather mules…"

The Traveller watched as two riders went galloping to the riverbank to round up their stock. They did this with much less trouble than either he or Dark had managed; he nodded his thanks.

Dark signed and told them of his mother's links to their people; the riders bobbed up and down in the saddle, smiling.

Lobo signed:

"Good guns. Fire many times. Look?"

He held out his hand to Viajero to receive the rifle. The Apache scowled, shook his head and aimed the rifle again. Lobo looked disappointed but noted the small metal cases lying on the ground near the ponies of the N'De and Cheyenne; these must belong to the guns. He said nothing.

Dark then signed:

"Take one mule – gift. Friends."

Viajero, still holding his rifle ready, nodded.

Lobo signed:

"One each man?"

Viajero cocked the hammer on the rifle and brought up the barrel further:

"No!"

He instantly regretted missing the chance to unload more of the animals that he loathed.

Lobo shrugged and backed up his pony. He spoke to one of his warriors and told him to cut out a good mule from the small herd and bring it with them. They watched as the Cheyenne and the N'De riders drove off the remaining mules and headed north.

The three other warriors, now focused on bringing home some meat, trotted off after the range cows at the riverbank. Lobo dismounted and draped a rawhide rope around the mule's neck. He also picked up the metal cases, shaking them free of dust. He would like to have one of the new rifles but he could possibly make a good necklace out of the metal tubes; he put them into his saddle pouch.

Screams from a wounded cow drifted up from the river as his warriors shot arrows into it; the meat would be welcomed back at the camp they shared with the Kiowa.

Lobo grimaced at the thought of going back – his people lived with the Kiowa out of necessity; they were too small and weak a band to exist by themselves on the great grasslands – but it was still demeaning to be beholden to another man. None of his people actually spoke the Kiowa tongue – they had to make do with hand sign. But he told himself as he remounted, for once, his war party had something to offer – meat, a mule and information.

---- o o o ----

Chapter Five

"Any mail for me?" asked the wolf skinner, cradling his Sharps carbine in the crook of his left arm. He felt an odd tingle of pleasure at speaking his own language for the first time in many months; living with the Cheyenne and speaking their lingo all the time was hard work.

He wiped his grimy right hand down the side of his buckskin shirt. It wouldn't do to get any letter dirty. He had come to Bent's New Fort on the Arkansas River to sell his wolf pelts and buffalo robes; he hoped too that his friend Henry Armstrong may actually have got around to writing at last.

"Name?"

The half-breed behind the trading post counter was fat and surly and blew wet snot out of his nostrils into his hand, wiping his palm on the counter.

The wolf skinner bristled with annoyance; he was tempted to smash the stock of his Sharps into the man's face to teach him better manners. But, breathing out calmly, he refrained – bloodstains on paper didn't look good:

"Carver - Pythagoras Carver," he said.

Baptiste Clauville sneered at the trapper's unusual first name while spreading four letters out on the counter and began to pick them up one by one, screwing up his eyes as he tried to make sense of the writing. He made sure that Carver could see the white man's scalp that dangled from a beaded band around his left arm as he shuffled the letters.

"It is unusual, no?" Clauville asked, his slight French accent betraying his ancestry and annoying Carver even more. The breed liked to take every opportunity to talk down to the likes of mere trappers; he might even short change him on his wolf skins too.

"How'd you mean?" growled the wolf skinner, with more than a hint of menace – the Frenchy was treading on dangerous ground.

"That someone like you – a common pelt trader – would ever *get* a letter…" the breed paused slightly "…let alone be able to read it as well." Clauville smirked and shrugged.

Carver looked at the breed with contempt – he had seen the beadwork on the armband and knew the tribe.

"I can read, write and I got my numbers, you Crow shit digger. And don't wipe your nose on my mail or I'll hang your scalp on my belt."

Clauville's supercilious smile faded and he started to claw at the letters on the table. Carver saw that the man's hands were caked with blood and brown earth – he must have been skinning a rabbit out back before he came in. Carver reached across the counter and pushed Clauville backwards so he staggered into shelves of canned goods. Tins clunked onto the floorboards.

The wolf skinner grabbed the folded and sealed papers and looked at each one, smiling when he recognised the coloured stamp with Queen Victoria's head on it and noting that Henry's handwriting was as bad as ever. He flung the remaining packets back on the counter:

"I've killed many of you buffalo stealers in the past – we Cheyenne consider you only as poor sport. None of you died well."

Carver said this in a mix of English and Crow so the message struck home. The breed's hand went to his knife but, noting that the trapper had cocked the Sharps, he just spat on the floor.

The wolf skinner let the hammer down slowly on the percussion cap in the rifle and went outside to read the letter, sitting on a pile of logs by the door.

He hadn't got past the second sentence of Henry's scrawl when, after a sigh of frustration and unfinished business, he stood up again and walked back into the trading cabin.

Clauville was bent over, picking up some of the tins that had fallen from the shelves; he stood up and drew his knife when he heard the floorboards creak. Without pausing in his stride, Carver walked up to him and crashed the iron butt plate of the Sharps into the breed's nose.

"Don't sass me again, you goddam gut eater," he said as he walked out into the sunlight.

---- o o o ----

Henry Armstrong's handwriting was hard to read – Carver's penmanship was much clearer - at least in his own opinion. Once, after they'd first gone to live in the Cheyenne village, Henry had written down his address in England and handed it to the wolf skinner. The Englishman had been surprised that Carver could read and write – many of the farmworkers on his father's estate back in Cumberland still hadn't mastered the art of it. He had been even more taken aback when Carver hooted at his poor writing:

"Jesus Lootenant! I'd kinda expected better from an educated man. It looks like a piss trail from a dyin' coyote"

Today, the wolf skinner tilted the page to catch the best light and decipher Henry's scrawl. It took a while but Carver absorbed the main points:

Father dead…estate to settle…mother taking over running land and tenants … Successful lecture tour speaking about his experiences living with Indians…asked to write a book…. illustrate with own drawings…

Carver laughed out loud at this – Henry had initially bluffed his way into the Cheyenne camp by sketching many of them in his journal; sadly, despite the different modes of dress and hairstyles, the faces of the portrait sitters all looked the same. Carver had asked if his art tutor was the same as his writing teacher.

...Bored at home ...current war in America...recrossing the Atlantic as soon as he could raise the money...join the cavalry and find glory...

The wolf skinner sat bolt upright – what the Hell was the boy thinking? Sure, Henry had been a good soldier – he had ridden with the US Dragoons under Harney against the Sioux in '55 and with Sumner against the Cheyenne on the south fork of the Solomon back in '57; they had met just after that battle and been friends ever since.

Indian-fighting was one thing but riding with Robert E. Lee or Sherman was another – Carver had no idea if Henry favoured the Union or the Confederacy and didn't really care. He had read newspaper accounts of the battles since 1861 – either from occasional passing pioneers on the Platte River wagon road or at trading posts where the mail came in. The killing made no sense – he couldn't imagine a war where close-packed ranks of infantry would charge into the blazing rifle muzzles of the other side; the cavalry didn't seem to have it any easier either. He shook his head and read on:

...combine war stories with Indian tales and write a book that would make them both rich...

Carver grunted with laughter. Henry had never been greedy or selfish – despite differences in their upbringings, they had been friends and brothers-in-arms.

Henry had never called Carver 'Pythagoras' and Carver preferred his friend's old rank of 'Lootenant' rather than 'Henry'. They had fought alongside the Cheyenne against the

Pawnee and Crow and had tried to steer the small band of Suhtai when dealing with incoming white men. Henry was well-respected in the tribe – he had come close to staying permanently with them when he'd bedded the widow of a dead warrior. But Carver was the one who'd stayed and married a Suhtai woman while Henry journeyed home some four years ago.

The wolf skinner was lost in idle thought when he remembered how long mail took to get from England. He checked the letter, squinting at the distorted scrawl of the last sentence:

...and finally, dear friend, sincere Christmas Greetings and may you have a prosperous New Year in 1864...

Jesus! That was over eight months ago – the boy could be here already or, worse, dead on some godforsaken battlefield. He turned the letter over – there hurriedly scribbled and at a sideways tilt to the rest of the letter was a postscript:

I've also taken a liking to doggerel to while away the boring hours...

Doggerel? Carver had no idea what Henry was talking about, the Englishman didn't really like dogs:

...so, I penned this after reading a newspaper article about a bartender shot dead for diluting his whisky:

Here lies Ernie Boone
Watered drinks in his saloon
Got six full rounds
From a Colt Dragoon

Good, don't you think?

Carver chuckled at the dumb verse – he'd be glad to see Henry again; the man was a mixture of education and foolishness. He missed that.

He folded up the letter and carefully slid it into a small oilskin packet to keep it dry. His wife, New Grass, had made it from an old waterproof coat that he had found abandoned on the wagon road. She had decorated it with pretty beadwork and though she couldn't decipher the written word on the papers inside, she accepted that her husband could exchange the contents of his heart with another without their enemies hearing them. New Grass had said she wished the Cheyenne had something similar.

Carver stood up and slung the Sharps across his shoulder and walked across to his horse and mule tethered behind the trading shed. He opened and checked his saddle bags to make sure he had all the correct goods in exchange for his wolfskins – powder, ball, percussion caps, hard candy, a swatch of pretty cloth and tobacco– it was all there. He saw the breed watching him from the back door, a bloody rag clutched to his nose, and remembered he had one thing left to do.

The wolfskinner walked up to the stoop and asked for a piece of paper; the breed was reluctant to help but a push from the muzzle of the Sharps persuaded him to co-operate. He and Henry had agreed that Bent's New Fort would be the place that they would both visit and collect any messages; they would rendezvous there if Henry ever came back.

Carver took the paper from the breed and, reaching out with one hand, took out the pencil from behind Clauville's ear. His note to Henry was short:

'Lt: I was here late summer of 64. Us folk will be camped up and around the Smoky Hill River for the winter. Wait until spring if snow too bad. PS – BNF is now called Fort Lion. PC'

He was smiling as he remembered Henry's childish poem which had cleverly included a firearm in it – a thing they both liked. He racked his brain to think of a suitable reply – the two of them always were competitive about the smallest things. Carver chewed on the pencil and wrote out some test lines on the board of the trading post counter. Clauville bristled but said nothing. Eventually the wolf skinner slapped the counter, pulled the sheet of paper and wrote:

Here lies George Carew,
Shot to death with a twenty-two
Poor George
Boo Hoo

Frontier poetry, By God! He folded the paper four times, putting it inside a small deerskin pouch that he kept in his possibles bag and pinned it shut with a sliver of elk bone, handing it to Clauville:

"This here's a letter for my friend – another white man – English, called Henry Armstrong. You lose it and I'll gut you like a pig."

Clauville was taken aback, not by the threat but because he recognised Henry's name:

"*Henri* Armstrong? I scouted for a man with such a name back in '55 – would that be him?" Clauville remembered a skinny but determined *Anglais* Dragoons officer who had ridden his troop hard down from Leavenworth to investigate the killing of a local trader all those years ago. Not him surely?

Carver was not inclined to discuss personal business with a half breed and, besides, he had other things to do. He turned round as he walked to the door:

"Just don't lose that goddam pouch Frenchy, 'less you wanna be twenty pounds lighter."

Carver was about to mount up and leave when he saw the procession below in the adjacent military post. He walked over to the edge of the compound. A line of ragged Indians was leaving the fort – some riding, some walking – a band was playing - some notes floated up on the wind - and the Indian leader leant down from the saddle and shook hands with a couple of the bluecoat officers.

He jumped as a voice spoke behind him:

"That's ol' Black Kettle, the peace chief of the Southern Cheyenne…"

Carver looked round quickly and saw a bluecoat cavalry sergeant standing behind him; Carver exhaled and shook his head. He was disappointed that a booted and spurred white man could approach from behind without him knowing.

"Jeezuz Sarge, you spooked me there. What's the Injuns doin' here at the post?" Carver thought it best to maintain ignorance about his own Cheyenne links.

"Well, at least a couple of those red devils have come to their senses – Black Kettle's just off to his own private reservation with some Arapaho…" The NCO took out a leather-covered hip flask and took a swig.

"They've been murdering white settlers and stealing stock for months now…it's a shame they'll get away with it."

Carver nodded silently. It was true there had been trouble along the Platte and the Santa Fe Trail and some Cheyenne had indeed been involved.

He recognised Black Kettle's name and whistled through his teeth – he was the leader of the *Wutapiu* band of the Cheyenne. Not a man well-liked by the rest of the People; three years previously he had sought peace with the white man and had signed a treaty that gave away Cheyenne hunting lands without authority or agreement from the Great Council. The rest of the tribal bands had disowned him; only cowards or the insane spoke to the whites.

Carver, though, had been pleased when he'd heard about the peace talks – it just might mean that he would never have to fight against white soldiers. That would be a difficult choice for him. After two Cheyenne wives in this life and living amongst the Suhtai, there was no telling where his loyalties might lie if it ever came to pulling a trigger.

"Where's the reservation they're goin' to? Looks like they're headin' to the Smoky Hill River country."

"No…" said the sergeant, tipping the flask to his lips again,

"…it's about forty miles away – up on Sand Creek"

Carver shrugged; he'd never heard of it.

---- o o o ----

Chapter Six

Pythagoras Carver walked across the lodge circle to the council fire; he had news.

Children clustered around him as though he was still a novelty, despite living amongst them for over five years.

"*Kah-vuh, Kah-vuh*" chanted the younger ones, pleased to be speaking their version of a foreign name as they held onto his fingertips. Carver, smiled indulgently, nodded and told them to settle down – the Suhtai men were going to speak of important things.

He looked nervously over his shoulder. Even though he had married a Cheyenne woman and had lived as one of them, he always felt uneasy leaving his rifles unattended in his tipi when he came out like this. It wasn't that he didn't trust the Cheyenne – after all, they had welcomed him and Henry Armstrong, into the camp after they helped defeat a Crow attack. It was just a deep, inbred suspicion that, as a white man, he shouldn't be so careless when he was not amongst his own kind. He could still never bring himself to hand a loaded gun to an Indian. Of course, some of the whites he'd met back in Independence and up on the Platte River Road also fell into that category.

"Kah-vuh! Are you going to the council?" It was a woman's voice, urgent out of the darkness by an unlit lodge and he walked over. It was Sweet Water, his sister-in-law.

"Yes," he said and wondered what she wanted; he waited for her to speak as her face caught the moonlight. She was a handsome young woman – Henry had been keen on her and lain with her when he had been here – but she was also one of the troublesome women warriors now. He tried to avoid being seen with her. He wondered where the Hell his friend Henry was now – despite the jostle with the Frenchy up at Fort Lyon, he missed speaking English.

"Our war leader will also be there," said Sweet Water, her eyes shining in the half light. "The first time we have been invited to the council fire…"

"I know," said Carver. "I asked for all war leaders to be there as well as our elders – I have news."

"Thank you" said the woman, resting her hand on his arm as she looked up at him. "Thank you for including the Forked Lightning Women – no-one else would have thought of it."

Carver smiled, patted her hand and walked away; he omitted to tell her that he'd only included the women soldiers because his wife had insisted on it. Her family ties were strong, especially with her sister – going along with some of her wishes made for an easier life.

A column of sparks rose into the sky outside the lodge of Bad Elk as someone pushed more wood into the fire; Carver could see figures hurrying towards it and quickened his step.

He took his place in the small circle of gathered Cheyenne and sat down, the firelight washing their faces in yellow and red light. Sparks flew into the blackness like fireflies. There was some joking, though it was subdued – no-one knew if Kah-vuh, brought good or bad news.

Bad Elk stood when all had assembled; he wiped the grease from his recently-finished supper from his lips and belched slightly. This was not a time for great oratory just a need to get Kah-vuh's news and perhaps make some decisions.

"Friends, our *veho* brother Kah-vuh brings some news from his people down on the Flint Arrowpoint River."

As always when Bad Elk spoke, the loudness of his voice startled them. His deafness was getting worse.

The Suhtai chief looked around the circle to see contented nodding though White Rain Woman, the Forked Lightning leader just waited silently. Bad Elk noted that she had forgotten to take off her pistol belt – a council of friends was no place for weapons. He grunted and sat down.

In the darkness, Carver grimaced slightly at still being referred to as a white man and the Arkansas River traders being considered 'his people' but took it in good part; he would always be an outsider. Bad Elk had not laid on any food to accompany his news nor had he produced a pipe to ensure truth was spoken but that was the chief's privilege. The white trapper shrugged and stood up.

"My brothers…" he began, before rapidly adding "…and sister," when he remembered the unusual presence of White Rain Woman.

"…when I was at the white trader fort, I was given a message from our other veho friend - Henry…"

There was much smiling and nodding as Henry's name was mentioned. Like Carver's, they recognised the English sound of his name.

Smoke on the Moon, the leader of the Striking Snakes soldier society was first to speak:

"Was *Hen-ree* at the fort – is he coming back to visit us?"

Carver shook his head, took out the letter and held it up for all to see.

Most of the gathering of leaders recognised what the white leaf in Kah-vuh's hand meant – they knew that white men could pass silent messages by making strange, track marks on the smooth surface. Several of the more curious ones had watched Hen-ree when he'd been in the village writing down something in his journal; they had been interested in the form that their words took when they appeared on paper.

"Hen-ree sends greetings to his friends in the Suhtai band of the People and wants you to know that he holds the memory of you close to his heart…" continued Carver.

There were genuine howls of joy from the small crowd – Hen-ree was a good man who had fought alongside them and helped keep cooking pots full in hungry times.

"…he says he is returning but doesn't know when he will get here as it is a long journey…"

There were sage nods of understanding in the firelight – Hen-ree lived far off, across a great lake that took many days to cross. Carver thought it best not to mention that Henry had said he was coming back to join the white man's war as a bluecoat soldier.

He was about to tell the gathering of his sighting of Black Kettle at Bent's Fort when they all heard shouts of joy from the edge of the camp circle. A small, bustling woman rudely swept into the gathering, sought out Smoke on the Moon and said:

"Our son and the Traveller have returned safely."

---- 0 0 0 ----

Chapter Seven

Viajero held up one of the bullets from the Henry rifles; the surrounding crowd looked on curiously. They had never seen one before – they recognised the lead ball in the top part but were mystified by the metal case under it. The Apache called it *'cartucho'*- the name the Mexicans had used. The crowd ignored the word– many couldn't understand him when he spoke Cheyenne, let alone a foreign tongue.

"It looks small…" said Broken Knife, the war leader of the Suhtai's Thunder Bears soldier society, "…can it kill?"

Viajero opened his mouth to speak but See the Dark took over the explanation:

"Yes, it kills…" and, though he had only seen it fired across a narrow valley floor as Kiowa arrows had hit the wagons of the riflemen, "…it flies over the distance of a well-shot arrow…"

"Possibly not one of yours then, my son…" Smoke on the Moon was never one to shrink from affectionate banter with his boy. There were hoots of appreciative laughter.

Dark took it in good part; he was used to it by now:

"Father, these guns mean that bows and arrows will become useless; this *'cartucho'* can be fired one after the other, faster than you can click your fingers."

The idea of a rifle carrying many, ready-to-fire cartridges in a tube under the barrel had been shocking to Viajero and Dark when the Mexicans had explained it. Even more puzzling had been the rifle's ability to fire one ball, eject the empty copper case and lever another into the breech in a single downward motion of the iron loop under the body of the gun. The whites were well named as *'veho'* – the word actually meant 'spider' but it also indicated a creature that was inventive and tricky.

The crowd suddenly became interested as the rifle's potential in battle struck them – many shots in a short period of time could kill many enemies. The soldier societies, children and some old men clamoured for a demonstration of its power.

Viajero now stepped back into the circle and held up his rifle; he and Dark had agreed to show what the rifle could do but they wouldn't waste ammunition, despite finding four boxes of it on the Mexican wagons. There would be only one demonstration.

Each man took five rounds from their separate wooden boxes and Dark handed his to the Apache.

Men moved around so they could get a better view as Viajero showed how to put ten bullets into the tube under the barrel. Warriors from the soldier societies, came up close to see how the gun worked. There was a buzz of anticipation, noisy children were silenced and all looked on.

The rifle was loaded in the blink of an eye – those Suhtai who already had guns gaped in disbelief. Broken Knife looked on quizzically - usually, it took a while to pour powder down the barrel, ram home a lead ball, then put a small copper percussion cap onto the nipple on the other end of the barrel. It was a difficult thing to accomplish when on foot – even more difficult in the saddle or during a battle. It was why he and many experienced warriors still preferred the bow – they could fire six well-aimed arrows whilst this was being done.

See the Dark now walked to one part of the circle and cleared people away from a live oak tree that folk usually sat under for shade. As the chattering line moved away, Crow Dress Woman, one of the Forked Lightning women warriors, dragged a reluctant, rangy dog to the tree and tried to tie it there.

It was a sweaty business as the dog refused to stand still – the crowd started to titter in embarrassment. Eventually a slim young girl called Star strode out to help her. Star had started to follow Crow Dress around after the raid on the Comanche and, though she was probably only fifteen summers or so in age, she was keen to join the women warriors. Star fastened the final knot as Crow Dress announced:

"It's a Crow dog…it followed us back with the stock we stole on our raid."

The male warriors looked at her in exasperation; this was not the time for idle boasting. Crow Dress, however, was unperturbed and with her hand on Star's shoulder, strode past Viajero to watch the demonstration.

The Apache picked up the rifle and threw it to See the Dark. The young Cheyenne would have the honour of showing his people this new gun.

Holding the gun vertically so all could see what he was doing, Dark cocked the lever under the gun and brought it up into the aim. Here, his lack of one eye didn't matter – his right eye automatically took in the sight picture of the rifle and he squeezed the trigger. Cranking the lever four more times, bullets flew and the dog, despite being over eighty paces away, went down in a welter of blood and yelping.

Dramatically – for See the Dark always loved attention – he called the Traveller's name, threw him the rifle and the Apache did the same thing – firing his five bullets into the inert shape of the unfortunate hound. Both walked forward to count the bullet holes in the dog's carcass. There were only nine. The Apache stood back and said solemnly:

"Perhaps it's not just the bow that you can't aim properly!"

Dark just grinned and reminded him that old men's eyesight, just like their sexual power, faded before that of younger warriors.

Meanwhile, the crowd went wild and yelled with joy – this was a white man's tool that would change battlefields for ever.

Women sang and swayed with pride that one of their own – oh, and not forgetting the Traveller – had been the bringers of great power to the Suhtai. Badlands Walking Woman – Dark's mother – sang her song to her clever son in her own high yip.

Bad Elk strode into the circle of happy, chattering villagers:

"Our two brave warriors have brought us guns that we can load when the grass is new and shoot until the snow falls…"

He was about to continue – though, those used to his oratory were moving out of range of his loud voice – when his wife shushed him and suggested they all eat.

Viajero caught the eye of Bright Antelope who stood with their daughter on the outer edge of the disintegrating circle. His daughter was smiling and clapping her hands in glee – she was proud of her father.

He was still nodding to his family when Dark walked up with the shattered body of the dog in his hand, its bloody muzzle leaving a bright red trail in the dust; grinning, he handed the skinny rear leg to the Apache:

"You'll be hungry," he said.

---- 0 0 0 ----

Chapter Eight

The Forked Lightning Women sat inside their lodge for their own small council and White Rain Woman looked around at her decreasing number of followers.

Outside the lodge, tending to an iron pot on the cooking fire, Star stirred the blackening meat. The lodge door was pinned open and eventually she took the pot from the flames and carried it into the lodge of the warrior women and placed it in the centre of the small gathering. She left the main lodge but sat cross-legged outside the door.

White Rain sighed and jabbed an arrow into the dirt floor, within arm's reach of them all, and, as leader, opened the talks, touching the arrow as their tradition required for each speaker:

"Sisters, there is food in the pot, eat now if you wish…"

Crow Dress Woman looked doubtfully into the small iron stewpot and took out an unrecognisable piece of meat and began to chew it, mainly out of politeness. She faced the door and called out:

"Little sister, do you want to eat?"

Star, perhaps wisely, shook her head. White Rain Woman's preparation of food was known to be poor – even her man, See the Dark, ate at his parent's tipi to avoid it.

Willow declined to eat too, as did Sweet Water – both mumbling an excuse that they would eat later. Blue Wing though, brought out her own wooden bowl and happily scooped the contents of the pot into it, tearing into the unnamed meat with relish.

"…we are only five in number now," continued White Rain, "…our sister, Looks Above, has decided to marry the young man who courts her under the blanket – she told me last night."

"She was too young to be one of our soldiers anyway," snorted Willow, though without the formality of touching the arrow.

Outside the lodge, Star leaned forward so she could be seen and coughed politely so that she could be heard; she was unable to speak however as she was not a member of the society, though she dearly wanted to be. The Forked Lightning Women ignored her.

Crow Dress Woman now leaned forward and touched the arrow:

"No…" she said "…she is just as old as Mouse was when she was killed; And Mouse was a great warrior."

As ever, when Mouse's name was mentioned, the three original Forked Lightning Women – White Rain, Crow Dress and Willow – all paused to remember their dead war sister. Tears often came as they remembered her. Mouse the song maker, joker and chubby friend to them all had indeed been a fierce warrior in the best of Cheyenne traditions. Her death on the war trail against the Comancheros and Comanches had been an unsettling time; the young woman writhing silently in agony before Maheo chose to release her from this life. But the guns that she had helped to steal on the raid had armed her sisters well and kept the small soldier society together. Now Mouse slept on a burial scaffold some way to the south; and though the women had often looked for its outline on a dimly-remembered hill, they had never seen it again and thought it may have blown down in a storm.

Sweet Water waited politely while the others' thoughts touched on their dead sister; Mouse had never liked her and when she'd tried earlier to join the Forked Lightning Women, Mouse had refused to ride with her.

Blue Wing belched noisily and put down her bowl. Sweet Water then reached forward to touch the arrow and looked at White Rain:

"Did you talk to Bad Elk about our next raid?" she asked.

"I did…" replied White Rain, "…but he didn't like the idea of it and has agreed with Smoke on the Moon and Broken Knife that none of their warriors can join us."

"We don't need them…" snorted Willow, "…we just need to find that Crow village again, find our Cheyenne relative there and bring him or her back."

Even as Willow spoke the words, the tricky nature of the task fell upon them all:

"It's a pity that Looks Above won't be with us – she would be good at finding the trail of the Crow and following it," said Sweet Water.

"She would also bring her guns – we'll need as many rifles and pistols as we can get if we get into a battle with the Crow," said Crow Dress; she held up Looks Above's weapons – left behind when she'd quit the society. The revolver and rifle with the five-bullet chamber looked rusty and uncared for. They would need to be cleaned before being used again. She would entrust that task to Star while they were away.

Blue Wing took out her bowl, re-filled it from the pot and listened to the dispiriting chatter as the problems seemed to mount – the Crow village would have moved by now – where to? They didn't know if they were looking for a man or a woman, someone old or young? The Moon of the Falling Leaves was close and it may be too late to go on a raid. There would be no forage for their ponies if they had to journey far…

Impatiently, Blue Wing burped and burst into song:

Don't try to hide
In the far-off mountains
Don't try to hide
On the seas of grass

We Forked Lightning Women
Will find you
And feed your flesh
To our eagles

The rest of the women stopped chattering and laughed – they had forgotten Blue Wing's talent for composing songs – just as Mouse the song maker had done. Blue Wing hadn't sung any new songs on their last raid against the Crow as it had been her first time in action and she had been shy. She belched again and White Rain smiled as she pulled the arrow out of the earth:

"Tomorrow – we ride tomorrow."

---- o o o ----

Chapter Nine

"We don't need any help from a goddam Englishman!" snarled the cavalry officer, stubbing out his cheroot on his boot heel resting on his knee. He spun the spur rowel on its pivot to hear it jangle.

"But Captain…" said Henry Armstrong, "…I've already ridden with American cavalry – with the 2nd Dragoons against the Sioux at Blue Water in '55 and with the 1st Cavalry against the Cheyenne in '57; I believe I acquitted myself well…"

"The First Cavalry? Most of those bastards were from the south and they joined the Confederates first chance they got; that asshole Jeb Stuart was one of 'em until Phil Sheridan settled his hash at Yellow Tavern 'bout four months ago."

Henry tried not to look shocked; he and Jeb Stuart, the languid Virginian, had been friends during the campaign against the Cheyenne. It had been a hard slog across Cheyenne country with few results to show in the end. The nine dead Indians after a rout on the Solomon River had seemed little compensation for the soldiers' hardships – Stuart himself had been badly wounded when they had broken the Cheyenne charge. And now his friend was dead.

"Still, you can always go and join the Rebs…" smirked the captain, "…'course, if we catch you crossing into their lines, we'll hang you as a spy."

Henry kept his temper as he sat and stared at the recruiter; this was not a good start to his new book of adventures – it would be hard to find glory if he couldn't even get into their damn Army. The hoped-for riches from prospective book sales dwindled into the distance.

He'd hit the same brick wall in New York as soon as he'd landed – no-one wanted to take on a foreigner at this point in the war. They were polite to him, of course, and explained if he'd come as a representative of the British government or even of his old regiment, he could join the Army of the Potomac as an observer. But fighting alongside or leading American troops was out of the question.

Henry's family links on the Army staff - who had helped him transfer temporarily from his English regiment directly into the US Army back in '54 - were of no help now. One suggested that he could try to head west - the war, he said, was more 'fluid' out there, though there were no guarantees. It had taken three weeks to travel from New York down to Fort Leavenworth – it may have been in vain.

Henry tried a new tack:

"What about your – er- irregular units? Militia, Volunteers or something – wouldn't they take any professional help they could get?"

Unexpectedly, the recruiter didn't dismiss it out of hand but ran his fingers through his long hair, sat back in his creaking chair and spoke to the ceiling:

"Those butternuts – the Confederates - are done Lootenant – you *are* a Lootenant right?"

"Well, I'm retired, sir - late of Her Majesty's Light Dragoons."

The captain thought the term 'Light Dragoons' sounded weak but kept it to himself.

"…the war is winding down Lootenant – the Union has the industrial muscle and numbers of men to grind the Rebs back into the Stone Age where they belong – this year or next, it don't matter – we'll win. Why do you want to join somebody else's fight?"

Henry sat up – he had rehearsed this part of the interview and prepared some of his answers on board ship as they had crawled across the Atlantic from Liverpool:

"Well, I abhor slavery, of course and feel that…"

"Jesus Christ Lootenant! There's not a man in the whole Union Army that gives a mule's fart about slavery – this is about our country, sir – our country!" the officer's voice raised in pitch as his anger broke loose. He stood up and continued, pointing his finger hard at Henry:

"…the Rebs want to split us in two – to make us two countries. To take the hard work and blood that *all* of us - all of us, mark you - put in takin' America back from the British – no offence intended Lootenant – and just ink in the Mason-Dixon line on a map so's to have their own damn turf with their mint juleps, cotton crops, black field hands and puppy-eyed southern belles – nah, to Hell with that!"

Henry was startled at the captain's tone – there was none of the dutiful emotion about denouncing slavery that he'd heard back home. He'd discussed the topic and the war in America with his cousin Langton, a politician, in his London club over claret and mutton chops. Langton had been evasive about his own support of the anti-slavery argument, instead, citing the economic benefits of southern states' cotton to Lancashire's biggest industry. Henry remembered snorting in disgust at his cousin's slimy tone and shiftiness as he left the club, his clothes reeking of cigar smoke and cooking fat.

A chair scraped across the floorboards and Henry watched as the captain got up and limped over to a tray with a glass decanter on it. The recruiter poured a stiff shot but didn't offer any to Henry. Then, as if remembering something, he stumped back to his desk and riffled through several documents before taking one out and reading it:

"Volunteers, you said? The Third Colorado are recruiting men for a 100-day enlistment – you could try them."

Henry perked up and smiled:

"Excellent sir! Are they here in Leavenworth?"
The captain snorted whisky down his nose with laughter:

"Nah, Lootenant, - you'll need to get to Denver!"

Henry's face fell – he'd never make it; Denver was hundreds of miles away. The Army officer saw that Henry's disappointment was genuine and took a different tack:

"Jesus Lootenant – you're awful keen to get yourself killed! What the Hell's wrong with you? Most of us in this war just want to go home. I lost my left leg with Custer's 1st Michigan, just outside of Gettysburg. As far as I'm concerned, I don't want to spread any other bits of me around this country."

Custer? Henry dimly remembered meeting a podgy youth with the same odd name at West Point when he was giving a lecture there after the Solomon Battle in '57 – he wondered if this was the same man.

The captain watched for a response from the Englishman but he could see he was deep in thought, trying to calculate how to get to Denver. He had one last idea:

"I'll try and send a telegraph message to Fort Lyon and see if they'll let you join the Third. There's a supply train setting out for there soon – you can ride with them but I'm not sure you'll get there in time."

Henry shot to his feet and shook the startled captain's hand, thanking him profusely. The captain backed away as Henry put on his old cavalry campaign hat and opened the door to leave:

"…and Lootenant? There's been Indian trouble out West; the Third won't be fightin' the Rebs – they'll be goin' after the Cheyenne."

---- o o o ----

Chapter Ten

See the Dark and Viajero watched as the Forked Lightning Women rode out of the encampment and headed north to find the Crow village they had raided and free the captive Cheyenne.

"They are taking a foolish trail…" said Viajero, "… they look for a village that has moved, to find a man or a woman they don't know."

See the Dark nodded glumly; he had spent the previous night in the lodge he shared with White Rain Woman and had found little comfort there. White Rain had been excited about her expedition into the mountains to find the Crow village – her warriors knew the place that the village *had* been and thought it should be easy to trail it to its new location. They would watch the village for a while and try to spot the captive. Dark had not been so sure, reminding her that the *Absaroka* people were watchful and Moon of the Falling Leaves was upon them, snow was possible – old tracks would be hidden and fresh tracks from the women easily discovered. She had shrugged off such difficulties.

Yellow Bear walked up behind them – he had an armful of plants for his potions – and stood with them:

"They asked me to bless them on their war trail," he said, scratching his skin as one of the plants stung him.

"And did you?" asked the Apache.

"I thought about refusing, but Maheo, our Life Giver, doesn't make any distinction between men or women – they are Cheyenne warriors - even if that is only in their own minds. So, I called on the *Maheyuno*, the spirit helpers, to keep them safe."

"My own God, *Usen*, would not be so generous…" replied Viajero, "…he protects the men and the men protect the women – it's simple."

The three men stood in silence as the five riders disappeared into the trees and headed towards the mountains.

There was a chill in the air and solitary leaves floated down on the breeze; Yellow Bear walked back to his lodge to prepare the potions. He had a good reputation both as a healer and a man who could select the right herbs and natural extracts to allow good things to happen. He had been given a fine wolf robe by one aspiring young warrior to make a love potion to aid his courtship of the girl, Star. So far, the youth's efforts with the eagle bone flute and blanket had been disappointing – Star had made it clear that she had ambitions other than marriage or children. The young man, however, aided by the persistence of youth and blinded by lust, wanted some sweet-scented smoke to create the right atmosphere when next he called at her family's lodge. Yellow Bear was keen to see if his plant choice worked and crawled under the tipi flap to begin his task; he sang a childhood song about nesting birds that his mother had taught him.

See the Dark pulled up his bear robe around his shoulders and walked over to his tipi; ducking inside he brought out his backrest of willow saplings and sat outside the door watching the vanishing riders. Viajero joined him, pulling a puma robe over his head.

"At least they are well-armed," said the Traveller.

"They'll need to be if they get into a fight with the Crow…" said Dark.

It was of little consolation to Dark that the Forked Lightning Women were the best armed warrior society in the Suhtai camp – each woman carried a revolver pistol and a repeating rifle with a similar revolving chamber, spoils of war for their part in the raid against the Comanche and their traders. The men in the Striking Snakes and Thunder Bears soldier societies had many less guns – it rankled then and it rankled now. When the women had returned from the raid, they had offered the spare rifles to those other societies to ease any hurt – whilst the warriors had taken them, it had mainly been with ill-grace. Masculine pride had taken a beating that day.

The Apache took out a pipe and checked the inside of the bowl, blowing through the stem to clear any obstructions. It wasn't a traditional Cheyenne or N'De pipe – it was of smooth, textured wood, curved, with a silver lid on the bowl; he had taken it from a white man he'd killed many moons ago. He sliced off some of the tobacco that he and Dark had looted from the Mexican wagon, stuffed it under the silver lid and lit the mixture. Dark had tried the veho smoking tobacco once and didn't care for it, mainly as it brought tears to his good eye and almost blinded him.

The two men sat in silence, each content to be in the company of the other. Dark said:

"Do you think those two Mexicans ever got home?"

"Who knows?" said Viajero "…we gave them a mule each and the fat one got his scalp back."

Both warriors chuckled, surprised at their own lenience that day. The fat Mexican had been far more scared than the younger one and had mounted his mule, clutching the drying circle of skin, blood and hair to his chest – he'd made wheezing, breathless sounds out of fear. Unfortunately, the mules that Dark and Viajero had left them were only used to a wagon harness and not men sitting on their backs – they'd brayed and bucked for a while as the warriors had looked on with amusement. The Mexicans eventually stayed afoot and led their mules away, southwest towards home.

The Traveller blew blue smoke into the air and enjoyed the calm that it brought; he'd looted many packs of cigars, cheroots and twists of tobacco from the wagons before they'd set them alight; he'd shared the spoils with the men of the camp when he'd returned. He'd been strict about one thing though – the whisky would be destroyed with the wagons – he had tried the drink once when he was a younger warrior and it had toppled him; it was dangerous to bring to camp. Dark had never tasted much of it but sipped a small sample as part of his share of the war prizes – he too spat it out when it burned his tongue, throat and belly. The spirits had exploded in the flames.

"At least our new rifles have extra ammunition..." said Dark, "...we may need it if those women bring the Crow back down on our village."

Viajero was surprised at his tone of distaste – White Rain was the woman that the young Cheyenne warrior slept with; perhaps all was not well in their lodge? He kept his own counsel.

Without any further prompting, Dark said:

"It's why we can't marry – both of us are warriors, she is not willing to give up the war trail and nor am I."

Viajero kept silent again. He and Yellow Bear had often talked about the difficulties of having women making their own trails in life; Yellow Bear was against it - without women bringing children into this world, tribal bands like theirs just got smaller and weaker - but the Apache was undecided. His own woman, Bright Antelope, was from the Mescalero people and had decided to follow him wherever he went after they'd first met. Indeed, she had tracked him from her grandfather's wickiups in the far southwest right onto the great grasslands when Viajero was on his life's quest, after the death of his first wife. Bright Antelope was a woman who knew her own mind.

See the Dark leaned sideways from his backrest, picked up a stone and threw it at a coyote that trotted hopefully on the edge of the camp in search of food among the cast-off pile of animal bones. The animal skittered away; its grey coat highlighted against the darker tone of the treeline.

"I think our time of being as one is over - we live in the same lodge but are apart," said Dark without any emotion, he was just stating a fact. The Apache nodded – he had no interest in the domestic lives of others – but, as he'd seen others do, he patted Dark on the shoulder to show some sort of sympathy.

"Perhaps the women wouldn't go off on these crazy raids if Bad Elk gave them something real to do…like the Striking Snakes or the Thunder Bears," he said.

Dark grunted, Bad Elk was his uncle – the brother of Smoke on the Moon:

"No, Bad Elk has done what he can, he's let them ride as guards when the village moved and forgiven them for going against his advice earlier…"

Viajero nodded; this was true – the Forked Lightning Women always *sought* advice before raiding but seldom took it; getting onto the war trail was more important than any possible consequences. When he had Dark had set off against the Comancheros and Comanches, the women had followed them to the country of the Texans despite their chief warning them against it.

"…but he won't let them go to war as part of our fighting warriors, like the Snakes and the Bears, because they …" See the Dark tailed off as he sought the reason, "…because they're just women, I suppose. It's not their place."

The Traveller was unconvinced:

"They fought well when we had our revenge raid against the Pawnee all those moons ago…they ran off the horse herd. To me – if women want to fight – and have guns – then we should let them."

Dark just shrugged – after all, not all *men* were warriors – he and Viajero were not members of any soldier society; they fought shoulder to shoulder as brothers because they chose to. Some men avoided the war trail as they knew it wasn't their calling – instead they made arrows, broke horses to the saddle or were lost in their own dreams. So perhaps not all women wanted to be married and raise children. It was a troubling thought for an instinctive warrior – Yellow Bear wasn't the only traditionalist in the camp. The young Cheyenne sighed again – his strength did not lie in his ability to ponder things – his head hurt now.

He moved back into the lodge, carrying his backrest as Viajero trotted off to join Bright Antelope:

"We'll need to test our rifles in the hunt and against our enemies – let's think on that!" he shouted to the rapidly disappearing Apache.

When darkness fell and the village rim deserted, a rider set out from the camp. She had stolen away from her parents' tipi, saddled her pony without alerting the guards on the horse herd and, with Looks Above's pistol round her waist and rifle across her back, set off for the mountains. Star didn't know about the love potion concocted by Yellow Bear and, even if she had, she wouldn't have cared - the war trail had sung its seductive song.

Whether they wanted her or not, the Forked Lightning Women would be getting reinforcements.

---- o o o ----

Chapter Eleven

The turkey vultures were a good signal, whirling on the warm air currents then lumbering out of the sky on heavy, beating wings and dropping behind a shallow escarpment; something rotting and dead was in the small canyon ahead and Big Bow knew that they had found them.

Raising up in his stirrups, the leader of the Elk Band, shouted to his warriors:

"The death birds have shown us the way! Ride fast to our brothers but don't touch them!"

The Kiowas needed no further urging and surged forward. They shrieked and yelled but their tone was mournful; they just hoped to chase away any ghosts that still lingered by their dead. Etsay and his Black Leggings warriors had not returned to camp after what was supposed to be a short raid on the white man's trail so a strong search party had been sent out to look for them.

Big Bow got there first and saw the scene of slaughter – all eight of his fellow warriors lay on the canyon floor; all had been mangled and dragged around by coyotes or wolves as the scavengers had fought over this unexpected meal. Hair and bones from skulls were scattered around each man – maybe bears had been here too. Two hulks of white men's wagons had crumbled to heaps of burnt timber and metal bones – there was no sign of the animals that had pulled the wagons, nor any white drivers. But though Big Bow and his warriors couldn't see them, they all knew that ghosts lingered – they would have to be scared away. He summoned Walks Many Tracks to the front of the mounted line and asked him to see off the circling spirits.

Walks Many Tracks was an old man and he had often seen death but nothing like this. After battles or raids bodies always needed to be buried right away but here – many days had passed and the wandering ghosts of the dead warriors would be reluctant to leave. He sighed at the difficulty of the task but took some sweet grass and sage from a pouch, lit a small fire and, with great courage, walked to each corpse and tried to chase off the spirits – waving the smoking bundle over their bodies and himself. The rest of the Kiowa stayed mounted, sang a loud ghost-chasing song and just watched him.

The old man finally found what remained of Etsay and called Big Bow forward. The pipe holder rode over and dismounted, but only after Many Tracks had told him it was safe; he called on the others to bury the dead quickly and search for any sign as to who had done this. He was apprehensive - normally women would wash bodies and comb their hair of the dead but none rode with them so those rituals would have to be abandoned.

The Kiowa chief looked around. There was no ground sign, of course – the constant wind, wild animals and the Kiowas' own ponies had muddled any tracks.

Big Bow mused on what he could see on the valley floor. The wagons had belonged to white men - maybe soldiers – and Etsay may have attacked them; the remains of some Kiowa arrows were still embedded in the fire shredded timber so they seemed to be part of the battle ground. But where the white drivers and their draught animals - horses, oxen, mules? - had gone was a mystery.

At last, the bodies were all buried; Many Tracks purifying all those who had pushed the remains into their shallow scrapes. The warriors trembled with the enormity of what they had done and several began a keening song of mourning – Big Bow joined in.

Two warriors, however, who had refused to touch the bodies or enter the ghost area but had scouted out further, came back with some interesting news – under the lee of an overhanging rock, untouched by wind or weather were four sets of tracks – two were boot prints of white men and the other two were iron shod mules. They were headed south west towards the white man's fort.

Big Bow heard them out and, working out pieces of the puzzle in his head, sent small parties to scout in other directions, away from the battle site.

The pipeholder then walked across to the wagons husks to see if there was anything he could salvage for his own use – sometimes white men carried iron tools that may be useful in war or hunting. He was breaking bits of charred wood from the wagon frame when he saw the small metallic tubes on the ground. He picked one up, brushed off the dust and ash with his fingers, sniffed it, licked it with the tip of his tongue and tried to decide what it was. There was a hint of burnt gunpowder from the inside of it but that could have been from the fire. Still, they were unusual so he collected as many as he could find and put them into his saddle pouch.

He had just remounted when a party of trackers returned from down trail; he waited to see what they had to say.

The youngest tracker was very excited:

"A broken trail but many mules with iron shoes and two unshod ponies, heading north – several days old."

Big Bow mused on this – they needed to get home and report it. The puzzle was still unsolved but the picture, like mud in swirling water, was starting to clear. He counted his warriors for the homeward journey; two were still out checking tracks.

Many Tracks had just shouted a final declaration to the spirits at the gravesite when the missing riders dashed onto the valley floor. They halted in front of Big Bow; they confirmed the mule and pony tracks but they had more:

"The riders of the unshod ponies dismounted under a tree – there were moccasin prints – one with upturned toes – *Chiricahua* maybe – and one Cheyenne."

Big Bow nodded his thanks. The disappeared whites may have killed Etsay and his warriors but an Apache and a Cheyenne had also been here at the same time. It seemed a strange alliance for an attack on the Kiowa but he would gather more information. Big Bow was determined to solve the puzzle and, more importantly, he would be seeking revenge.

---- 0 0 0 ----

Chapter Twelve

Henry Armstrong tilted his old Army campaign hat against the snow flurries and spurred his horse forward as he nudged the scrawny steers of the beef herd into the pasture at Fort Lyon. It was mid-November and though he'd outfitted himself for winter, his clothes seemed inadequate against the keening wind and blizzards now whipping across the Arkansas River. He missed his warm buffalo robes that he'd had when camped with the Cheyenne.

He suddenly felt tired – six weeks on the Mountain Route of the Santa Fe Trail riding a hard wagon seat had made his back ache; he'd been happy to volunteer as a cattle drover just to get back into the saddle again.

Living a harsher but simpler life on the American Plains had once seemed natural when he'd lived for over a year in a Suhtai tipi - but three years in England had made him soft and forgetful.

Of course, he remembered some things; the bachelor officers' quarters in Fort Leavenworth had been his home back when he'd been on active duty with the US Army and he remembered some parts of the Arkansas River; even his vocabulary of Cheyenne words hadn't entirely deserted him but the acceptance of the vast scale of the country and distances to travel had been a rude re-awakening. America was just so bloody big…

At home in his late father's library, he'd looked at maps of the Great American Desert - or as much as was known then – and, as far as he could reckon, the entire island of Great Britain was only just as long as the Yellowstone River. And, as the Englishman scraped snow from his face, he knew it wasn't just distance - even the weather itself was a sharp reminder of being under endless skies.

England, with its railway system and network of passable roads was smaller and easier to get around. Henry had never been one for the detail of commercial life at home but even he knew that the stock and produce from his remote Cumberland estate now got to distant markets in good time and business could be conducted within days rather than months. His English house, only a stone's throw from the invisible border with Scotland and considered almost inaccessible ten years ago, now seemed much more connected to daily life.

It had been good to live at home for a while but America had made him restless – cold, stiff and saddle sore that he was, he was pleased to be back.

Henry dismounted and unsaddled his horse to hand it back to the Sergeant in charge of the military remuda; they had been reluctant to loan him a mount until he'd casually mentioned his service with the Dragoons and Cavalry.

Last time in America – when his family still had money – he'd been able to bring out his own tall, grey gelding. What the animal had lacked in recognised breeding in England, it had certainly made up for in stamina – unlike many horses bred for the Dragoons and Cavalry, the grey had adapted well to the prairie grass and hard-to-get grazing when he'd lived at Leavenworth and with the Cheyenne.

The Sergeant inspected the returned horse as the first of the supply wagons rumbled into the post over the iron hard ground:

"Don't worry Sergeant – it's still got four legs; one at each corner – I checked," said Henry. The Sergeant smiled tightly at the poor joke:

"Nah, no need for checkin', mister – I can see you know yer way round a saddle horse. Where's next for you?"

Henry thought it best to keep his plans to himself until he'd found out what the new regiment of 100-day enlisters in the

Third Colorado were up to. If they were indeed setting out to hunt down the Cheyenne as the Leavenworth recruiter had said, then he would bow out.

"Just some hunting, come Spring, I think. I'm hoping to meet up with a friend here."

"Well, you sure got enough firepower there..." said the sergeant, nodding at the Englishman's two rifles," ...but you'll need to be careful, the Indians are on the warpath and won't take kindly to some white man shooting down their game."

"I'll be careful, Sergeant – thank you," said Henry as he hoisted the two canvas rifle cases across his shoulder and, dragging his saddle over the dirt, walked across to the lead wagon to retrieve his few sparse possessions and the boxes of ammunition. Now, he would need to buy a horse, supplies and a pack mule for the next part of his journey; he patted his money belt to make sure the silver dollars were still there.

Encumbered by all his kit, the walk up the escarpment to the trading post was difficult but a helpful infantry Corporal gave him a hand, hoisting the saddle on his shoulders. After the usual small talk about who he was and what he was doing there, the Corporal said:

"Just look out for that Frenchy trader mister – he'd take the coins off your dead eyelids if he could."

Henry thanked him for his concern and said:

"Well, we English have ways of dealing with the French – just remember Waterloo."

The soldier looked puzzled: "Who's Walter Lu – a Chinaman?"

Henry laughed and patted the young man on the shoulder as farewell; still chuckling, he dumped his kit under a lean to as shelter from the increasing snow and pushed open the door.

He didn't recognise the trader at first as the breed stood with his back to the counter loading tinned goods onto the shelves. But the man whirled round when Henry spoke:

"Er, any mail for me – Armstrong, Henry Armstrong?"

"Ah, *Lootenaung* ! I heard you would be coming…" The French accent sounded dimly familiar to Henry.

"It is I, Baptiste Clauville, at your service…" He looked disappointed that Henry didn't recognise him even when he announced his name.

"I scouted for your troop back in '54 when we investigated the death of that …"

"Of course, *Monsieur* Clauville – the dead trader, near the Platte!"

Henry stepped back to look more closely – he recognised the Crow armband with the white man's scalp on it but that was about all. This man was fat and bloated though seemed to have the same air of tetchiness about him as the one he remembered. They had clashed on the trail over some now-forgotten social misdeed and Henry, as the Officer Commanding the troop, had put him in his place.

"You've put on a few pounds *Monsieur* – too much good living I imagine. And your nose seems a bit more crooked."

Clauville looked dismayed and his hand flew to his face to touch the scar made by Carver's rifle butt:

"Ah *oui*, some madcap wolf skinner on the rampage about a week ago – I took care of him though…"

Henry grinned at the mention of a wolf skinner – and then remembered:

"A wolf skinner, eh? And you took care of him? Hmmm…"

If Carver had been the one bashing Clauville's ugly mug then there was no way that the breed could have bested his friend – not unless he shot him in the back.

"Any mail for me?" said Henry brightly, smiling as the small skin pouch was handed over.

---- o o o ----

Chapter Thirteen

Star rode cautiously as she followed the Forked Lightning Women. There had been some flurries of snow and though these had cleared, the ground was hardening quickly. Soon she would lose their tracks – she would need to get closer to the women's war party but to time it right so that White Rain Woman wouldn't send her back.

So, caution would prevail for now; Star dragged her buffalo robe up around her shoulders and kicked her pony forward as she entered the mountain country of the Crow.

Dusk was falling as she entered the forest of lodgepole pines – the trees were close together so snow was light on the ground and the carpet of needles showed the scuff marks made by the women's ponies. The sign looked fresh so Star dismounted and rested her horse – she was closer than she thought; she would ride alone for another day then announce her presence to the women. She hoped they would be glad to see her.

High on a rocky promontory, a mountain lion screamed. Star shivered and unrolled her buffalo robe bed under the pine cover.

---- o o o ----

Viajero swung up into his saddle and tried to avoid the reproachful gaze of his wife.

"You are just returned from one raid and now you go off on another - just as the snow falls…," said Bright Antelope.

"What about your daughter and me?" she wailed. The Apache cut her short:

"You have enough food for much of the winter and I'll be back soon. Say a prayer to Usen for me."

He slid his new rifle into the saddle bucket, patted the extra bullets in his possibles bag and trotted his horse over to where Dark was waiting for him at the edge of the village.

Dark tried to ignore the outcry from Bright Antelope but it was embarrassing; he was glad that he had not married if this was what it meant. Men should be able to do what they wished without interference from women.

Out of the advancing dusk, his father, Yellow Bear and Broken Knife walked up to his pony, waiting until the Traveller had joined them.

"My son," said Smoke on the Moon, "This is a dangerous time to go on a raid – the Moon of the Popping Trees will soon be here. Your horses will weaken without grazing when the snow comes."

Dark listened dutifully and nodded as Viajero swung his pony alongside.

"Father, we mounted our big revenge raid on the Pawnee in the winter, all those moons ago. That worked well…"

Smoke nodded but said:

"There were more of us in the war party then and we had a plan; youngsters brought along our spare horses, stripped bark for forage and provided hot food on the trail home. All our preparations fitted together – that was why it worked."

Dark was about to argue when he saw his father fold his arms and stare off into the distance. There was no more to be said – his advice had been given but a warrior could decide his own destiny and not even a father could interfere.

Yellow Bear stepped forward to the pony, patted Dark on the knee and said:

"I have had no dreams of danger about your raid – perhaps all will be well. I have prayed to Maheo for your safe return…" Turning to Viajero he looked up at the Traveller and smiled:

"As for you - you do your own praying!" Oddly sullen, the Apache jerked his chin upward in acknowledgement.

Broken Knife had stayed silent – he was an austere man and emotion rarely figured in his judgments. He had no comforting words for their quest:

"Your trail is the trail of the weak-minded. Those women you follow are crazy too – you are well-matched!"

---- o o o ----

The grizzly was hungry and irritable; it grunted angrily as it pushed through the mountain thickets. It hadn't eaten enough over the past few days; game was scarce, snow was here and he needed to go into his long sleep. He had chased some wolves from the carcass of a drowned elk some time ago but his body told him that he needed more food in his belly to support him through the no-eating time - until the new grass and freshly-born animals arrived.

He crushed a sapling with his front paw, stood on his hind legs and raked the bark of a tree – the noise carrying down to the floor of the small valley. Somewhere far below, in the thick brush, an animal made a nervous noise and the grizzly heard it.

He stopped and sniffed the wind. There it was – just a faint tang on the breeze. The bear dropped back onto all fours and trundled off in search of the scent. It may well have been just a passing scent but it contained all the essences he recognised - blood, bone and sweat; it was prey.

---- o o o ----

Chapter Fourteen

Little Snake's wounded leg had healed – not completely, but enough to walk with only slight stiffness. This was fortunate as he now needed all the speed he could muster. Something was happening at the southern edge of the Crow encampment and attention was diverted – there were shouts of warning, some shots and a drumming of ponies' hooves. Little Snake didn't know what it was but knew that this was the time to take his freedom back.

Straight Hair, the old Nez Perce woman who'd been looking after him, slipped him a skinning knife and said:

"Go! Take a horse and get out!"

Little Snake hesitated; the main horse herd was some distance off but he knew that many Crow warriors tied their best hunting or war ponies outside their lodges; he would look for one of those.

He ran stiffly across the middle of the village circle, past screaming women and children being led away from the danger by old men, his head whipping from side to side until he saw a pony still tied up outside a painted tipi.

No-one stopped him or questioned what he was doing. As he ran towards the flapping tipi cover, he recognised the painted symbols on the skins – it was the lodge of Many Bulls, Red Horse's father. No matter, a horse was a horse.

Little Snake jumped astride the pony and immediately fell off the other side; it had been so long since he'd sat on a proper mount that his injured leg couldn't steady him. He thumped onto the hard earth and shouted in pain.

The tipi flap whipped open and, shrieking defiance, out strode Red Horse's father. He had been in the middle of painting his face to meet whichever enemy was attacking his village and now this thief was outside his lodge. His bow was across his back but, dropping the paint gourd, he pulled his hatchet and bent over Little Snake, arm upraised – this miserable Cheyenne dog would be his first kill today.

The blade fell swiftly - but Little Snake was just as quick and he scuttled under the pony's belly. The horse, still tied to a stake and panicked by the shouting and shooting, reared and plunged in fear, crow-hopping from side to side. It barged Many Bulls who was trying to get round behind it to close with Little Snake. The warrior fell over onto his back and the young Cheyenne knew he had only once chance to get away.

Many Bulls wriggled on his back trying to avoid the plunging hooves of his pony until a stray blow from a rear hoof stilled him for a moment.

Little Snake took out his skinning knife – it was too short in the blade for a killing wound by stabbing so, leaning over the stunned warrior, he sliced downwards through Many Bulls' deerskin shirt, then deeper into the softer flesh across his stomach. Plunging his hand into the reeking hole he'd made, Little Snake grabbed a warm clutch of entrails and disembowelled the Crow chief.

Yelling his own song of triumph after defeating a warrior, Little Snake mounted the still fearful pony, now spooked by the blood and death throes of its owner, kicked his heels into its flanks and galloped out of the village.

A saddened Straight Hair watched him leave; she nursed a faint hope that the boy would turn round and rescue her but, no, he just thundered off on Many Bulls' fine pony, shrieking with joy that he was free.

She knew she would never see him again.

---- o o o ----

Star was awoken by the screaming of her pony; she had not lit a fire in case the smoke was spotted by the Forked Lightning Women, or worse, an enemy.

The bear had rushed the tethered animal, grabbed it by a foreleg and crushed the bone. The horse crashed onto its side, threshing wildly with its hooves as the bear sat on top of it and started to eat it alive.

Star grabbed the guns from under the fur robe and ran towards the bear, thinking it odd that she wasn't afraid. At twenty paces from the grunting, blood-slathered bear she fired two quick shots from her revolver, both missed. The bear stopped, looked at Star, then continued to rip at the pony's flesh.

The girl ran closer and fired the remaining four bullets into the unmissable target, she heard the thud of the lead balls as they went through the thick fur and into flesh. The bear fell off the horse carcass onto its side, making a noise as though it was winded. The young Cheyenne woman whooped at her victory but her joy was premature.

Slowly the bear got up again, roaring, angry and in pain from its wounds it loped towards Star. The young woman knew enough not to run - bears could run fast and climb trees – so she unslung her repeating rifle and backed away slowly as the bear got closer.

With her back against a tree, Star steadied her aim as Crow Dress had taught her. The bear reared up on its hind legs – it was much taller than a man – and roared its defiance, its hot stinking breath wafting over the scared girl. Star cocked the hammer and pulled the trigger. The copper percussion cap snapped a sharp report but the fouled chamber that carried the spark to the gunpowder was clogged – the gun didn't fire.

The bear slashed downwards with a massive claw, ripping Star's face open, the white bone and teeth of her jawline exposed in a spray of blood.

The bear though, made the same mistake as Star; thinking her dead or no longer a threat, ambled off to eat more of the twitching pony. Star was an inexperienced warrior and unfamiliar with guns but she knew, badly wounded that she was, that she must finish off the bear in case it came back to check on her.

She hauled herself to her feet, re-cocked the rifle and, though the gun barrel wobbled with the effort of keeping it steady, pulled the trigger and shot the bear in the rear. The animal roared in pain and surprise, fell forwards and, groaning with the effort and unsteady on its feet, turned round to face her. The bear's large diamond shaped head swung backwards and forwards as it watched her through glittering eyes. Star knew she couldn't stand another charge by the bear – it was now or never.

 Sweatily, she thumbed back the hammer again on the rifle. This time she staggered forward and fired, the rifle muzzle almost touching the snout of the grizzly. The lead ball smashed through its front teeth and out of the back of its skull, snapping the spine on its way. The bear fell heavily at her feet, its bulk making the ground shake. The girl fell to her knees, the bear's spraying blood mingling with her own.

It was only then that Star felt the pain of her wound, dropping the rifle and frantically pushing the flap of flesh back across her jaw. Blood pulsed out, gushing between her fingers.

She was getting cold and fainted. She didn't hear the pony galloping up.

---- 0 0 0 ----

Chapter Fifteen

The Crow couldn't believe their encampment was being attacked by women; and they all seemed to have guns.

Children fled screaming from the mayhem as shots and the drumbeat of pony hooves rumbled over the hard ground. Mothers gathered up their smaller children and ran towards the surrounding forest while men tumbled out of family tipis with weapons and tried to get to their horses. Dogs barked. Old men and younger boys came running into the village, alerted by the shooting and yelling. Some of the boys had been out hunting for small game and had bows at the ready – they fired angry but ineffectual arrows at the intruders as they raced by.

White Rain Woman led the charge with a sweating spare pony galloping behind her; Willow was at her side – she needed a steady shot to clear any resistance she might encounter and Willow was good with both pistol and rifle. On the other side of camp, Crow Dress led Sweet Water and Blue Wing to run off the pony herd. All the women shrieked with fierce joy, tinged as it was by fear.

"Where's the captive!?" yelled Willow as she shot down a warrior who rushed at her. White Rain didn't answer but kept galloping towards a small cooking fire outside a shabby tipi. The leader pointed ahead:

"There!"

A figure knelt at the fire, there was the Cheyenne slave! The Forked Lightning Women had watched the camp for two days before attacking. Though White Rain had made them wear Crow moccasins to disguise any tracks the villagers might find in the snow, the women had been dismayed by the amount of activity both inside and outside the camp – children playing, hunting parties coming and going, Crow women gathering grasses and tree bark for winter pony forage. They could have been discovered at any minute.

Spotting the captive had been hard – most of the Crow looked as the Forked Lightning Women had imagined *any* slaves might look – undernourished and thin. It had been the keen-eyed Blue Wing who'd spotted the tell-tale sign – the plan was brought forward; the sooner it was over the better.

Willow leapt off her pony dragged the surprised old woman to her feet by her deerskin shift:

"We've rescued you - come!" She said this in Cheyenne but saw a puzzled look on the woman's face; she didn't understand her own language, perhaps she'd been a prisoner for too long.

Willow grabbed the necklet that the old woman wore - a poor ornament of a broken Cheyenne arrow suspended on a sinew string - and held it up in front of the crone's face:

"See – our striped arrow. That's us -get on the horse!"

Straight Hair had no idea what the woman was saying – she recognised the hairstyle and pony markings from her youth when their people sometimes traded in more peaceful times. She was even more surprised to be bundled up across the woman's saddle cantle and taken off in an undignified manner. She didn't protest though – the necklace that Worm had given her seemed to have a magic all of its own. Now, she too was free.

---- o o o ----

Crow Dress's attack pushed ahead at the same time – they could hear Willow shooting on the other side of the camp. Birds wheeled overhead and somewhere a horse screamed in pain

The three women galloped out of the treeline into the grazing pasture; many ponies were already having to paw at the ground to get any nourishment. Their heads were up - spooked by the flying birds and distant, alien sounds.

The pony herd was a disappointment; it was much depleted and hardly worth the danger she had exposed them to. Ponies were already thin – the herd looked worn out. Still, they needed to be scattered to prevent pursuit

Crow Dress Woman was wearing the skin shift that named her – dyed dark red with many rows of elk teeth across the front. Her father had taken it from a Crow woman's tipi many years before. She smiled at the irony of attacking a Crow village dressed as one of her enemies; she was happy just to be in action.

"There's not many horses for a village this size"" yelled Sweet Water.

"No matter – just run them off!" replied Crow Dress

"I'll try over this hill!" shouted Blue Wing before Crow Dress could forbid it. The young woman galloped off, joyfully singing her war song.

"No!" yelled Crow Dress, "…just stampede them!" But she was too late, Blue Wing ignored her. She shrieked in irritation and reined towards the clusters of alarmed animals.

Blue Wing was still in sight of Sweet Water and Crow Dress when she fell out of the saddle and crashed onto the ground, where she lay winded. She had an arrow in her side and raised herself up onto her elbow as a returning Crow hunting party crested the hill and charged towards her.

Wounded she may have been but the young warrior raised her pistol and fired at the charging Crow; she hit a horse in the chest and it staggered, stopping suddenly and pitching the rider over its shoulder. His companions couldn't avoid him and charged over him, trying to get to the wounded woman.

For a heartbeat, Sweet Water was unnerved but dug her heels into her pony's flanks and rode towards her wounded war sister.

A Crow warrior reached her first, dismounted hurriedly and was about to drive a hatchet into Blue Wing's head when Sweet Water crashed her pony into him. The man was flung sideways and lay still.

Sweet Water leapt out of the saddle and tried to heave Blue Wing back onto her pony but she was too badly injured, the arrow waggling back and forward in her flesh each time she was moved; the girl yelled in pain.

Blue Wing couldn't stand or help herself to get mounted; Sweet Water, grunting through gritted teeth, tried in vain to get her into the saddle; the young woman's legs collapsed and she became a deadweight – a frozen liability to herself and others on the battlefield.

In a moment of clarity, the young song maker remembered she was a Cheyenne warrior. She became calm and just said:

"Go, sister – leave me!"

Sweet Water had no breath left to answer her but by now, firing covering shots to keep the advancing hunters at bay, Crow Dress had joined them.

Both women hauled Blue Wing onto her pony saddle – she couldn't sit astride but lay belly down across the saddle seat and tried to endure the pain as the arrow jolted and plunged deeper inside her. The three galloped away from the village, scattering horses and mules before them.

Blue Wing, fading into unconsciousness, looked behind the plunging rump of her pony and could see that the Crow were catching up – Sweet Water was finding it hard to lead her pony by its headrope. They would all die if she slowed them down.

Though not the leader of the war party, she had her own responsibilities. So, with a short prayer to Maheo, she pushed herself out of the saddle and fell off her horse, its rear hooves cracking her face as she slid under it.

She was singing her death song when the Crow caught up to her.

---- o o o ----

Chapter Sixteen

Little Snake dismounted and took in the scene quickly – keeping a cautious eye on the bear in case it wasn't dead. He knelt beside the girl, whose face was badly ripped open, to see if she was still alive. She was still breathing but it was shallow and laboured.

He walked quickly over to her fur robe bedroll and saw the bow and quiver of arrows. He laughed out loud when he saw the distinctive stripes of Cheyenne markings on them – he ran his finger over the additional arrow marks; he had never seen the forked lightning emblem on any arrows before. The wounded girl was obviously one of his own people though he couldn't tell which band she hailed from – but why did she have so many guns? He gathered the pistol and rifle and laid them out by the girl; the rifle may have one shot left in it but, never having fired a gun before, Little Snake wasn't sure.

He laid the robe next to her on the ground and rolled her into it; snow had started falling again and breath stood out in whitish grey plumes from his mouth. He had watched Straight Hair gather moss and leaves to help with his own wound, so he tried to do the same. He lay the girl on her back; the half mask of her face fell back into place then and it seemed a good place to start.

The cold air slowed the blood flow so he scraped moss from the bark of trees and packed it into the gaps between the lines of flesh where the claws had raked her; the sight of her closed teeth in a pink and white jawline upset him. She moaned in pain. He tutted in sympathy and drew the robe higher around her neck; he was cold too but the wounded girl came first. They needed a fire and food.

He walked back to the dead pony and rummaged through the saddlebags – the girl had been well-prepared and had brought a buffalo horn with a smouldering ash of dried punk inside. He opened the buffalo horn and blew gently on the ashes, they flared briefly and glowed red again, the warmth seeping into his palm; they could have a fire.

Little Snake used his small skinning knife to cut a thin steak from the pony's rump and stood up with it dripping bloodily onto the ground.

It was then that he saw the two warriors watching him.

---- o o o ----

Viajero raised his rifle and pointed it the scruffy youth who was obviously about to rob the inert Cheyenne girl; the boy froze, a piece of pony meat in his guilty hand.

The Apache re-slung his rifle across his back and drew his war club – no need to waste a precious bullet on such a poor specimen. He walked over to the youth who seemed rooted to the spot; Viajero stared at him – the boy wasn't afraid. He raised his arm to strike him when See the Dark shouted:

"Wait!"

He saw the look of relief on the youth's face when he heard the Cheyenne word.

Little Snake frantically tried to remember his own language before these strangers killed him; in the end he pointed to himself and signed:

'*Medicine Arrow People.*'

"I don't think so," said Dark out loud, noting the boy's haircut and poor clothing – obviously a Crow. They would deal with him later once they had found the Forked Lightning Women. He walked over to the motionless girl and stared down at her – it was shocking to see a woman so badly injured though he made no move to help her.

"Ask him if he's seen any women warriors," said Viajero sarcastically, nettled at being denied a kill.

Dark nodded, disregarding the tone in the Apache's voice.

Little Snake gained some confidence by understanding the conversation and prepared his words even as Dark asked the question in hand sign:

"Yes, I think they are attacking the Crow village north of here," he said, pointing down the trail his own pony had made.

Both Viajero and Dark were astounded by the Cheyenne words flowing from the youth's mouth – perhaps he *was* Cheyenne after all. Both men remained suspicious however:

"How did the attack go?" asked Dark, guiltily realising for the first time that he wasn't concerned about the safety of White Rain Woman, merely for the success of his own folk against the Crows.

"I don't know…" said Little Snake honestly," …I stole a horse during the shooting and escaped – I was a prisoner."

Viajero interrupted:

"Then what are you doing with her?" He nodded towards Star, still wrapped in the fur robe.

"I heard shots and rode over here and found her," replied the boy. There was silence as the two warriors mulled this over.

"Where were you escaping to?" said Dark. Something about the young man gnawed at him. The Forked Lightning Women were looking for a Cheyenne captive in a Crow village – if this was the one, where were the women?

"South, to find my people. I am a Suhtai of the *Tsis-tsis-tas*."

Dark said testily:

"Just because you understand my language, doesn't mean you are one of us! You may be a Crow spy."

Little Snake wanted to shout at these two slow thinking men but refrained – they could still kill him despite the tribal kinship he had with one of them. He churned through memories when he was a boy:

"No. I was in Twisted Wolf's band – we stayed apart from the rest except when we gathered for the buffalo hunt in summer or dedicated the Sacred Arrows."

Dark was amazed, though Viajero had never heard of Twisted Wolf. But Twisted Wolf had led the Suhtai a long time ago, many summers before the Traveller had joined the Cheyenne:

"Twisted Wolf was our chief until the Pawnee raid, many summers ago…" Dark began.

"I know! I know! I was captured in that raid by them and traded off to the Crow. I am Little Snake!" The youth jumped up and down with excitement – Viajero sniffed irritably at the display.

See the Dark however became calm; the name he knew, though didn't recognise the boy's face:

"I was called Otter then – you are the one who put an arrow into my left eye."

---- o o o ----

Chapter Seventeen

Henry was trapped in Fort Lyon and bitterly resented it.

He knew he should have set out earlier to find the Suhtai but getting a horse and mule at a military post had taken time; it was wartime and animals were not for sale. He'd slept on the floor of the draughty trading hut and tried to keep his distance from Baptiste Clauville; the half breed obviously had no friends on the post and looked on Henry as an old saddle companion from the past.

Still, the cunning Frenchy had at least manged to get him a horse and mule from an unscrupulous Quartermaster. Now some arrogant, Johnny-come-lately officer had arrived with his regiment and closed down the post – no-one allowed in or out.

He railed at the sturdily built, bearded Colonel who was keeping him there:

"Who the Hell are you, sir to make a prisoner of me – I'm a free born Englishman and I demand to be on my way!"

The Colonel slapped his rolled gauntlets into the palm of his hand and nodded to the Sergeant of the Guard.

"Be quiet Mr Armstrong! You stay at the fort until I say you can leave. My name is Chivington - I command this post and the entire District of Colorado – while you tread my soil sir, you'll do as I say."

The Colonel's eyes drilled into Henry and he stared back. The blue coated officer was obviously someone important but he also had the look of a zealot.

Henry tried a new tack:

"I have ridden in your Army sir -with the Second Dragoons and First Cavalry; on both occasions against the Indians."

Chivington stared back at him:

"Those were both Regular Army units, Mr Armstrong – my men are all brave Volunteers from this very territory…"

The officer pushed his hands through his beard and walked to the door:

"You Regulars rarely waged war on these savages harshly enough. We have to clean up after you and kill them all. Our country needs to be civilised, sir!"

There were footsteps outside and Henry saw a thin-faced Captain reporting that all troops were in the saddle. Chivington, look back from the door frame:

"Sergeant! Keep Mr Armstrong here until noon tomorrow, then let him go. I have God's work to do…at Sand Creek!"

---- o o o ----

Chapter Eighteen

Sweet Water was about to turn her pony around and pick up Blue Wing when Crow Dress Woman galloped up:

"Leave her – we don't have time! Let the spare pony go!"

Sweet Water, eyes afire with anger, reached out to slap Crow Dress across the face but she was too far away:

"That girl fought well and deserves to be saved!" she shrieked, though she could see that Blue Wing was now lost; the Crow pursuers had stopped to drag her, screaming in pain, back to the village. Two of the Crow fired arrows at them but the shafts fell short.

Crow Dress didn't mind Sweet Water's violent reaction – the girl's first proper raid against the Crow, when they had successfully stolen the horses and mules, had probably been too easy; none of the Forked Lightning Women had fallen. Now, they had a casualty and that was hard to deal with. Crow Dress remembered the lingering death of her friend Mouse on their way back home after the raid on the Comanches and her own sorrow – all the Forked Lightning Women had sung the warrior mourning songs on the long trail home. But, now – as she was in charge – Crow Dress had things to do:

"Sister…" she laid her hand on Sweet Water's arm," … we need to find the meeting point on the back trail and see if we can find the others."

The women kicked their tired ponies back into motion and rode south.

---- 0 0 0 ----

White Rain Woman and Willow galloped into the arranged meeting point, Straight Hair still across the saddle cantle of the Hunkpapa girl and White Rain leading the spare pony.

The old crone had been very quiet and, at first, Willow thought she had died. But she had hauled herself off the pony's neck and stood, smiling her toothless smile at the Forked Lightning warriors. She signed who she was:

'Pierced Nose people. Slave. Thank you.'

Willow groaned out loud:

"We've rescued the wrong captive!"

White Rain, rolling her eyes in disbelief, dismounted and looked back up the trail. No sign of the other three yet but, fortunately, no Crow pursuit either – Crow Dress's group must have scattered the horse herd.

She turned back to Straight Hair, gulping as she did so – this would take some explanation back in the Suhtai camp; the men would never let them forget it. She walked across and held up the broken arrow necklet in front of the old woman's face and signed:

'Where? Who?'

Straight Hair replied:

'Boy. Medicine Arrow people. Escaped.'

This gave White Rain some comfort but it was a small blessing only – their attack had, at least, allowed the real Cheyenne captive to get out of the Crow village. Of course, returning without any proof of success had just made the raid futile.

White Rain remounted and signed to the old crone from the saddle:

'Go home.'

Straight Hair replied and pointed to the spare horse:

'Pony? Me?'

White Rain shook her head and led the animal out of the clearing. Willow rode up alongside and said:

"You're making her walk home? She's just an old woman!"

Without looking back, White Rain replied:

"Yes, but she's not *our* old woman."

Straight Hair shrugged, pulled her shift around her shoulders and set off north. As a slave, she was used to walking everywhere – the Crow never allowed her to own a horse. Still, her knowledge of the mountain slopes she had trodden as a girl and young woman may come in useful as she sought out the Nez Perce.

The old woman had disappeared into the treeline when Crow Dress and a weeping Sweet Water rode up, ponies lathered in sweat. Crow Dress reported to her leader:

"Our sister Blue Wing fell in battle! The Crows are rounding up their ponies and won't be far behind!"

---- o o o ----

Chapter Nineteen

Little Snake rode with the girl, still wrapped in her fur robe, in his arms, and followed Dark's directions to the Suhtai encampment, a three-day ride away. Snow fell more heavily and lay in white swathes outside the treeline; the sky darkened and the air chilled.

The one-eyed Suhtai man – Little Snake still remembered him by his child's name of Otter – and the dark-skinned warrior from the far southwest had not given them any food or weapons. He understood this; they were on the war trail against the Crow and couldn't spare any. But the girl would need to be fed soon, if only to get warmth into her body. The cold had stopped her gashed face bleeding for now but the movement of the pony made her cry out from time to time; she seemed to have no strength to speak. He couldn't even ask her name – he hoped she would live.

The boy felt as though he should know her – they were both from the same small band though she was a couple of summers younger than him; maybe they had played together. The girl moaned a little and started to stir in his arms. Little Snake was worried she might fall off the horse and hurt herself so he reined his pony into a stand of live oak and looked back up the trail.

There were no signs or sounds of pursuers; he dismounted and carried the girl from the saddle to a patch of dry and clear ground under a long, overhanging branch back in the daytime darkness of the trees.

A pool of stale water stood in a small muddy hollow, scummed with leaves and twigs. Little Snake broke the surface ice and pushed this away gently with his fingers and cupped his hand into it and took a drink – his face wrinkled as the muddy grit swept over his teeth and down his throat. He coughed and retched slightly, though he was smiling to himself as he balanced up his situation – hungry – Yes; thirsty – Yes; cold – Yes but Free! His heart leapt at his change in fortune.

Under the tree bough the girl moaned and raised her arm. Snake cupped more water in his hands and knelt beside the girl, trickling the brown drops into her open mouth:

"What's your name?" he asked. The girl croaked something but the effort defeated her.

"Don't worry – I have my own name for you – you are Bear Killer!"

---- 0 0 0 ----

See the Dark and Viajero rode at the front of the attack on the pursuing Crow. They both stayed in the saddle and saw for the first time how much better the repeating rifles were than their old single shot carbines. Controlling their ponies with just their knees, both men found they could keep the rifles up to their aiming eye and just crank the underlever to reload – almost without thinking.

Their first volleys made the Crow stop their charge and ride into the trees, away from the zinging bullets.

Two enemy warriors fell from the saddle and lay in the trail, wounded and writhing in pain; White Rain, close behind the Traveller and Dark, rode up and finished them off with her pistol. Whooping with delight she slid out of the saddle and scalped them, tucking the bloody locks into her pistol belt. Returning home with no released captive might just be offset by carrying enemy war trophies:

"Sister!" she yelled at Willow, "Get as many scalps as you can – we need all the glory we can get!"

Willow, ever practical, dismounted and ran over to her ecstatic leader:

"There is no time – we are heading towards a Crow village and they'll be mounting up as soon as they can – we need to help your man and the Traveller. Get your rifle, the men are over there!"

Viajero and Dark had dismounted inside the treeline and shot at any movement coming from the fringe of the Crow village – they could hear the confused and angry shouts of the enemy as orders were given, the neighing of terrified horses and the loud screaming of women and children as they tried to escape this attack on their homes.

Three of the Crow warriors had decided not to look for their stampeded horses but to charge the enemy on foot. They looked for the gun smoke still curling through the trees and ran hard towards it, yelling their death songs. Dark and Viajero obliged and shot them down.

Willow and White Rain had arrived beside them and the drumming of hooves back along the trail signalled that the tired ponies of Sweet Water and Crow Dress had caught up. All the women now joined the firing line – there was a lot to do.

A group of Crow boys, not yet warriors, ran to the treeline, leapt over the bodies of the fallen warriors and dived into the bushes as bullets followed them. Some were armed with smaller bows and their arrows were meant for birds and small game but they now became a threat. At the same time, six mounted Crow charged out of the village towards the Cheyenne group.

Crow Dress saw the boys first as they crashed through the bushes to get to her, the first two carrying only knives. They were brave but foolish – to save ammunition, she drew her hatchet and buried it in the face of the first youngster and seeing the second one pause – a look of horror on his face – she calmly shot him down with her pistol, the bullet smashing through his mouth and out of the back of his neck. Blood spattered the pine needles and thin winter grass. The other boys paused and dived into the cover of the underbrush; they would be more cautious in their approach to these deadly women.

The mounted Crow had timed their attack well – they were halfway to the treeline when first Dark, then the Traveller, paused to re-load. The women saved them – all grabbed their rifles and fired as swiftly as they could into the close packed group of riders, bringing down three of them and unhorsing a fourth.

The remaining two stayed mounted and charged into the treeline, one being swept out of the saddle by an overhanging branch. He lay winded as Sweet Water finished him off with her revolver.

The last warrior seemed surprised by the presence of so many armed women and, in a bad miscalculation, ignored them. The Crow's horse panicked inside the closeness of the trees, plunging and braying with fear. He was the only one who carried a gun – a rusty pepperbox revolver – and he fired at the Apache. Two bullets tore chunks off the tree bark; Viajero looked up but continued to re-load his rifle.

Willow saw the intrusion into their firing line, ran across to the mounted warrior and stabbed him in the leg before hauling him out of the saddle and cutting his throat. The Traveller saw that she'd probably saved his life and he raised his chin in thanks as he slid the last bullet into the rifle magazine. The Hunkpapa girl was delighted at the recognition of such a fierce warrior and without knowing why, blushed.

There was a lull in the firing and Dark yelled:

"Get to the horses – we've fought our battle today!"

Dark and Sweet Water were last to bring up their ponies and were just about to swing into the saddle when the Crow boys, lying silently in the close brush, fired their small bows.

Two of the arrows, stuck in Dark's back and he yelled out in pain; his pony kicked out in alarm as two more arrows went into its flank. Sweet Water took an arrow in her cheek but managed to get into the saddle, blood gushing down her face.

Atop his pony, Dark was twisting and stretching his hands down his neck but couldn't reach the arrows so she rode back behind him and pulled them out. The unexpected pain made him yelp. She tutted unsympathetically and then pulled the arrow out of her own cheek.

More slim arrows sailed out of the bushes but only hit the horses. White Rain dismounted and, handing her reins to Willow, strode grimly towards the twitching bushes; she was joined by Viajero – both with hatchets in hand.

Most of the boys had fled in fear but three stood their ground, arrows gone but knives out. Viajero didn't pause but cleaved the skulls of the nearest pair. White Rain had to run to catch the last one but she grabbed his long hair, pulled the boy to his knees and looked down at his scared, dirty face. She spat at him before curving the axe across his neck, almost beheading the boy. She walked out of the brush past Viajero:

"When you find a nest of snakes, you have to kill them all," she said in a quiet voice.

---- o o o ----

Chapter Twenty

Henry saw the small foot sticking out of a riverbank hole as he approached the creek; the foot was wearing a moccasin beaded in a Cheyenne pattern. He dismounted carefully, pausing to recall some words from his past with the Suhtai and called out:

"I see you – are you hurt?"

There was no reply so he walked over and looked inside the hole. The foot belonged to a child and she was dead; Henry hissed air through his gritted teeth at such a sad sight.

Spotting the shoe – pale against the dark sand – had shocked him. Though two days behind, he had followed the trail of the Third Colorado Volunteers up to the Cheyenne reservation on Sand Creek, a place he had never visited before with Bad Elk's band. Clauville had told him that Black Kettle's people, the Wutapiu and some Arapaho and northern Suhtai were up there; perhaps they would know where Bad Elk's band was. He assumed the soldiers had just gone up there to see that the Cheyenne had stayed put in their allotted place. But this?

As tenderly as he could, he pulled the body from the hole and lay the child on top of the frozen, churned earth on the river bank and looked at the wounds. The girl's body had slashes down the back and the wrist of one hand was only still attached to the arm by shreds of skin. She had possibly crawled into the hole to escape her attacker. Someone must have pursued her to the hole and shot her as she lay inside – a bullet hole went from an entry wound under her chin to the bone shattered exit in the top of her skull.

His four years at home in England had blunted his outdoor skills; there, he got his information from newspapers and mail – now he would have to read the ground. Carver was always much better at this than him but the foreboding he felt made him concentrate. He inspected the tracks on the bank and around the flats at the hole entrance. Tell-tale marks of shod horses and footprints from a white man's riding boot confirmed who had pursued the girl and killed her. These were soldiers' boots. His anger rose as the slash marks now made sense – they were from a cavalry sabre.

Henry buried the girl as best he could in the freezing sand – the shovel he carried on his pack mule ringing out metallically in the cold air. His Christian instinct told him to say a few words at the graveside but his mind was blank with cold and anger. He felt guilty that he didn't wrap the girl up in his saddle blanket to bury her. But, the practicalities of life, now he was back on the Plains told him that he may need it himself and the child was beyond comfort. Instead, he repeated some words in Cheyenne that he'd heard Yellow Bear speak at another funeral all those years ago when he'd lived with the Suhtai:

"Maheo! This child's trail in life was cut short. Let her spirit ride alongside you until we all make camp together again…"

He then added his own words, feeling guilty as he knew he was condemning one of his own kind:

"…and pursue her killer and let her take revenge."

He crumbled some chunks of frozen sand onto the grave mound and placed a twist of tobacco as offering.

Henry shook his head at the futility of his actions as he retied the shovel to the packsaddle.

Religious belief was a mystery to him. Attending services at the family chapel on his father's estate had never raised even a glimmer of faith in him - about the afterlife, God or any of the other totems that Christians were supposed to believe in. The estate's vicar – a robust and outspoken variant amongst his largely docile and quivering fellow travellers – had noticed his cynical boredom and, tweaking his ear, marched him outside to hiss:

"Boy! One day the Good Lord will send a bolt of lightning to strike you down as you go to church."

Henry remembered the smell of port wine on the clergyman's breath as he slapped away the hand and said:

"Good! It'll mean I don't have to listen to bastards like you anymore!"

He was smiling at the memory as he went back to the grave mound, patted the soil and remounted.

Back in the saddle he looked at the trail ahead – the lines of shod horses dispersing towards a distant skein of remaining, upright lodge poles, some still smoking from the cavalry's revenge fires.

This was Chivington's doing – attacking the Cheyenne and killing children – it may have been the fat zealot's vision of God's work but Henry knew there would be Hell to pay.

---- 0 0 0 ----

Bad Elk's camp was in turmoil. Dog Soldiers – though they had not been present for the bluecoat attack - brought news of the fight at Sand Creek had ridden hard into the Suhtai circle, yelling their anguish and shrieking for revenge. Bad Elk, seeking to calm his frightened people, walked into the melee of drumming hooves and spittle-flecked Dog Men and told them to leave.

"No! There are battles to fight! Give us your warriors..." cried one, heavily painted with black and white jags of lightning across his face, "...we must find these women-killers and rub them out!"

Bad Elk said nothing as the man reined in his pony and then spurred it towards him; the horse, a fine bay mustang, pranced relentlessly as it approached. Bad Elk was unarmed and afoot but no over-painted troublemaker was going to make him move. The Dog Soldier brought out a hatchet from behind his war shield:

"If there are no men here – bring out your women – I hear they fight on behalf of the Suhtai!"

Without warning the Dog Man stopped his pony suddenly and looked beyond Bad Elk.

"If you want to see the power of the Suhtai, friend, then keep moving towards my brother – you'll be dead before you can raise your axe!" growled Smoke on the Moon.

Bad Elk, startled by the interruption, looked round to see a quiet semi-circle of his band's Thunder Bear and Striking Snake soldiers with bowstrings drawn and guns pointing at the Dog Man. He smiled:

"Thank you and your fellow Dog Soldiers for the information…" he said, straining to keep the sarcasm out of his voice as the Dog Man shifted uncomfortably in his saddle at the loud voice and stinging words.

"…I will consult my People and we will act as we see fit – just like you and your Lakota friends do. I hear that the Great Council never approved your attacks on the white settlers – and those attacks brought the bluecoats upon us!"

Bad Elk had never liked the Dog Soldiers – courageous, yes but unrestrained, unmindful of any of their actions on the rest of the Cheyenne and, worst of all, intermixed with Sioux warriors that he regarded as bad company.

The Dog Man glared but swung his pony round with a defiant yell and galloped off to join his departing companions.

Smoke on the Moon nudged his pony forwards, leant down from the saddle and placed a brotherly hand on Bad Elk's shoulder:

"Our father would have been pleased with your bravery just now but our mother would have been astonished at your tact!" he said laughing. Bad Elk grinned, relieved at the departure of the Dog Men.

"Broken Knife and I will take our warriors out to see if the pony soldiers' are coming from Big Sandy Creek. I'll send a messenger back to report which way they are going. It may be wise to get the People out of danger…" said Smoke, though instantly regretted telling his brother what to do next – Bad Elk was a wise man and would already have a plan.

As expected, Bad Elk acted swiftly – he ordered the village to pack and move north, closer to the Tallow River. It was a hard decision to make in winter – finding a camp ground with all the required timber, water and forage was hard enough at the best of times when scouts could look around at leisure. Now they would have to take what they could find.

Deep in thought, he walked back to where Burnt Hair, his wife, was dismantling the lodge.

"Will the pony soldiers attack us?" she quailed. He smiled reassuringly and said:

"No, we'll be long gone if they are coming this way."

He sat down and watched her collapse the lodgepoles and fold the skin tipi sections onto a travois tied behind her pony. He made no offer of help – this was women's work and, he reasoned, he would only get in the way. He regretted that his pipe and tobacco were probably packed into one of the *parfleche* containers – a smoke would enable him to think. He got up to rummage inside one when a woman's voice called out, shrill with alarm:

"My brother!" – it was Red Shawl Woman, mother of Star the absconded girl warrior. She caught his arm and blurted out an incoherent tale about her daughter returning, wounded by a bear, accompanied by the Traveller and 'those women' – she meant the Forked Lightning Women, Red Shawl was not a believer in their new found freedoms – and a rescued captive. Oh yes, and the Crow may be following them on the revenge trail.

Bad Elk sighed and sent the woman on her way – he would get the full story later when she'd calmed down; though the information about the pursuing Crow would need to be verified. She hadn't mentioned See the Dark, his nephew – he hoped this was just an oversight.

A young boy, on his way to round up the pony herd for the move north, passed by on his sorrel mount. Bad Elk called him over and told him to ride after Smoke on the Moon and tell him to send some scouts out towards Crow country, to see if any danger approached from that direction. The boy, delighted to be released from a routine task and given something important to do, galloped off, yipping with pleasure.

Bad Elk sat down and, elbows on knees, and held his face in his hands – everything seemed to be happening at once. If the Iron Sky hadn't yet fallen, it certainly seemed to be pressing hard on the top of his head.

---- o o o ----

Chapter Twenty-One

Lobo stood in front of the Kiowa chief and tried not to be afraid; he had never been to the campfire of Big Bow before and wasn't sure why he'd been summoned. He'd have nothing to say to Big Bow as he couldn't speak his language but he'd see what he wanted and try to help – his small band of Kiowa Apache depended on co-operation with their more powerful allies.

Big Bow motioned him to sit and, to Lobo's surprise, leant over to the fire and passed a cooking pot full of roasted meat, signalling him to eat. Lobo grinned and nodded – the meat was good and the Kiowa Apache always seemed to have too little to eat – it was a welcome change to fill his belly. Big Bow waited patiently while Lobo ate – the Kiowa nodding encouragement and exuding calm.

Another Kiowa man, that Lobo recognised as Hair Stands Up, walked up and sat beside his chief; Big Bow nodded in greeting and spoke some words to him. Lobo watched as Hair Stands Up pulled a skin pouch from his belt and loosened the sinew that kept it closed. Whatever the contents were, Lobo wasn't to see them yet. He wiped the grease off his lips and said his thanks – one of the few Kiowa words that he knew.

Big Bow nodded and smiled – Lobo was reassured, perhaps he had done nothing wrong? He breathed out in relief.

Suddenly, Big Bow pointed to the neck decoration that Lobo was wearing – the Kiowa Apache warrior sat up in surprise; did he want paid for the meat? Lobo untied the necklet and passed it, jangling metallically, to Big Bow who signalled that he didn't want it as a gift but signed:

Necklet – where from?

Lobo held the necklet in his hand and looked at it – he'd kept the copper cartridge cases that the N'De man had fired from his new gun over a moon ago. One of his warriors who was good with metal had formed it into a decoration to wear. He signed:

'Picked up. Apache man. New gun. Left them behind.'

Big Bow watched closely and nodded. Hair Stands Up opened the pouch and tipped out some of the same cartridges onto a red blanket. Lobo was puzzled – had these Kiowa met the same man? Big Bow signed:

'From Kiowa fight. Tracks of Apache and Medicine Arrow man. New guns.'

Lobo sat bolt upright – he could actually help! He signed:

Yes. Medicine Arrow man there. Stone eye. His mother of my people. Both new guns. Many mules.

Big Bow:

Heading towards Apache lands or Cheyenne?

Lobo confirmed they'd gone north, towards the Cheyenne country.

Big Bow:

They killed my warriors. We find them when Moon of the New Grass comes.

The Kiowa chief sat back contentedly – he'd received some criticism from his own people for not avenging the deaths of Etsay and his Black Leggings warriors right away. He'd kept the peace by saying he needed some more information – the Kiowa would have to be patient and trust him.

Now he knew he had taken the right decision – those copper tubes had been important; he was glad he'd picked them up. They needed to find the Cheyenne band that contained a one-eyed warrior with a Kiowa Apache mother, an Apache man and those new guns. It shouldn't be too hard – the Cheyenne were generally friendly and would not suspect his motives.

Revenge would come with the Spring.

---- o o o ----

Chapter Twenty-Two

Cold Moon was new to the Thunder Bears and was pleased to be on the war trail so soon after his purification ceremonies. The young man didn't know any of his fellow warriors well as he'd married into Bad Elk's Suhtai band only one summer ago. Still, personal glory in any coming battles with the bluecoats would make up for any lack of deep comradeship. He shrugged deeper into his bearskin robe and guided his pony along the jagged creek bank.

He, like many of the People, had been rattled by the disruptive entry of the Dog Soldiers into the village circle, screaming for revenge after the Sand Creek fight. Cold Moon had watched the Dog Soldiers' craziness with distaste. The cool and calm dispatch of Suhtai warriors to their tasks by Broken Knife and Smoke on the Moon suited him better and he was happy to be in the saddle, riding slowly through cold mists towards Sand Creek to bring in any survivors and destroy the white horse soldiers.

It had been a long ride to reach Sand Creek and winter still lay heavily on the land; scattered snow drifts lay in sheltered places and the air was chill. Packs of wolves with bloodied muzzles walked past the warriors, unafraid and sated – it was a bad sign. A bank of white fog slipped over them as they approached the creek.

He rode into the roiling clouds of river mist as all his flanking riders disappeared from view; Broken Knife, somewhere ahead, called out to them from the greyness:

"Keep in earshot; I can see the lodgepoles of Black Kettle's circle now."

Off to his left, Cold Moon could hear neighbouring hooves sliding and grating on the frozen earth so he reined his pony towards the sounds. A black jagged shape arose and suddenly he was in a treeline with wet, low-hanging branches brushing his face. His horse, spooked by the mist and trees, whinnied in alarm. Another horse nearby grunted and a mule brayed.

A mule?

Cold Moon was puzzled as his brain raced for answers – they had brought no mules. But he was not going to summon help on his first war trail with his new companions – it would be embarrassing if it turned out to be nothing more than a stray from the devastated village. Instead, he spoke:

"Friend?"

There was a reply, but it was a poor version of his native tongue:

"I am a friend of the Cheyenne!"

Cold Moon was spooked and heard the rattling of low branches as the speaker came towards him; he cocked the hammer back on his trade gun and backed his pony out of the treeline and onto the creek bank. The mist rose and out of the stand of timber walked a man wearing a soldier hat and leading a horse and mule. The man was white!

Cold Moon shouted a warning to the others, wherever they were:

"Veho! Veho!"

He looked around to see where his war companions were but the mist had only cleared where *he* was. Ahead, from where the torched lodgepoles jutted above the grey smoky carpet, there was a confused jangle of voices. Cold Moon must warn them again. The white man came towards him, waving his arms and shouting something.

He braced the stock of the gun against his hip and fired; the veho staggered under the impact of the bullet and went down. Cold Moon charged, ecstatic that his would be the first kill of the war trail – it would seal his acceptance and status early. He drew his hatchet and leapt off his horse.

---- 0 0 0 ----

Henry Armstrong was only dimly aware of two fights going on above his head. He lay face down where he'd collapsed when the bullet had hit him, tearing the muscle through his right shoulder. There was not much blood but it hurt like Hell.

Someone was sitting, straddling him across his back, shrieking like a demon. A blow from a hatchet sliced through the collar of this bearskin coat but didn't connect with bone or flesh. He tried to turn his head to speak, to tell his attacker he was a friend but the warrior seemed unable to hear him. His face was pushed further into the frozen ground

A clatter of pony hooves and a sudden shouting melee over him relieved the weight off his back as the attacker was dragged off to one side. Henry was roughly flipped onto his back and he looked up into the painted face of Broken Knife. The leader of the Thunder Bears didn't seem pleased to see him:

"Today is not a good day to be wearing soldier clothes," he said, flinging Henry's wide-brimmed campaign hat into his face.

---- 0 0 0 ----

Chapter Twenty-Three

The Englishman's return to the Suhtai village, hunched over his saddle horn and in pain from his shoulder wound, wasn't the happy homecoming he'd expected. Broken Knife had refused to take the time to make a travois to ease strain on his wound, so he'd made Henry ride back with the Thunder Bears after their scouting of Sand Creek.

Broken Knife's warriors were angry. They had found only bodies and body parts – a grim harvest in the winter cold. There was little they could do. Some of the Thunder Bears had relatives amongst Black Kettle's *Wutapiu* band and didn't know what had happened to them.

Henry knew many of Broken Knife's warriors, and they knew him, but the scar of the massacre of Black Kettle's village hung over them like a pall of funeral smoke. There had been no joyful shouts of recognition when they'd pulled Cold Moon off him or cheerful criticism of his poor language skills as in times past. Instead, they had been sullen and silent – only grudgingly leaving their saddles to hoist him onto his horse. They had ridden at a hard pace to get home to prepare for the big revenge trail against the whites and, when they finally reached the Suhtai circle of lodges, left him on the ground when he fainted.

Many of the younger children, unaware that this veho had once lived amongst them ran screaming for their mothers who charged out to protect them carrying hatchets and knives. The women didn't care about recognising Henry, just protecting their children from a strange white man in a soldier hat. Only Carver's intervention saved him:

"Stop it, you fools!" he yelled as he sprinted to Henry's side, laying him on his back so they could see his face.

"Don't you recognise our friend, *Hen-ree* who helped save the woman of Smoke on the Moon from the Crow and filled your bellies with his hunting rifle when hunger stalked our lodges?"

The women paused; one of the older women pushed through the line of muttering females and walked over to Henry, who was coming out of his faint and winced as the pain of his wound caught up with him:

"Yes, it is our friend *Hen-ree* but his red face hair is gone – maybe that's why we didn't know him."

Relieved at any excuse to hide their embarrassment, the women agreed that the veho's face had changed and walked back to their chores, herding their children from him.

New Grass arrived at her husband's side and handed Carver a buffalo robe from their lodge bed. Carver helped his friend stand up, threw the robe over his shoulder and helped him back to his family tipi:

"Lootenant, I'm mighty glad to see you again but you need to grow your damn beard and lose that hat!"

"Good to see you too, Mr Carver. Your poetry is bloody awful by the way."

---- 0 0 0 ----

BOOK TWO

'The hatred of many enemies is a sign of Cheyenne greatness.'

(Broken Knife, leader of the Thunder Bears soldier society)

Chapter Twenty-Four

See the Dark and Viajero had tired of riding in the mass of warriors and pushed their ponies out in front. They had to canter for a while to break free of the noisy throng:

"We'll scout ahead," he told the Apache.

"No need for scouts with all those…" grunted Viajero, flicking his hand vaguely to the rear.

That was true, thought Dark – the huge war party didn't need to stop and worry about enemy strength or if the signs were good for a fight – they just rolled over anything in their way. He likened the massed warriors to a grinding stone – crushing all before it; there could be no glory in that.

The young Cheyenne disliked fighting alongside people he didn't know – and there were many of those. Too many in Dark's opinion. Warriors from most of the Cheyenne soldier societies were in the war party as well as Lakota and Arapaho. The Suhtai miliary societies were there of course – Smoke on the Moon leading his Striking Snakes and Broken Knife his Thunder Bears. They were somewhere back in the crush of riders. Though Smoke was his father, Dark had learned to leave him alone to command his warriors – he didn't want to ruin any pre-battle medicine rites that they had performed; especially if it got his father's warriors killed.

Viajero, of course, just disliked other people in general and being assailed with their constant chatter and never-ending war songs in alien tongues made his head ache. The Dog Soldiers were some of the loudest. His own N'De people cherished silence – noise either warned enemies early so they could flee or it brought enemies to you before you were ready.

The Apache had joined the Cheyenne on the early revenge raids in midwinter as the news had come in about the massacre of their people at Sand Creek. Though he would never *be* a

Cheyenne, his sense of home and family with the Suhtai had required his unquestioning help and so he gave it.

Out of earshot of the others, both men had discussed the latest ride against the *vehoe* - the war bands had joined together yet again to attack more whites but food was short, ponies tired and, since an attack some days ago on an isolated ranch and a lone family wagon, there were few whites to kill. It was a wearisome business but they would need to stay until they thought revenge had been served.

The Apache seethed with discontent – neither he nor his young war brother had taken part in any close fighting – they had taken part in the charges against the whites of course but, by the time they had reached the enemy in the crush for personal glory, all the other warriors had made their kills or counted coup. It was galling and frustrating but it was a duty that had to be done until someone ended the revenge trail. Complaining about it had to be done with care or not at all.

Still, outside of the main throng, talking openly was possible. See the Dark spurred his pony up alongside the Apache:

"One of the Dog Soldiers wanted to trade for our new rifles," he said.

The Traveller grunted and asked:

"And what did you say?"

"I told him they had nothing we wanted…"

The Apache nodded in approval. Dark though, as usual when he had too much time on his hands, wasn't done:

"…I also said that Yellow Bear had told us that your God, Usen and Maheo had combined their magic to bring the rifles to us. And if anyone tried to steal them, they would die a lingering death!"

Viajero looked at the younger warrior with astonishment and shook his head with mock sorrow at the blatant lie:

"Well, what will probably happen now – now that you have disrespected both of our Great Spirits – we'll end up as vulture food long before our time – so, thank you!"

Dark snorted with laughter, leaning off to one side in the saddle as the Apache swiped a hand at him. Disrespecting the gods – even in jest - could bring bad medicine when least expected.

Viajero hoped that his friend would not have made up any more tales that the One God would not find funny. The young Cheyenne though was obviously in a chatty mood:

"I was pleased that my uncle kept the Forked Lightning Women at home – it wouldn't be a respectful thing to do to allow them to mix with all the other soldier groups on a real war trail."

Viajero nodded:

"Maybe, but some of those women have already been on more war trails than many men."

"Yes, but I heard that the Kit Foxes and the Elkhorn Scrapers refused to ride if the women joined us," said Dark.

"Well, that's *their* problem…" said the Traveller, "…as for me, I think they fought well against our enemies – especially the tall, stringy one."

"Ah, Willow," said Dark knowingly. There had been talk that the Traveller was looking for a second wife. Most people thought that Mouse might have been his choice. But Mouse, who had always been affectionate to the Apache, had been killed on the war trail against the Comanche; Dark had assumed that her death had made the Apache lose interest in any other woman. But, the Hunkpapa girl, Willow? That was a revelation…he would tease the Apache some more when the time was right.

"It is good that *Hen-ree* came back to us – that idiot Cold Moon almost killed him." said Dark.

Viajero and Dark had both called into Kah-vuh's lodge to see Hen-ree before they took to the war trail again. The white man was pale and thin – he didn't look healthy without his beard.

"Hmm," said the Apache, "I saw he had two new rifles like ours – but he didn't have the gun that you gave him when he left."

"I know…", answered Dark proudly, "…that rifle now hangs in his lodge in his own country – he says his friends often ask who we are. He tells them our names – we are famous."

Their ponies had slowed to a walking pace and the noisy war throng in the rear was coming back into earshot. Both men spurred their mounts to a trot to increase the distance again.

Two pronghorn antelope sprang out of a gully and dashed away – two dust-coloured blurs against the broad, yellowing sweep of the grasslands. The warriors steadied their spooked ponies.

Viajero said:

"With those new guns, Kah-vuh and Hen-ree should have joined our war trail."

"No…" said Dark, "...we are killing whites – they would be fighting with their own kind – of course they are not here."

The Traveller just grunted but wasn't convinced; he had no convictions against killing anyone – enemies or his own people - if they needed to be rubbed out.

"At least Hen-ree gave us presents – did you bring yours?" said the young Cheyenne. The Traveller nodded and seemed mollified by the reminder. He reached around into his possibles bag on his hip and held up a small wooden carving:

"It is a good gift. Hen-ree remembered my spirit creature – it is a good likeness. They must have skilled woodcarvers in his country."

The Apache looked closely at the detailed tool work on the carved horned lizard then put it away again. He nodded in satisfaction.

"Did you bring your gift?" the Apache asked.

"Of course…" said Dark, patting his medicine bundle around his neck, "…it's in here."

No man could see the contents of the young Cheyenne's precious bundle as disaster would befall the owner so he didn't open it - but Viajero had seen the gift anyway when Hen-ree had handed it over.

"I have seen glass beads before but never a glass eye."

"Yes," said Dark, "The colour matches my good eye. I took out the stone eye you gave me and wore the glass one once – to show my mother…"

"What did she say?"

"She screamed and said it was witches' work. Then she burst into tears – she said I looked like a boy again."

Viajero smiled but noted that Dark's stone eye was now back in the boy's head where it belonged; after all, they were off into battle and he knew the young Cheyenne treasured the confidence it brought. That gift had sealed their friendship many moons ago.

See the Dark smiled ruefully as he remembered his mother's reaction when he told her of the gifts Hen-ree had brought – she had never been comfortable with the white men in the village.

Still, he'd thought of a way to taunt the Apache some more about Willow and opened his mouth to say it. But the Apache had stopped his pony.

"Hah!"

Viajero was looking dead ahead.

It was only then that Dark, concentrating with his good eye, saw the rider– a solitary Indian some ways off, coming towards them, unhurried and constantly checking the ground. Viajero called to Dark who rode up alongside; both men dismounted, hurrying to a rocky outcrop to see if the man was friend or foe.

The rider got closer – Dark, though his one eye was inflamed from lack of sleep, could eventually see by the rider's spiked scalplock that he was a Pawnee. The man was wearing a white man's linen shirt and carrying a rifle, sitting astride a *veho* leather saddle. He and the Apache cranked a bullet into their new rifles at the same time and were about to shoot when the rest of the war party crested a ridge behind them. The warrior mob shrieked their war cries when they spotted the intruder on their war trail.

The Pawnee stopped his pony abruptly as the swarm of his enemies came into view, churning the slopes into dust.

A breakaway group of younger, inexperienced warriors dashed out of the mounted crowd and urged their reluctant ponies towards him. The Pawnee fired a quick shot from his rifle before reining his mount around and galloping off eastwards. The bullet hummed over their heads and smacked into the earth behind them.

Dark and the Traveller thumbed their rifle hammers down – no need to waste ammunition - and snorted in disgust as the group of yelling and bored youngsters set off in pursuit.
Dark watched as the Pawnee's fresher pony gradually outdistanced the fading mounts of their young men.

He mused on what they had seen – what would a lone rider be doing out here equipped with so many goods of the *vehoe*? Probably a scout for the bluecoats or a hunter for other whites that brought food to night camps. It was hard to tell. Whatever it was that the Pawnee was heading back to, he just hoped that it would make a good target for a successful attack so that their dead brothers and sisters at Sand Creek could be finally avenged. And – as he silently acknowledged to himself – it would also mean that they could all go home.

---- 0 0 0 ----

Chapter Twenty-Five

"Goddamn trail jumpers!"

Jubal Tallentire was short in stature and temper. Patience was fine for preachers or women sewing quilts but it didn't sit well with the captain of a westbound wagon train. He had good reason to curse out loud.

He stood up in his stirrups, using the height of his big grey gelding to get a better look. The view didn't make him any more amenable. The grass north and south of the trail had been chewed and trampled. And it was recent. Cropped stems, yellowing in the summer heat stretched out for a quarter mile or more on either side of the wagon road. A roaming buffalo herd *could* have stripped this grazing but a cold trickle of reality in his belly told him otherwise.

Nudging the flanks of his horse with his heels, he slowly crossed the broad trail looking at other signs. He found no comfort there. Splashes of cattle dung were no more than a day old and fresh ruts from iron-rimmed wagon wheels, cloven tracks of oxen and boot prints from teamsters had churned the soil leaving a darker, reddish-brown hue on the dusty surface. Another wagon train of emigrants, bound for California or Oregon or some other goddam place, was ahead of him.

Tallentire snorted in frustration; his aim to lead the first wagon train across the Plains at the ending of the War of the Rebellion had misfired. Lee's surrender at Appomattox had been only been signed a few weeks earlier, but Tallentire's 's calculations to get in front of any competitors by an early jump-off from Council Bluffs had failed. From here, and on along the Platte River Road, his wagon train would pay the price. The cattle and wagon teams ahead of him would have first chance at any available grass, his own pioneer column would be a poor second. They would eat the early-bird trail dust all the way to the Rockies.

He spat at the new tracks and arched his back to relieve the stiffness brought on by too long in the saddle. The leather creaked under his shifting body weight. He eyed the spoiled ground in disgust. A move of a wagon train depended on available pasture and water; it was Tallentire's job to find it and this wasn't a good start.

Then, as if that wasn't enough, there was the goddam Indians; news up from the telegraph office in Independence – before they'd even crossed the Missouri - had brought dire warnings from Fort Laramie. There had been a lot of Indian trouble along the wagon roads since the New Year. Large war parties were reported to have attacked and killed settlers, railroad workers and soldiers alike. The wagon boss had tried to stay in a cheerful frame of mind when his fearful company of pioneers asked difficult questions about their safety.

Jubal Tallentire was rarely alarmed; he had already considered his choices. Indian attacks on wagon trains were rare; too many guns in too many hands usually kept the red devils away. His own column of forty wagons was a moving fortress – fifty, even a hundred braves would be stupid to chance their luck in the open. Reassuring folk of that quieted some of their anxiety. Still, all weapons were now kept close by their owners and more night guards became the new reality for his company.

Lost in thought, he pulled his hat brim down to shade his eyes. The unusual early summer heat seemed to draw the moisture out of his skin. His throat was already dry but a pull at his water bottle would have to wait. His horse snorted the rising dust out of its nostrils. Now, as he sweated into his saddle leather on the edge of the Plains, Tallentire bitterly recalled some damn Scotch poet saying about the plans of mice and men coming unstuck. The bastard had been right.

He jerked out of his reverie, turned his grey horse round and looked eastwards, back along the rutted track. He couldn't see his column yet and stifled his irritation. This was not an occupation for an impatient man. Still, discipline was holding up well and the pioneers were settling into the routine of trail life.

He shaded his eyes from the sun and looked eastwards again. A column of dust rose into the blue sky as the canopies of the lurching wagons crawled into view. Hell, they were still a couple of miles back. That was the trouble with fine weather, it made the pilgrims dreamy and overconfident. Children would be sent to pick berries or wild flowers, women would visit each other's wagons, cattle would be allowed to graze where they wanted, drovers would catnap and the iron-shod wheels would slow to a crawl and defeat the day's purpose of cutting down the miles to trail's end.

Frustrated, Tallentire dismounted, loosened the cinch on his saddle and, holding on to the head rope, allowed the gelding to graze on what remained of the summer grass. The grey picked fastidiously at the grass stems. The wagon captain watched and grunted in contempt. These big American horses didn't fare well on prairie grass, they needed a daily feed of oats to keep them in condition. One of these days he would trade the damn thing in for a sturdy Indian mustang.

A cloud of flies descended onto the grey's flanks and hocks. The horse flicked its tail in annoyance. Tallentire took a sip of warm water from his tin canteen, rolled it around the inside of his mouth and spat it out into the tangle of grass roots.

He pulled the head rope of his horse and the grey walked to him. The noise of the approaching column drifted to him on the breeze as he tightened the cinch on his saddle. The sound of singing drifted up to him – a hymn, he thought – then he remembered, today was Sunday.

 He crouched down again using the shade of his tall horse to keep cool and whiled away the minutes before he would have to remount.

An adventurous steer was out in front of the column, followed about half a mile back by a young drover, embarrassed by his failure to keep the animals in check.

The steer spotted Tallentire hunkered down behind the horse, rolled its eyes in alarm and defecated energetically. Tallentire stood up, threw the reins back over his horse's neck and sighed. What better travelling companion could a man need than a four-legged shit sack? The next fifteen hundred miles suddenly seemed like a long way.

He held onto his saddle horn and hauled himself up; it was only when he'd regained his seat that he noticed the swirl of dust off to the west – right in the path of the approaching wagons.

A single rider was spurring towards him –Tallentire squinted at the image; it was John Iron Rope, the column's Pawnee scout who'd been riding a half day ahead to find water and grass. The Indian was waving his rifle, his spiked scalp lock flattening against the crown of his head as his pony came at a dead run towards Tallentire.

The Pawnee slid his horse to a halt:

"Indians coming – Lakota, Cheyenne – many!"

"Painted for war?" asked the wagon boss, trying to be calm.

"Yes…" replied the scout, circling his mount to look westward again.

"How many?"

John Iron Rope stopped his horse prancing and looked directly at Tallentire:

"Many - like maggots in a dead buffalo."

The wagon captain kept calm but spurred back towards his column; John Iron Rope couldn't explain in numbers used by whites but he never exaggerated - his mobile fortress may soon get a chance to prove its worth.

---- 0 0 0 ----

Chapter Twenty-Six

"Jesus, Mr Carver, steady on. That hurt!"

"Stop moanin' Lootenant – you're like an old woman – just stand up and straighten yer arm out," said the wolf skinner, jerking his friend's arm in no gentle fashion.

"That wound was a through and through – didn't nick the bone, went in above the armpit - you were lucky."

"Bollocks," said Henry as he pushed his right arm into his shirt sleeve. It was an effort and he steadied himself on the lodgepole:

"I need to unpack my camp gear and move out of here – your wife is getting tetchy with me."

"Nah, New Grass is happy to have you here – same as me."

Carver stood in front of Henry and put his hand on the other man's shoulder:

"Thanks for the new rifle – we'll test it soon. You must be made of money now yer Poppa's met the Great Spirit."

"Well, any money I had from my father's estate is gone – so I'm penniless. Just a poor, poetic soul wandering life's highway…"

"Yeah, I wouldn't count on yer 'poetry' makin' you a livin'" said the wolf skinner unsympathetically.

"Well, I was quite impressed with yours, Mr Carver. I've been thinking about this – we should publish a joint volume of our doggerel that can be used on gravestones. I was thinking of 'Tombstone Tragedies' as a working title. What do you think?"

"Jeezus, Lootenant, you need to get laid to take your mind off this crap."

Henry grinned and pushed past, flipping back the tipi door flap and sat down outside in the sunshine. Carver joined him, pulling his willow backrest away from the cook fire and stretching himself out. They sat in silence for a while – happy to be back in each other's company.

Henry fumbled in his pocket and brought out a small hard-backed notebook:

"Here's one I did in New York – in a restaurant…"

Carver groaned and put his head in his hands while Henry read out loud:

"Here lies steak chef
Vincent Blair,
Faced a shotgun
For a dare
Now he's peppered
Medium rare"

"So, my friend, you can see the main poetic elements of each of these – a name, a firearm or weapon and a death – Tombstone Tragedies, see?"

"God Almighty!" snorted Carver. "Poetic elements? We're in a goddamn village full of savages and you're spoutin' poetry."

Henry smiled – he knew his friend well. Once left alone, he knew Carver would be furiously trying to outwit him with better rhymes. His friendship with the wolf skinner had taken many strange turns but none as daft as this. There was a pause.

"Not everyone's pleased to see me back…" said the Englishman, "…Badlands Walking Woman, of course – she's never been very appreciative of my magnetic personal charm…"

"Yeah, I wonder why," countered Carver sarcastically.

"…And Sweet Water – she's a bit distant. As though we'd never lain together before…"

"Well, she's been a warrior for a while now," said Carver, "She won't be wantin' to give up her free life just to be at your beck and call."

"Oh absolutely, dear boy – we talk of course, but that's all. I must admit though, my pride is a little hurt."

Carver smiled at the Englishman's expressions – it was good to talk in his own tongue again - but it reminded him of more serious things:

"New Grass asked me the other day why I didn't call you *Henree* like all the Suhtai. She asked me what my friend-word meant…"

"Friend-word? Oh 'Lootenant' you mean?" said Henry; "So what did you say?"

"Well, for now I just said it was something I'd called you when we first met – it was what white men did before they became true friends and I don't like lyin' to her. But I'm gonna call you Henry from now on – whether it sits easy with you or not."

"Of course it does my dear friend – just reassure me I don't have to call you Pythagoras – I'd die of embarrassment," laughed Henry.

"It's serious, hoss. Someday one of these Indians is going to link that name with you bein' a pony soldier – even if it was a long time ago. Then we're both for the peeled skin and the anthills. Sand Creek should make us both more cautious."

"Got it Mr Carver…" said Henry flourishing a mock salute, " …what do you want me to call *you* then? 'Mister' sounds a bit formal."

Carver lit his pipe, stared into the distance and said:

"My mother used to call me 'Pye'."

"Not a bloody chance!" snorted the Englishman, "…I'll sound like a waiter with a damn dessert trolley – 'Apple Pye anyone?'," and laughed so much that his wound hurt again.

---- o o o ----

"Those Forked Lightning Women hate men," said Badlands Walking Woman as she stretched forward to scrape the elk hide thinner; it was a good skin and would make an excellent shirt for her husband when she'd dressed it properly. She dropped the shreds of flesh and fat into a pot – there would be soup later.

Bright Antelope wasn't so sure:

"They are young and strong-willed, yes but they are proud of finding a new trail in life for women to follow – I once thought about being one of their warriors…" she hesitated, "…long before our daughter came along, of course." The Mescalero woman sighed in envy, cut up her newly snared rabbit and wiped the steel blade on the grass.

Badlands merely grunted in disbelief. Bright Antelope kept her own counsel but remembered when the newly-formed Forked Lightning Women had returned from the fight against the Pawnee winter camps on the Loup River. They had made a name for themselves as warriors that day, running off the pony herd, trampling Pawnees under hooves and killing any who got close to their hatchets. Theirs had been a wild glee, shared by Bright Antelope, – a triumph over an enemy as they'd extracted retribution for an earlier raid on the Suhtai that had killed many of the band's fighting men. Despite much criticism, White Rain's women warriors refused to disband and re-join the marriage pool. Bright Antelope didn't blame them – her own marriage to Viajero was strained as he followed his own warrior's path. Their daughter was always asking for her father and she had no real answers to keep the girl settled or distracted.

Burnt Hair kept silent on the matter of the women warriors; her husband, Bad Elk needed to keep the peace in the band between dissenters and supporters. The Forked Lightning Women had gone off on a badly-planned raid against the Crow last winter and had been roundly criticised when it had failed, especially as Blue Wing had been killed and the young girl, Star, had lost most of her face to a bear. Burnt Hair sought a new topic – talking about the women always brought division:

"I was pleased to see that the other *veho* has come back to visit us," she said.

Badlands pressed her lips together in distaste. She had always harboured the view that the white men - *Hen-ree* and *Kah-vuh* - had some evil motive for living with the Suhtai. She had tried to prove it to her husband but failed – Smoke liked them and would not hear a word against them. She also knew that she was in a minority in the whole village – the white men were popular because one of them had taken a Cheyenne wife and both of them had fought against enemies of the Suhtai. Still, her suspicions held:

"The one they call *Hen-ree* is only here because he was shot by one of our warriors. He was lucky that Broken Knife recognised him in time."

Burnt Hair was surprised at Badlands' bitter tone:

"Those men saved your life– you should be more grateful!"

"I only say what I see – Broken Knife told my husband that they'd found him at Sand Creek after the pony soldiers had attacked Black Kettle. Don't you think it strange that the veho had been in that very place – right where all that killing took place - and was wearing a soldier hat? Neither of them has joined the war party to fight the whites while our menfolk are risking their lives for revenge! I wonder why?"

"It's what *our* men do…" countered Bright Antelope, "…that is their purpose in life – they hunt to keep us fed and make war to keep us safe. Those white men did the same for us when they needed to and no-one wants them to fight against their own kind if they don't want to."

The Mescalero woman gathered the rabbit pieces, brushing off the strands of dried grass that had stuck to the red flesh, put them in an iron pot and stood up:

"And the soldier hat? He wore that when he was here many moons ago – long before the fight at Sand Creek! Your bitterness makes you blind as well as crazy!"

Bright Antelope checked any further outburst and held her tongue - Badlands Walking Woman had been the first in the Suhtai to offer any real welcome to her and Viajero when they first joined the village; she had been kind and patient as they overcame the language barrier between them.

It had been Bright Antelope that had originally collected the round black stone from her Mescalero lands; the same black stone that now sat in the eye socket of Badland's son. There was real friendship and a sacred bond between their families but they would drift apart if this conversation went on. She walked away. Burnt Hair, glad of the excuse, joined her.

But Badlands wasn't finished:

"You mark my words well. *Hen-ree* has found out where we are and will bring more soldiers to kill us all. He gave my son that glass eye so he can see when we are weak!"

---- o o o ----

Chapter Twenty-Seven

Buford Magill looked along the sights of his long Springfield rifle at the approaching horsemen and found himself smiling in anticipation of the coming fight. He'd had much experience – along with over a million others - at estimating military strength in the field. The War between the States had been a hard taskmaster. He knew what a full regiment of cavalry looked like.

Despite his southern name, Buford Magill was a Maine man, though he was always quick to say that his Daddy was a Texan, born and bred; he'd been killed by the Comanche long before the war started and his mother had moved back north to her native state. So, Buford had no compunction with closing and killing his Reb countrymen as his regiment swept down from Little Round Top with the bayonet. But today, the regiment-sized group of riders wasn't cavalry – they were Indians, maybe a thousand of 'em. No telling what the outcome might be. He licked his thumb and cleared some dust from the notch of the rear sights.

"You ready there, Mister Magill?" asked the wagon boss.

"Sure am, Cap'n – it's nice to be able to stand up and load the rifle behind cover for a change. Comfier like."

"I agree…" said Jubal Tallentire, "…these wagons make a good fortress – we'll be fine."

"That's a lot of Indians out front though…" said Magill, "…never seen so many. Still, I ain't never been on the Plains before."

"If it's any comfort Mister Magill, I've done this for nigh on twenty years and I don't recall war parties this size either. Ol' John says quite a few have guns – progress, I guess."

Tallentire kept a wary eye on the massed Indian horsemen – these were probably what all those panicky telegraph messages in Independence were warning about. At first, his settlers were spooked and despairing but, after helping align the wagons into a defensive box shape, their fears seemed to ebb away and all now stood to arms – tense but uncomplaining.

The riders milled about; if the Indians had some sort of plan, it was lost on Jubal Tallentire. They were still almost a mile away – too far for any accurate shooting; they would need to be a lot closer for any of his pilgrims to be able to hit anything. As if to oblige, the Indians rode ever forward.

"Who are they anyway, Captain?" asked Magill.

"Well, Ol'John says they're mainly Cheyenne, a good chunk of Sioux and some Arapaho. Those Cheyenne have real beef about the Army massacring their people last year. It must be a big hurt – they've been on the warpath for months. That Chivington has a lot to answer for."

Magill was about to reply when the Indians suddenly broke ranks at a half mile out. A small group galloped forward and charged the wagon lines – as they got closer, neither Tallentire nor Magill could see a single gun in any Indian hand.

---- o o o ----

"Those young ones are going to be rubbed out," said Viajero as he watched the glory-hunting youngsters try to make their first kill.

"The Dog Soldiers sent them – to teach them the ways of battle – I think that's one of the Dog Men leading them," said Dark, shading his good eye with one hand.

Both he and the Traveller had ridden to the flanks for a chance to get in close to the halted wagons – they could see the stock and draught animals from the wagons inside the squat defences of the whites, milling about as the tension rose.

As the novice warriors closed on the whites, puffs of white smoke spurted from the wagons, the boom of the shots followed close; several riders fell out of their saddles and crashed into the churned earth. Not all were dead; one stood up and tried to catch a passing pony with an empty saddle only to be shot down by a double shotgun blast from the wooden walls.

Despite the losses, the young men whirled their ponies and charged again – at first firing arrows at the more difficult targets between the gaps in the wagons but then deciding, after some hurried talking out of range of the guns, to fire volleys above the canvas tops and drop them into the less-well defended far side of the square. This caused some whites to drop – the young men whooped with joy - so the hated whites could be slain, even behind formidable barriers! A shout of encouragement went up from the main body of the war band.

Dark was elated; it was an unexpected moment of victory against a well-armed and well-defended enemy:

"Those boys will have earned their war honours today!" he yelled to Viajero above the noise. The Apache just shrugged – charging against heavy odds wasn't his way; better to wait until nightfall and creep in close and kill them with the knife. He flinched as Dark stood up in his stirrups and yelled his war song close to his ear.

There was a drumming of hooves on Dark's left and he was surprised to see his father ride up with his Striking Snake warriors backed up by some men from the Kit Foxes soldier society. All had bows drawn with arrows nocked; the arrowheads were wrapped in dry grass or cloth.

Above the yelling and chanting Smoke shouted to his son:

"We're going to get close enough to shoot our fire arrows into the wagons – Broken Knife's boys and the Arapaho will do the same on the other side. Any whites that come out - kill them!"

Father and son exchanged an affectionate glance but there was work to do…

Dark nodded and shouted the plan to Viajero; the Apache waved his gun in agreement. At least now there may be some targets in the open to use their rifles on. Smoke rode on, followed by his screeching warriors, dust shielding them from view. Unprompted, the Apache rode after them and Dark followed; for the first time in this fight, both could hear the noise of bullets flying past them – they were in killing range now and needed to be careful.

Dark watched as Smoke's warriors rode behind a shallow mound, circled their ponies and lit their arrows from a buffalo horn with smouldering hot ashes inside. Viajero grabbed Dark's sleeve as he went past:

"Not too close, little brother – those fire arrow men make a good target standing still…"

As if in agreement, a volley of accurate fire swept from the wagons and emptied several saddles – there were cheers of encouragement from the *vehoe*. Dark shouted to his father but could only watch as the Striking Snakes broke up and rode towards the guns, firing their flaming arrows into the canvas and woodwork of the whites' wagons. From the other side of the wagon camp came another volley of fire as smoking arrows arched into the sky and plummeted into the wagon tops – Broken Knife was completing his part of the plan too.

Dark's pony became restless – anxious to be in the battle, feeling the tension of its rider - and it snorted and leapt with shallow jumps, especially when bullets hummed past. It was hard to control the animal and keep his rifle ready for action. But, despite several fires starting, there were no whites to shoot.

The main war party remained mounted, out of the range of the guns, and just waited.

---- o o o ----

Buford Magill was actually enjoying the fight with the Indians; in his experience of battles in the late war, standing up behind a barricade and reloading at leisure was almost a luxury. Charging shoulder to shoulder into levelled Reb muskets on some battlefields, as heavy lead slugs tore lumps out of the Maine men was no way to fight – those boys didn't want any goddamn general to say later that they'd died well. No Sir – they wanted to fight clever and *live* well.

He was in his practised rhythm - tearing open the paper cartridge with this teeth, tipping powder and ball down the barrel then ramming the charge home - when his wagon exploded beside him. Magill knew that it was only a couple of small barrels of coal oil but it was enough to set the woodwork on fire and caused him to move outside the cover that it had given. There was no time to douse the flames – others were in the same predicament. Canvas coverings now smouldered and burst into flames; sparks flew and settled on other wagons.

Black smoke roiled over him as he coughed and stumbled away from it – he was joined by three other men and a woman, all with tears streaming down their faces, as they loaded their guns again.

---- o o o ----

See the Dark and Viajero didn't have a good view of the wagon camp as they circled their ponies, keeping out of gun range. They knew that many fires were burning but the smoke covered the battlefield and the main war party, whilst restive and noisy, still hadn't moved in for the kill. Indeed, a small herd of buffalo had crested a hill some distance off and some of the war band tried to ride off and hunt them, only to be whipped back into place by others. Dark didn't blame them – food had been short and discipline over the large group of fighting men, all out for personal glory, was hard to maintain.

Suddenly, one wagon, off to the left of them, burst into a sheet of flames and whites were stumbling outside of the defensive walls – *now* it was time for them to attack. Both warriors spurred their horses towards the staggering figures.

At last, out of the corner of his eye, Viajero saw the main war party move forward – horses jumped into motion, warriors waved their shields and weapons; loud battle cries carried over the distance. The war party surged ahead, picking up speed as many prayers were said, eagle-bone whistles shrieked and death songs sung. Even Viajero was impressed with the colour and power of the sight. But he and Dark needed to kill their enemies now before the others ruined it! At least this time they were close.

Both men chambered rounds into their rifles at a dead run, their ponies pleased to stretch out and do their work. They rode in an arc to use low cover until they could close with the whites, round the low rise where the fire arrow men had lit their shafts.

The whites were easy to kill; two short volleys from their new rifles and four bodies crumpled to the ground, some still twitching as they stubbornly clung to life.

Viajero leapt from his pony and used his stone club to smash the skulls of a woman and a fat, bald man - though this was hard as his pony reared and tried to drag the reins from his hand. The woman had a beautiful necklace of green stones around her neck. He thought that Willow, the Hunkpapa girl, might like it so he tried to rip it off but the plunging pony threatened to break loose so he paused. He was about to bludgeon the third man writhing in the soft dust when he noticed that Dark wasn't there.

A burst of heavy but measured firing from the front of the wagon defences told the Apache that the main body was now attacking, screams and yells split the air – but from whites or his own kind, he couldn't tell.

He leapt back into the saddle, leaving the skull-crushing unfinished and, using the height from his horse, looked round for his war brother. He spotted Dark's pony standing back in a hollow but the young Cheyenne wasn't in the saddle – Viajero was sure that he hadn't been hit so where was he? He galloped across the short stretch of ground.

---- o o o ----

Buford Magill had seen the Indian crush the heads of the other folk on the ground and tried not to writhe in pain; playing dead might be better. Mrs Ashton and her husband had screamed a lot as blows from the stone club had descended in rapid succession. They were soon quieted though. Oddly, the short dark Indian suddenly stopped his attack and rode off – Buford didn't care why – he was just relieved to be alive.

Sparks and ash from burning wagons fell onto his face and the sound of gunfire still echoed from the front of the wagon defences. Ponies thudded past him though he couldn't see if the riders were white or red. He pulled himself up until he was leaning on one elbow; as far as he could tell he'd been shot three times and blood oozed from his left thigh and side. Pain came from the right side of his neck and red streaks on his exploring, powder-singed fingers confirmed the wound.

The sun cast his shadow on the ground, and he saw in his silhouette that strips of blackened canvas had caught in his hair, some sticking up, some hanging down – he looked like a goddamn Indian! Still, things could have been worse – Magill forced a smile.

A groan from the prostrate body of the third man brought Magill back to his predicament, vulnerable on the outside of the wagon defences. He craned his neck to look round at the man – he had seen him before at the campfires but didn't know his name. His throat was smoke-parched and he was unable to call out. At least the groaning man still had his Colt Dragoon in his hand – Magill had no idea what had happened to his Springfield rifle. The firing on the wagon lines had faded away – perhaps the attack was over?

Nathan Bolt had lived up to his name during the war – he had scuttled away from his regiment during the battle of Shiloh and stayed out, shacked up with a whore in Indiana until Lee had signed the surrender. Now some goddam red savages had stopped him getting West to where easy money could be made and one of them had the damn gall to sit on the ground just across from him! Well, Damn You mister! He raised his Colt and fired into the man's spine.

Buford Magill's life force slowly flickered out – the final sparks in his brain told him nothing; he had been killed by a man he didn't know, in a place he didn't know, on a date that would never figure on any tombstone. He just wished his mother knew where he was.

---- 0 0 0 ----

Dark was kneeling by his father's body and looked up as the Traveller came to find him. Smoke on the Moon had been shot through the head, streaks of his blood mixing with the red battle paint of the Striking Snakes. The bullet had gone in through his left cheek and punched out of the right side of his head – he would have been dead before he fell out of the saddle.

Viajero dismounted swiftly but saw the young Cheyenne's' tears of grief and stood back. The boy had been cradling Smoke's head in his lap but was now rocking back and forth on his haunches, wailing inconsolably. The Apache was always at a loss when it came to grief – he was sad for Dark of course, the boy had just lost his father. But he had died as a warrior should – in battle against his enemies – so there was a sense of satisfaction of a life's aim being accomplished. He could shed no tears for Smoke on the Moon, just as he'd shed none when his own family had been killed by Mexican raiders back in his own country, before he had met the Cheyenne. Death could be a long or short ride along life's trail. Tears didn't help.

The Apache looked across to the wagons – white men were shouting and ripping burning canvas from metal frames as they separated the devastated wooden frames from those still serviceable. He shook his head – the *indaa* would never stop coming here.

As the smoke lifted, he could see that the main war party seemed to be gathering again – back in the place they had charged from. Several of their number still lay sprawled around the wagon camp – there would be many to mourn back in their home villages.

Shots still came out from the wagons, some in their direction. He and Dark were still vulnerable in the hollow:

"Are there any rituals we can do for your father? We need to be back in the saddle."

Dark just grunted and hauled Smoke's body over the cantle of his father's pony. Then he remounted and said:

"No, we'll just go home."

For once, in any fight, back as far has he could remember, the Apache felt relieved.

---- 0 0 0 ----

Chapter Twenty-Eight

Dark said little as he led the pony away from the battlefield. He had wrapped his father's body in his bear robe and, as there were no trees here to make a travois, tied him head down across the saddle cantle with rawhide rope. He had cleaned Smoke's head wound with dry grass, though a trickle of blood still fell on the ground, marking their route, as they set out on the trail home. It was an ignominious way for a famous warrior to travel – even in death. He hoped Smoke would forgive him in the next life.

He knew he was already disobeying his father's wishes – Smoke, like many other Cheyenne fighting men, had always said that if he was to die in battle, his body should be left there; no-one should risk themselves to bring it to another place. Coyotes and wolves would benefit from the food and his remains would be scattered over the country he loved.

Indeed, had not the hated *vehoe* not been so close, Dark may well have done what his father had wanted. But flesh-eating animals were one thing – white men were another. He knew that the pony soldiers had chopped up the remains of Black Kettle's people after the fight at Sand Creek – rumours from the *veho* towns told of purses being made out of Cheyenne women's breasts, necklets made from the bones of children's fingers and hatbands made from skin cut from the dead had shocked them all. Dark would make sure that no such indignity would happen to his father.

Two other Striking Snakes, both married men, had been killed in the wagon fight but their bodies lay under the guns of the whites and couldn't be recovered. Dark hoped that the whites would leave them alone and move on to wherever it was that they were going.

His decision to take his father's body home seemed to have been some sort of signal for the large raiding party to split up and move back to their own encampments. Some of the younger warriors had howled at the plan and wanted to continue on alone. The war weary pipeholders of the raid – and they were many – had left the decision up to them but warned them about being tracked back home so that avenging pony soldiers could find them again. After some reflection and angry talking, most agreed and rode sullenly homewards in disconsolate groups. A few, desperate for recognition, left to find other trophies and plunder. See the Dark ignored their plaintive whining – he was anxious to take his father back to the Suhtai encampment.

Viajero rode silently behind his young friend, pleased that none of Broken Knife's Thunder Bear soldiers or the surviving Striking Snakes had decided to accompany them on their sad, homebound ride – at least it would be quiet. He looked up to the darkening sky; it was odd, in late summer, to be following the north star towards the Powder River country away from the Suhtai natural homeland south of the Tallow. He knew that Bad Elk had moved his village up there so that the Cheyenne warriors could attack the whites in the north, along the iron tracks of the white steam machines and the wagon roads. It was unfamiliar country – he hoped Dark wouldn't get lost.

A drumming of hooves made him turn around. Two of Broken Knife's warriors rode up to Dark:

"The back trail is clear – no whites are following us. Our pipeholder wants us to press on quickly to the land of our cousins…Bad Elk's village is there."

Dark just nodded – the warriors were very young, they seemed scarcely out of childhood. Their eyes showed their tiredness but they were upright in the saddle and proud to have fought on the war trail – Dark hoped that they may have had better luck at collecting battle honours than he or the Traveller had.

He tried to smile, but as usual when his stone eye had been in its socket for too long, merely managed a grimace. The boys tried not to look shocked and rode off.

Viajero watched them go – he did not exchange any greetings or farewells with them. The boys would reach Bad Elk's band first and spread the word of the Suhtai losses. The Apache doubted that they would bother to notify his wife that he was safe, not that he had asked them to do it. His White Mountain brethren had been of similar mind – men took to the war trail because they wanted to – Usen would always decide which ones came back and those who never did. The feelings of family didn't come into it. He would have to grit his teeth and silently accept the wave of grief that would accompany them into Bad Elk's village on their return.

See the Dark and Viajero rode on, silhouetted against the darkening sky as the stars rose up from behind swathes of thin cloud. Normally, after a battle – as the excitement had faded and fatigue took over – the pair would have discussed what they had done with Dark deliberately exaggerating his deeds and courage just to see the Apache react. But the death of Smoke cast a grim pall and stopped any talk.

As the moon came out, the Apache stopped his pony and unsheathed his bow, bent the frame to attach the string and nocked an arrow onto it. Dark stopped too – there had been no warning of any enemies from the Traveller, though their horses were now sidestepping nervously.

Out of the darkness and into the moonlight, the young Cheyenne saw why – around fifty paces behind them a small pack of prairie wolves padded along, sniffing the air as the blood scent from Smoke on the Moon's body reached them. They smelled the carrion on the pony and they were hungry.

The grey semicircle, seeing the rider halt his pony, stopped too – unsure of what to do next. To Dark, the wolves, like the two Thunder Bear soldiers, seemed young and inexperienced.

Viajero settled their indecision by putting arrows into the two leading animals. The wolves screamed in pain and whipped their muzzles around, arching their spines to try and grip the arrows to pull them out but, after a while, crumpled exhausted into the sage brush. Encouraged by such weakness, their companions fell onto them and ripped them apart in bloody chunks of fur and flesh.

The Apache now spurred his pony to catch up with Dark – in the pulses of moonlight, the boy seemed brighter than of late.

The young Cheyenne looked at Viajero and said:

"Wolves are just wild dogs – there's probably a meal for you back there."

In the darkness, the Apache smiled grimly – it would take a while longer but the boy was coming back from his grief.

---- o o o ----

Chapter Twenty-Nine

"What the Hell are those Kioway doin' way up here?" growled the wolf skinner.

"No idea, old man," said Henry as they dismounted from their ponies and unloaded the buffalo meat. New Grass put the heavy joints onto a worn elk skin and dragged them off to the lodge. She too eyed the Kiowa uncertainly as the small party of warriors talked in sign language to Bad Elk.

"They're way off their own huntin' lands…" said Carver "…they usually stay 'round the Arkansas with the Comanche."

"Maybe they're lost," said Henry, as he stared at the small mounted band of strangers.

Carver snorted in disbelief:

"Nah, they want somethin'." He watched as Bad Elk was joined by Yellow Bear. Carver hesitated then walked off to his lodge, pulling Henry by the sleeve – the sight of white men in camp could arouse suspicion among the visitors.

Hair Stands Up stayed in the saddle and greeted the other Cheyenne man who'd just walked up.

Yellow Bear signed his welcome but remained wary as he watched the sign talk between Bad Elk and the mounted group.

Both the Suhtai soldier societies were out of camp on the Sand Creek vengeance raid so few warriors were around to defend the village if it was needed. The Kiowa weren't enemies of the Cheyenne – at least for now – they and the Comanche had helped feed and shelter the People when they'd fled from the bluecoat soldiers after the fight at Turkey's Creek eight summers ago. But the story of the Kiowa leader – a search for stolen war ponies - didn't ring true and one mounted stranger, who was staring intently at the criss-crossing sign talk, wasn't a

Kiowa. This smaller man was much less prosperous, with patched clothes – he seemed ill at ease being in Kiowa company. Yellow Bear thought that he couldn't understand what the other Kiowas said around him.

Lobo sat uncomfortably in the saddle – this was the third Cheyenne camp they had visited in the past ten days and the lies of Hair Stands Up made him nervous. Big Bow's mission to find the killers of the Black Leggings soldiers last year had been entrusted to one his deputy chiefs; Big Bow remained at home waiting for news. Their search now seemed a rude and dangerous intrusion when the bulk of the Cheyenne were out fighting the whites – the people remaining in the village seemed tense and suspicious. The Cheyenne even had white men in their village – he had seen them before they slipped out of sight – traders or trappers maybe? Still, he had to concentrate on his task now - Big Bow had ordered him to ride along with Hair Stands Up to identify the men he had seen with the rifles and mules.

Suddenly Lobo was aware of a tugging at his leggings and looked down from the saddle; a short, fierce-looking woman was speaking to him. It took him a while to realise that she was talking in his own tongue:

"Na-ishan-dina?" she hissed.

"Yes, I am" he replied, "who are you?"

"I am one of your people; captured by the Medicine Arrow people when I was just a girl," said Badlands Walking Woman. The man in the saddle smiled as she stumbled over long-forgotten words:

"Are you a slave? - do you want to be rescued?" he said, hoping that they wouldn't have to fight their way out of the Cheyenne village.

Badlands snorted with laughter, she was one of the most forceful women in camp with two famous warriors as her kin – so no, she wasn't a hostage:

"Come and eat," she said.

Lobo hesitated then realised that one of the things he and the Kiowa had been looking for - a Kiowa-Apache woman living amongst the Cheyenne – was now holding the bridle of his horse. Perhaps she would lead them to the Apache and the stone-eyed boy.

He dismounted and, ignoring the surprised looks of the Cheyenne camp chief and Hair Stands Up, walked to the woman's lodge and sat outside next to the cooking fire. The woman dished stewed meat from the cookpot into a wooden bowl and told him to eat – Lobo never refused food and ate hungrily. They talked as he ate – she seemed keen to know where they had come from and what he was doing in camp with the Kiowa warriors. Lobo was evasive and, to fend off any questions about Hair Stands Up's lies, he asked her about her family.

It was while they were talking that a commotion broke out at the southern end of the camp circle. Bad Elk and Yellow Bear took their leave of the Kiowa and hurried down to see what was happening – women were wailing, children, reacting to their mothers cried and dogs barked. Old and young raced down to the source of the noise and amplified the panic – the sounds weren't joyous.

Bad Elk struggled to part the growing crowd of people and to make out what had caused the upset.

Then he saw the small, dejected war party walk their undernourished ponies into camp – Broken Knife and a straggle of Thunder Bears and Striking Snakes were there but he couldn't see any sign of his brother, nephew or the Traveller – a rising black cloud of doom encircled his heart and he pushed through the tense bodies to hear the worst.

Hair Stands Up was annoyed – it wasn't polite to abandon visitors in camp but something bad had obviously happened to the Suhtai. He and his warriors had come a long way north to find Cheyenne camps. His chief, Big Bow's demand for information for his vengeance trail was still clear – they would track down the killers of the Black Leggings boys, even if they spent all summer doing it. Now, abandoned in mid-conversation with the Suhtai, Hair Stands Up would try a different village downstream.

They reined their horses to leave, leading Lobo's mount in the direction he had gone with the woman. Suddenly, the same woman, her face stiff with fear and a meat knife still in her hand, rushed past them and down to where the ill-tidings had come into the village. They saw Lobo looking puzzled at the cooking fire and motioned him to get into the saddle:

Once mounted, Lobo looked around guiltily and signed:

"We have found them,"

Hair Stands Up, nodded and smiled with contentment. Big Bow would be pleased. Not only did his chief now have a target for revenge but, if he had judged the swirl of activity correctly, the Suhtai had just lost warriors on the war trail and would be even weaker.

---- 0 0 0 ----

Chapter Thirty

Carver had sent New Grass down to talk to the returning warriors, judging it best for Henry and himself to stay low until they knew what was going on. Henry disagreed, shrugging off the wolf skinner's restraining hand and flipped back the skin lodge door.

He was met by Badlands Walking Woman coming back from the death news. She was wailing loudly and cutting her hair; two long black braids lay on the ground behind her as she tugged at remining tufts and sliced them off, wisps blowing into the wind. She had slashed her legs and rivulets of blood seeped into her moccasins. The Englishman stepped forward to offer comfort but she looked fiercely at him through red-rimmed eyes and snarled as she raised her knife to him.

Carver had come out behind him:

"See, Henry? None of this – whatever *this* is - is your fault. But Injuns git mad real fast and no tellin' how they might act if they see us there. Sensible men stay outta the way. We'll wait until we can hear from New Grass and weigh up what it might mean."

Henry drooped his head and hissed his frustration – doing nothing didn't sit well with him – the armies he'd served, both British and American – had always frowned on indecision and inactivity. But Carver wasn't finished:

"In the meantime, load your rifle and picket your pony close to hand – takin' our leave in a hurry might be needed."

---- o o o ----

Bad Elk sat and took in the camp's deep despair. The village remained in loud turmoil for an entire day as the returning warriors told their stories of the long raid. Not all had returned together and one of the Striking Snakes they thought was dead had turned up wounded but alive the next morning. This had given some hope to those in mourning – perhaps their relative was on his way back too?

But, at dusk two days later, the arrival of See the Dark and the Traveller, with the body of Smoke on the Moon across the saddle, removed all doubt about any survivors. The loss of five warriors of his band's fighting strength was a serious blow and had unsettled the Suhtai.

Bad Elk felt the same surge of helplessness that he had experienced after the Pawnee raid many years ago – an unease brought on by the sudden weakening of their ability to survive. True, some of their warriors had returned but their ponies were thin and needed rest, arrow quivers were empty and powder and ball were in short supply. All would need to be replenished.

His sister-in-law seemed to be going crazy with grief. Badlands Walking Woman seemed stunned by having to deal with her dead husband's corpse; usually it would have been left on the battlefield, buried under rocks or on a platform up a tree. She wailed far into the night – a keening, alien sound that rattled nerves further. Then, suddenly, she stopped shrieking and practical matters seemed to have taken over.

He had walked past her tipi to hear her cooing, as if to a child – through the open flap he saw Badlands brushing Smoke's hair smooth with a porcupine quill comb and sang her love songs to him as his flesh grew even colder. The couple's other son, Flea, sat right in the shadows of the lodge, wide-eyed and petrified by his mother's signs of madness.

Bad Elk found it hard to adjust to his brother's death – Smoke had seemed invincible in battle and wise in peace. It had been Smoke who had persuaded him to take on the role of chief after their last chief, Twisted Wolf had been killed during the Pawnee attack many moons ago, in the same year that Dark had lost his eye. Their battle losses had been much worse then but

Smoke and Broken Knife had steadied the younger hot heads and forced the band to work together to survive the winter. Then, at least, despite his new burden of leadership his brother had been by his side to encourage and advise. The hole left by his death was deep.

He sat with his head in his hands by his campfire and moaned in despair and grief. No amount of food brought by Burnt Hair, nor offers of his pipe and tobacco would calm him. He raged at Maheo for giving him such a great weight of responsibility – no mere man should have to bear this alone.

Distance from familiar country was one of his fears. His Suhtai people were far from their homeland, so Smoke would not even be buried in his own country. Though Bad Elk was relieved that the long raid, punishing the whites for Sand Creek, was over and he was satisfied that their trip to the Powder River had been necessary to support the war bands – he was unsettled by just being so far north.

Though the country they were staying in was beautiful and buffalo had been plentiful, the long war trails by the warriors had meant that less hunting had been done and the meat supplies were already starting to be stretched. He knew the whites would be out looking for them – the journey back to their Smoky Hill country would be full of peril.

Yellow Bear walked up and sat down beside his friend – they had always found each other to be wise company. This was not the time for talking though; the spirit diviner just put his hand on Bad Elk's shoulder and patted him gently.

After a while, when his chief had stopped rocking back and forth, Yellow Bear said:

"The burial scaffold has been erected and your brother needs to be laid on it – your people are waiting."

Bad Elk nodded without looking up, then stood and straightened his back. He walked across to the hill by the riverbank with Yellow Bear and silently entered the howling circle of Suhtai mourners.

---- o o o ----

The Forked Lightning Women stayed discreetly at the edge of the funeral ritual for Smoke on the Moon while his brother and son led the mourning. They watched as the leader of the Striking Snakes was laid to rest with all due ceremony – he was wrapped in a buffalo robe and had his weapons and amulets hung from the wooden cross pieces of the scaffold. Dark brought Smoke's war pony into the circle, led it under the platform then killed it with a knife to its neck. The pony crumpled to the ground, blood gushing from the wound. To make sure that his father could see the stars that marked the trail to Maheo and the next life, Dark had exposed Smoke's face to the winds and the robe remained open to the sky.

Yellow Bear chanted incantations to summon the spirit helpers and wafted sage grass smoke from a burning taper then watched as the Striking Snakes soldiers performed a ritual dance to show respect to their dead pipe holder.

Broken Knife, aloof as ever, watched with detached interest – those young Striking Snakes would need to choose another leader soon – none seemed ready for it.

White Rain and the original women warriors had all liked Smoke – he had been fatherly towards them and, though he was a traditional Cheyenne and had been hesitant about their soldier society, he had not blocked it. Indeed, he had welcomed them onto the war trail against the Pawnee when the time came for revenge. They all wept unashamedly and hoped Maheo, the Life Giver, would see Smoke arriving in the next life and give him plenty of buffalo to hunt.

It was Willow, perhaps because she was an outsider from the Sioux, who spoke an uncomfortable truth:

"We will miss the father of See the Dark of course, but the death of five of our Suhtai warriors means that the soldier societies are now weaker…"

White Rain always went quiet when Dark's name was mentioned; it was true that they had made, and occasionally lived in, a lodge together but the indecision about marriage between them was an obstacle. Still, she had deliberately sought him out to comfort him in his grief and he had seemed grateful.

"So?" growled Crow Dress – a note of warning in her voice; the Hunkpapa girl was not known for her tact.

"Now they'll really need our help!" replied Willow, a little too chirpily for the occasion.

White Rain caught up to her and slapped her across the face with the back of her hand – it was an insulting blow and Willow drew her knife. Both women were now experienced warriors – the fighting spark strong in both of them. White Rain had not taken her pistol or rifle to the funeral but squared off in front of Willow regardless.

"*That's* all you can think of?!" shrieked White Rain, "…one of our finest warriors is being sent on his death journey and all you see is an *opportunity*?"

Willow, head cocked to one side as she kept a wary eye on her leader, remained calm but moved her knife to its fighting position; no-one slapped her and got away with it.

Sweet Water, her face still scarred from the small arrows of the Crow boys in the fight last year, grabbed Willow's arm:

"No! If we fight amongst ourselves, then our enemies will have won a greater victory."

Breathing heavily, both women faced each other. Eventually, each putting a reconciling hand on the other's arm. Sweet Water was right, this was not a time to fight between warriors and friends.

Willow was about to speak when a strident voice shrieked across the clearing; it was the wife of Smoke on the Moon:

"Enemies? The *vehoe* are our enemies and you…" Badlands pointed at Sweet Water with a trembling hand caked with blood from slashing her arms, "…have lain with one and your sister is married to one! They bring poison and folly to the camp – they turn the heads of our children with gifts and games. They raise dust between us so we can't tell friend from foe. Their people have killed my husband – both those white snakes should leave and you should go too! You are not true a Cheyenne now."

Willow snorted with laughter, pleased at the distraction from being slapped:

"Sister – you are not a true Cheyenne either. Just like me. If all the non-true Cheyenne rode out, our camp would be empty!"

White Rain laughed. It was an exaggeration and all knew it but the humour took the sting out of Badland's words.

Willow had only been very young when See the Dark's mother had been brought into the Suhtai circle, spitting and furious at her capture from her southern grasslands people. Everyone thought she was crazy then and avoided her – especially the men. Perhaps she was headed down that same trail now she had lost her husband?

Sweet Water put her hands on the shoulders of her friends and pushed them away from Badlands Walking Woman, back towards their lodge. Her own thoughts stung her - she had only lain with *Hen-ree* a few times before he went back to his own country; they had been close but had not planned anything beyond those occasional nights. One of the attractions of *Hen-ree* was that he *wasn't* a Cheyenne - the white man had never lectured her about Suhtai traditions or counselled her away from her warrior life so she was always relaxed around him.

Now he was back the old affections had returned but she was concerned that he was being vilified by some – all out of his hearing, of course. There did not seem to be a threat to his life – yet – but she would keep an eye on the troublemakers just in case.

---- o o o ----

New Grass was shaking when she brought the news. Hidden in the treeline she had watched Badland's screaming outburst against Hen-ree and her husband. The woman had seemed like a rattlesnake in a pony herd, striking out at anything that came in her path. Even, worse, she was starting to persuade others that the presence of white men in camp was the source of their troubles; the families of the other four dead warriors were the first to take her side.

She reported the events to Kah-vuh with tears in her eyes. Betrayal by some of the tribal women hit her hard – she had washed clothes at the creek with them, helped them sew hides for their lodges and had brought back children who strayed too far from camp. Now…this.

Carver nodded and patted her shoulder affectionately and passed his pipe to Henry:

"What d'you think hoss?"

Henry drew on the sumac mixture and wished it was a cigar:

"Well, Badlands has never liked *me* – even before Smoke was killed. But he was the one who held her in check – now he's gone we've lost an ally - anything might happen…"

The Englishman coughed as the blue smoke caught his lungs; tobacco and talking never mixed:

"…of course, I could always leave the camp and you could stay. That might ameliorate things…"

Carver didn't know what 'ameliorate' meant but assumed that if Henry decided to ride out, things might settle down; he was unsure though.

New Grass sat just inside the door of the lodge and waited until *Kah-vuh* had time to translate some of the men's talk for her. She had seen Hen-ree's cautious preparations for riding out; even worse, her husband was doing the same. She was nervous now in case they had to flee the Suhtai circle and leave the rest of her family.

---- o o o ----

Chapter Thirty One

In defiance of Badlands Walking Woman, Sweet Water deliberately sought out Hen-ree, walking over to his temporary canvas shelter just outside the main Suhtai circle and, uninvited, sat down beside his cooking fire wrinkling her nose as she looked inside the iron cookpot:

"Bad Elk says we will move the camp tomorrow; he says the widows will be allowed to share a lodge. Hunters will share some of their meats with them. We are going south to our own country at last."

Henry nodded in approval. It was typical of Bad Elk to choose a wise and humane way to ease the widows' loss of their main food providers. Carver had told him of war widows in other Cheyenne bands being ejected from their husbands' tipis and all the dead man's property being given to the poor. Sometimes, in the winter, they starved to death.

"Does your face heal well?" asked Henry and leaned forward to trace the light scars on her cheek with his finger. She did not draw away from him.

"Yes, they were only arrows meant for small birds but those Crow boys were good shots."

Henry smiled:

"Well, I'm pleased you survived it – it sounded like a stiff fight."

Sweet Water smiled shyly; it was the first time they had spoken as fellow warriors. There was a pause.

"What are you cooking?" she said.

"Elk...I think!" said Henry, prodding the simmering, unknown lumps with his hunting knife. She nipped a piece of meat with the fingers and tasted it, laughing:

"You should name this meal after our leader!"

Henry looked puzzled.

"Because it's bad elk!" she hooted.

A joke from Sweet Water! Henry grinned as she leaned closer:

"Perhaps you can share it with me – and also your ..." she waved a dismissive hand at the scruffy canvas shelter, "...lodge."

Henry gritted his teeth; he wouldn't lie to her:

"I'll share anything with you that you want – but I may not be here much longer..."

---- o o o ----

White Rain Woman knew where Sweet Water had gone – they had discussed it before her war sister had headed across to the veho's lodge. She had just been on the verge of giving advice against it when the younger woman put her hand on White Rain's arm and said:

"I know what you are going to say – not to make things any worse for Hen-ree or myself..." she tilted her head up defiantly, "...but I don't care and nor does he!"

White Rain shrugged - Sweet Water could make up her own mind and choose what she did in life - and was about to turn away when the girl added her own advice:

"You should go over and talk to See the Dark. Comforting him after his father's death was good but he still eats with his mother! He looks…" she paused as she chose her next words carefully, "…ragged and not well cared-for."

White Rain nodded dumbly in agreement. Dark, despite being a well-respected warrior in the tribe, showed few signs of wealth or prosperity. Yes, he had a string of fine ponies, a lodge of his own – though it was still unpainted with any of his spirit signs – fine new guns and plenty of food. At one time, Badlands had always lavished attention and care on her son but, as her bitterness and unpredictable nature grew, this had lapsed and Dark had the look of a pauper. Even the flesh around his stone eye looked sore.

The Forked Lightning leader watched Sweet Water walk away then went back to their soldier society lodge – there were things she needed to collect. Whether she would make the next move for love, she was still unsure but, as she reasoned to herself, at the very least a Cheyenne warrior needed some help and she would give it.

---- 0 0 0 ----

Chapter Thirty Two

Carver and Henry stayed mounted while they watched as the two regiments of infantry, each heading in a different direction, marched past each other on the Platte River Road. Boots scuffed the dust and it settled on slung muskets and backpacks, turning blue uniforms greyish white. Some of the soldiers halloed to them and the Englishman raised his hat in polite response. There was some jeering and catcalling between the NCOs in each column, though it all seemed amiable.

"What the Hell…?" said Carver out loud.

Henry smiled, recognising the banter:

"Galvanised Yankees…" he said, pleased to be imparting some wisdom to his friend instead of the other way round. Carver still looked confused so Henry pointed to the eastbound column,

"…Confederate prisoners of war who signed up to soldier on the frontier for the Union instead of fighting their own comrades or being in a prison camp. I assume they are being mustered out."

He had heard the term back in Fort Lyon before the Sand Creek fight. It seemed to fit.

"Galvanised Yankees eh? Sounds like a good deal for those boys," said Carver who had favoured neither side in the War; he belonged to neither North nor South – he was a westerner.

Henry was about to reply when an officer on a horse trotted up and shouted:

"Silence in the ranks! Company Commanders, rest your men by the side of the trail and let these damn Rebs be on their way!"

The departing eastbound column jeered at the officer's pomposity and swung past with increased vigour.

The westbound columns halted in a series of poorly executed drills – and, though Sergeants roared, the men simply fell out of line and collapsed in small untidy heaps as the heat haze shimmered.

The mounted officer, snarling in silent rage, spotted Henry and Carver and reined his horse over to them; it hadn't been a good display of military efficiency in front of these civilians.

"Good morning gentlemen – Colonel Henry Carrington of the Eighteenth Infantry at your service." The man gave a short, symbolic salute from the brim of his hat.

Carver just raised his bearded chin in acknowledgement but Henry proffered a full salute in return, his palm facing the officer:

"Ex-Lieutenant Henry Armstrong at *your* service sir!"

Carrington looked startled at the accent and the English-style salute; he stared at Henry:

"Did you serve, sir?" he asked, bristling slightly at the gesture.

"Not in *your* war, Colonel but I did serve in your Dragoons and then the 1st Cavalry against the Indians before the current … er, unpleasantness," replied Henry, amused to see how quickly the man took offence.

"You boys goin' far Major?" asked Carver.

"It's Colonel actually sir…" replied Carrington with exaggerated politeness to emphasise the importance of his rank and task, "…and we're bound for Fort Laramie in the first instance. Then we'll garrison posts along the Bozeman trail – to protect settlers from Indians."

Carver snorted rudely with laughter:

"Not sure how you can protect anybody from Injuns from inside a fort! Where's your cavalry?"

Carrington pointed back along the trail in silent triumph and, as if in reply to Carver's mischievous question, a dusty column of blue coated horsemen appeared and dismounted raggedly beside the resting foot soldiers. Behind them, some distance off swayed the canopies of Army supply wagons.

Henry winced when he saw the horsemen; not one rider had loosened the cinch on his saddle to ease wear on the horse's belly but flopped into the patches of greasewood at the trailside and pulled hats over their eyes, most of them didn't even keep the reins in their hands. These were not trained cavalrymen – and no match for Indians. Carrington noted his concern:

"I know, I know Mr Armstrong – your service in our mounted regiments does you great credit and I can see that you seem unsure about the quality of my detachment of mounted soldiers but we in the Eighteenth Infantry can adapt to overcome all challenges – including staying in the saddle!" He laughed at his own little joke.

Henry remained silent but saw that Carver was watching the approach of one of the infantrymen. The man was very young and carried a Civil War surplus rifled musket as his weapon. He had a piping voice that made him seem even younger:

"Sergeant says we gotta git movin'"

Carrington stared with irritation at the lack of salute or respectful address but said nothing – he waved the boy away. Carver growled:

"Major, sorry *Colonel* - you got yer foot soldier boys with old guns goin' to sit behind fort walls on the main trail up to the

Injun Powder River country. And yer mounted boys don't know what to do with their horses - Red Cloud's Sioux'll have you for breakfast!"

Carrington winced at the harsh words – his own lack of fighting experience in the War of the Rebellion always put him on the back foot. He had stayed behind a desk for the entire conflict, a fact often pointed out by his critics. Still, he had been privy to some strategic chat before he had left his comfortable quarters in Fort Kearny; this would hopefully silence the impudent frontiersman:

"Mr er.. what's your name?"

Carver grinned and growled:

"Skinner – Wolf Skinner." Henry shook his head in mock dismay.

"Well, Mr Skinner…" said Carrington, inexpertly trying to control his horse as a wind got up and a dust devil swirled under its nostrils, "...we are part of a greater plan to clear the Indians from between the Platte and the Arkansas and allow our country to have a clear and peaceful route west - a corridor if you will - so we can expand to the Pacific, where we need to be. So, we will keep Red Cloud's Sioux, the Cheyenne and any other damned dirt digger from upsetting that scheme. My colleagues along the Arkansas will do the same. Treaties have been signed sir – I believe the savages will not prevent our work..."

The Colonel paused in his explanation as all three heard shouting from the ragged column; a mounted officer rode up and down the blue lines, haranguing soldiers back into two ranks, ready to resume their march. Henry could hear their grumbling from where he sat in the saddle.

The new officer, his one silver bar glinting on his uniform, rode up to join them:

"Colonel, the men have rested enough and they're drinking too much water. We need to stretch our legs to get to Laramie. Let's be off!"

Henry listened quizzically to the Lieutenant's attitude to his Commanding Officer and watched as Carrington blanched at the public display of disloyalty, his teeth set in a grimace of disapproval. Once again, there didn't seem to be an ounce of respect in this man's tone either. Henry knew that disrespect and ill-discipline among the officers made soldiers uncertain and weak. This infantry regiment seemed an ill-formed and unhappy body; if it ever saw action against the fighting Cheyenne or the Lakota, disaster seemed likely.

Carrington unclenched his teeth and, in an odd gesture, leaned out of his saddle towards Carver and Henry and shook each of them by the hand:

"I must take my leave of you gentlemen and go off to build my fort in the wilderness."

He smiled a tight smile, knowing that his own weakness had been displayed. Turning to the officer, he said:

"Very well, Lieutenant Grummond – lead the column out please."

Colonel and Lieutenant rode back to their soldiers and resumed their march along the Platte. Carver looked at Henry:

"I know damn all about soldierin', hoss but that just seemed plain wrong."

"You're right my friend…" said Henry, "…back in my old regiment, my CO would have horsewhipped me out of the saddle if I'd addressed him like that. I have a bad feeling about our infantry friends."

"Damn right…" agreed Carver as he watched a whirl of vultures flying above the column, using the warm air to gain height, "…mebbe those birds know more'n we do."

---- o o o ----

Badlands Walking Woman grinned a savage smile of satisfaction: she had been vindicated. The two white men had been caught in the act. She waved for Bad Elk to come and look.

Bad Elk sighed in annoyance – the widow of Smoke on the Moon still caused upset even after her husband had died. But the camp chief was busy – moving his people out of the Powder River country back down to their homeland on the Bunch of Trees River took time. He couldn't wait to get there either – it hadn't been easy mixing in with their northern cousins who had lived with the Sioux for so long that they now dressed, fought and often spoke like them. Life shouldn't be this difficult.

Snarling in frustration he left the slow-moving column of Suhtai and set out for the distant ridge where the troublesome woman frantically signalled.

His sister-in-law was standing in the stirrups – excitedly pointing to the valley below. Bad Elk suddenly saw the marching columns of bluecoats and stopped – he didn't want to be seen nor risk the Suhtai to a sudden attack if the soldiers realised that they were being watched.

"The *vehoe* can't see you, they are smothered in their own trail dust!" shouted Badlands. Bad Elk gingerly heeled his pony forward and reined in his horse alongside her. He craned his neck to get a better view.

"Well?" he said.

"There, there! On the other side of the soldier lines – there you see the treachery that lives in our village!"

Bad Elk looked at where Badland's finger pointed – it was a small group of horsemen, two in blue coats and two dressed like hunters. He recognised Hen-ree and Kah-vuh, of course – he knew how they sat in the saddle – it was important to be able to tell friend from foe whenever they returned to the village. They had supposedly gone off hunting – to share their catch with the Striking Snakes widows – though Bad Elk could not see any meat across their saddles. What they were doing talking to the soldiers he had no idea.

"It all makes sense now…" said Badlands, her face glowing with righteousness. "I said they would bring more soldiers to us after the fight with Black Kettle's people. Now here is proof!"

"You'll notice the bluecoats are walking north, whilst we are headed south – what proof is that?" Bad Elk replied whilst keeping an eye on the group below. He was about to ask another question when the woman shrieked and pointed again:

"Hah!"

Even Bad Elk saw it – the handshake – a white man's sign of friendship and peace. He had shaken the hands of both *vehoe* when they first came to live with the Suhtai. The gesture seemed rooted in good faith – why Hen-ree and Kah-vuh would want to exchange such sentiments with enemies of the Suhtai, he couldn't tell.

One thing was sure though, Badlands wouldn't take any advice from him or wait to reveal the white men's secrets to her growing band of believers. His sister-in-law was a difficult and unstable woman but maybe she had a point.

---- 0 0 0 ----

Chapter Thirty Three

Willow had been right; the loss of the Suhtai warriors on the long raid had resulted in more responsibility for the Forked Lightning Women. Gaps needed to be filled and they now rode alongside some of the remaining Striking Snakes soldiers as a screen to protect their southbound column of families and stock.

The Hunkpapa girl felt happy – the bad luck of one was the good fortune of another; she sat upright on her pony with rifle on her thigh and pistol in her belt. Her war sisters, in arrowhead formation behind her, trotted their ponies a little to keep them supple.

She smiled to herself – riding ahead of moving stock was much better than trailing it at the rear and eating their dust. But the real responsibilities would come when they were allowed to fight alongside the men, though even she – optimist that she was – could not see this happening soon.

Hooves sounded on the hard-packed earth behind her and Little Snake rode up:

"Sister, my chief, Broken Knife wants you to hurry the column along – bluecoat soldiers are near, Bad Elk has seen them."

Willow looks sceptically at the skinny youth and growled in her strange accent:

"If my war sisters and I hadn't rescued you from the Crow last year, neither your hair nor your tongue would be so long. It does not sit well that an experienced warrior –and I mean, me – is instructed on what to do by an untested boy."

Little Snake flushed hotly:

"I am not untested!" he yelled, "I killed Red Horse and then his father, a Crow chief, as I escaped…" spluttering to a silence before remembering:

"…and I only used a skinning knife!"

Willow looked levelly at the boy – he was right of course; he had indeed killed Red Horse and Many Bulls – but she was enjoying her new confidence as a warrior and decided to tease him a little:

"A skinning knife, eh? Just as well it wasn't a bow and arrow as that didn't work out well for poor See the Dark, did it?"

The reminder of his poor bowshot that cost See the Dark his left eye stung the boy and Little Snake didn't react well. He barked his defiance, barging his pony into hers and slapping her across the back of the head. In reply, Willow thumped the youth in the face with the steel butt of her rifle and he fell out of the saddle.

He scrabbled at his pony reins and just managed to keep it from running off as he staggered to his feet. Willow sat calmly in her saddle, pointing the muzzle of the rifle at the young Cheyenne.

"Sister!" someone shouted; Willow looked round to see the Traveller trotting up to join them.

The Apache reined in his pony and looked at the impassive girl – she was a force to be reckoned with, no doubt, but moving camp with whites close by was a tense time and distractions like settling scores could undermine them all.

"He's not the enemy…" he said, motioning Little Snake to remount, "…we may need all the warriors we can get – try not to kill any of ours."

Willow was about to answer when he held up a hand to silence her. Turning to Little Snake he said:

"This woman has killed Pawnees, Comanches and Crows; she has stolen their horses and guns – respect is due."

The young Cheyenne bowed his head while Willow listened, blushing slightly at the praise – not because she thought it wasn't deserved but because it came from the Traveller, himself a formidable and respected warrior.

Viajero watched the girl's face redden – the young Hunkpapa woman was impressive and would make a good wife, even if she *was* taller than him. He hadn't mentioned marriage to her at all – though their mutual admiration was becoming well known in the Suhtai camp. Still, he reasoned, there was no hurry as the lanky girl had no other suitors that he knew of – he would wait.

But, as ever, Usen the Life Giver would always prompt him in his guilt, the Apache knew that he already had a woman, though they had never formally married; one that got more demanding by the day as well as a daughter whose girl child ways had become tiresome. He would need to think about it – raising the topic of a second wife with Bright Antelope would be tricky and, if she had a knife in her hand, probably dangerous.

He would talk to Yellow Bear over a pipe of *veho* tobacco – the medicine man may have some calming potions that worked for the unpredictable women of the N'De.

Viajero reined his pony off to the right and trotted off to the flank where he and Dark normally rode when the Suhtai moved. As instructed by Broken Knife, the column was now moving quicker with all the available ponies being used as mounts for women and children and the Apache threaded his way through them, barging the slower ones out of the way.

As usual, without offering or getting any greeting, Viajero took his place alongside Dark as they silently pushed on towards the home in the Smoky Hill valley.

---- o o o ----

Lobo had been left alone and his heart was bitter. He and the Kiowa scouting party of Hair Stands Up had been shadowing the Cheyenne column – staying well to the west where they couldn't be seen, just below the skyline but keeping track of the Suhtai to see where they would camp next. The encampment was heading south, closer to Kiowa country and easier for Big Bow to take his revenge against the killers of his Black Leggings warriors.

Lobo could tell though that Hair Stands Up had grown weary of the need to be on the trail; the man seemed anxious to get back to report to his leader.

In truth, Lobo could also tell that all the Kiowa in the scout party had tired of *him* – tired of the constant need for sign talk between them and tired of being away from their warm lodges and the food cooked by their women. The Kiowa were indeed fearsome warriors but, now that he had seen them up close and on a tribal mission, Lobo was now much more scornful of their ability to take a few hardships.

Lobo had woken up one morning to see the Kiowa already mounted and ready to go home. They looked down at him as he shook out his bedrobe; Hair Stands Up had signed:

'You are Kiowa eyes now. Follow Cheyenne. When closest to our country, come and tell us.'

With no word of farewell, the Kiowa had reined their ponies south and headed off towards the Arkansas.

Lobo had snarled at their ingratitude and selfishness.

No-one had offered to remain with him on the quest and they had left none of their food. Though he had not actually seen the stone-eyed boy and the man of the N'De again, the Kiowa Apache woman he had met boasted that the boy was her son and the man was of the White Mountain people who camped with the Suhtai. None of these things could be coincidence – it had been he, Lobo, who had found their elusive quarry. Without his cunning, Big Bow still wouldn't know where they were.

Hair Stands Up would probably go home and claim the credit for finding their prey. If Lobo now failed to shadow the village properly, *he* would be held responsible. The warrior threw down a piece of jerky in disgust. Those arrogant Kiowa would have to pay a price for demeaning a man of the *Na-ishan-dina*. He was tired of living on their sufferance – a change was long overdue and, though he had no idea how to do this, Lobo decided that he would bring it.

The air was cooler now as the late afternoon darkened into evening. The sun was dropping behind him as he dismounted and pulled a buffalo robe over his shoulders. He sat down and leaned back against a rock, watching as the distant Cheyenne halted, now hard to make out in the brief glare of the sun's dying rays, unloaded their travois of tipis and poles to make camp.

Lobo picked up his discarded slice of jerky, blew off the dirt and ate it – his short rations and the chill of the surrounding rocks reminding him of how the comfort-loving Kiowa had scuttled off home.

The far activity of the Cheyenne had now ceased. There was no tell-tale woodsmoke and only a few tipis had gone up. The Medicine Arrow people must be making a cold camp – ready for a quick move when dawn came. He and the Kiowa had seen the bluecoats marching up the Platte trail and stayed well out of their way; it made sense for the Cheyenne not to produce tell-tale smoke columns to bring the soldiers down on them.

Bitterness about his treatment by the Kiowa grew, though any actions he took against Big Bow's people - and Hair Stands Up in particular - had to be balanced against any retribution *they* might take against his small group of Na-ishan-dina.

Lobo knew that his warriors couldn't defeat the Kiowa in battle – even if they mounted a surprise attack – there was just too many of them.

If the Spirit of the Grasslands was on his side, then Hair Stands Up *may* be killed in any attack on the Suhtai – the ones he had seen were well-armed - but it was a dangerous gamble and he couldn't count on it. He needed many guns or warriors to help him break the Kiowa – but only the advancing whites had that power. He needed a plan. Lobo shook his head; thinking was painful and made him hungry. The weight of all decisions that he had ever made as tribal leader was never heavier than it was now.

For now, he would watch the Suhtai camp until it was within range of Big Bow's revengers and then decide what to do – his desire to please the Kiowa chief by betraying the Cheyenne location had withered away. Maybe the two white men he had seen inside the camp could help though he didn't know how.

It was while he was shading his eyes, looking into the setting sun and musing on these things, that an answer came to him.

---- 0 0 0 ----

Chapter Thirty Four

Henry sat on his pony and looked into the valley; he shrugged his neck deeper into his coat collar as a light rain spattered onto his hat brim. The bustle of activity in the Smoky Hill valley was a surprise, especially this far west. As well as the smoking locomotive pushing a flatbed wagon laden with sleepers, ties and rails in front of it, large tents were being assembled trackside and men swarmed in all directions. The shouted instructions of track foremen and the metallic clang of hammers on iron spikes carried up to him on the hill:

"Those railway boys have worked hard getting the line this far!"

Carver agreed:

"You're right, hoss. They were nowhere near here last year. No wonder ol' Bad Elk moved the camp up nearer the Saline – too much happenin' down here."

As they watched, a column of wagons rolled along the Smoky Hill trail heading further west; a small troop of cavalrymen rode in front and mounted men fanned out on each flank.

"Those boys ain't takin' any chances with them wagons – musta been Injun trouble down here."

Henry nodded and was about to speak when he noticed one of the flank riders break off and ride slowly up the hill towards them:

"A visitor I think, Mr Carver."

"Yup," said Carver and cranked a bullet into his rifle as it lay across his saddle cantle.

The Englishman tutted:

"He's a white man, Mr Carver…no need for such precautions…"

"So are *we* hoss – but he ain't in uniform like those bluecoats. Just could be one of those days when any polite yakkin' about yer army career won't do us much good."

Henry smiled but said nothing – Carver seemed to worry about everything these days; still, it would do no harm to pay attention to the approaching stranger. The man approached them unhurriedly, he carried a long rifle cradled in his left arm, though he slid the gun into his saddle bucket to keep it out of the rain. The fringes on his buckskin coat blew in the breeze and his wide hat brim repeatedly blew down over his face

Henry could see that the man was young and the hat seemed too big for him but he was smiling as he fumbled to stop the brim blocking his view:

"Damn hat! Wedding present from my wife – I told her the wind would lift it all over Kansas unless I tied it down!"

Henry smiled and nodded; Carver raised his bearded chin in greeting. The young man untied the leather thong from under his chin and took off his hat so the strangers could see his face:

"Good afternoon gents – Bill Cody – army scout along the Smoky Hill trail – out to Fort Hays."

Henry got in first, knowing Carver would decline to answer:

"Good afternoon, Mr Cody – delighted to make your acquaintance…"

Carver hissed at the flowery language.

"…Henry Armstrong and er, Mr Carver – just two wandering adventurers along the trails of the Great Plains. We are from nowhere and going to nowhere in particular."

Cody smiled, noting the English accent but also noted that the two travellers seemed to have no camp equipment, pack mules or any food supply that would help them on their wanderings in Indian country. Their answer as to their intentions was as vague as it had been poetic. Still, as long as they didn't pose a threat to his supply wagons, that was their business. He nodded to their rifles:

"Those are fine firearms gentlemen – do you ever get to use them?"

Carver growled at the young man's impertinence but Henry intervened:

"Just for hunting sir, just for hunting but they enable us to be well-prepared for any eventuality…like Indians…"

"…or curious army scouts," snarled Carver.

"Excuse my friend sir – we haven't spoken to another civilised white man for weeks – he forgets normal politeness."

"That's quite alright Mr Armstrong – scouting for the Army will probably not help my social standing either." Both men laughed and Henry spoke:

"The railway seems to have made great progress, Mr Cody – where is it bound?"

Cody shrugged: "Denver, I think – though it could be China for all I know!" He paused, leaned forward in the saddle then continued:

"You gentlemen livin' a basic life in your wanderings? You got tents or food? I only see a bedroll on your saddles. Don't look like a comfortable way to see our great country."

Henry felt Carver bristle at the questioning and quickly replied:

"Oh, we are camped nearby Mr Cody – nothing much, but enough for us. We just rode over to see the famous railway."

Cody crammed his hat back on his head:

"My apologies for the questions sir – that's the problem of being a scout, I guess. I just keep lookin' at the sign to see what it means and where it may lead. No disrespect intended; we are a free country after all…"

"None taken, Mr Cody," said Henry; Carver's growl of 'Speak for yourself' went unheard.

The Army scout looked down at the railroad, Henry thought there was a glint of sadness in his eyes:

"One thing I do know is that those damn machines will soon fill this country up with people. Same pattern too – soon as we want to move west – trappers, soldiers, settlers, farmers and then the Goddam lawyers! This…" he gestured with a dismissive hand into the bustling valley, "...just brings 'em quicker. Those wild places that you both enjoy - that *I* enjoy - will soon be gone. Injuns too. Make the most of the wilderness while you can my friends!"

Cody waved in farewell and slid his horse back down the crumbling slope and re-joined his companions on the flank of the wagon column.

Carver and Henry watched the riders disappear. The locomotive in the valley blew a warning hoot on its whistle; iron wheels screeched on new rails and couplings clanked as men, grading the ground ahead with picks and shovels, gave way to the track layers. The rain blew up into a squall and the workers were lost to view.

"Well, that's another hundred yards gained for civilisation," said Henry, tilting his head to stop the water going down his neck. But Carver had already turned his horse north, back to Bad Elk's camp on the Saline and didn't hear him.

Neither man saw the small warrior on his pony just below the skyline of a nearby spur as he reined off behind a hill to hide.

Despite his many fears, Lobo had now seen how the whites from the Suhtai village could help him. He just needed to get close enough to talk to them.

---- o o o ----

Chapter Thirty Five

Broken Knife rarely spoke out at the council fire – he could count on the fingers of one hand the number of times he had done this in the past. Then, he had been content to let Bad Elk, Yellow Bear and Smoke on the Moon discuss tribal matters, but the death of the leader of the Striking Snakes had forced the Thunder Bears' pipeholder to take a more active part.

The loss of the warriors on the vengeance trail weighed heavily on his mind – Suhtai battle strength had been cut down and he was now the remaining experienced war chief. He looked around the semi-circle of faces, flickering in the firelight of Bad Elk's lodge, and realised how much he missed the presence of Smoke on the Moon. They had often been rivals when it came to selecting up-and-coming youngsters for their soldier societies – but it had been done with mutual respect. Broken Knife knew what his limitations were and was able to admit that Smoke on the Moon had been a more mature man than he. Now he must be a thinker as well as a fighter; Bad Elk and Yellow Bear had asked for opinions and he must give one:

"Friends, our grief for our lost brothers still hurts us all but we must act swiftly to make sure our people are protected by the warriors we have, until we are strong again…"

There were nods of agreement and grunts of approval. Bad Elk just stared into the fire but looked up to make sure that folk didn't think he wasn't paying attention. Talk of military strength always brought thoughts of Smoke to mind.

"…The Striking Snakes need a new leader – I have asked See the Dark to do this but he prefers to fight alongside the Traveller instead. All men may make their own choices about their war trails and we must respect his…"

More nods of agreement and Yellow Bear patted Bad Elk's shoulder in consolation – Suhtai war leadership in that family would end here. Broken Knife continued:

"...I spoke to the remaining Snakes soldiers two days ago and told them to select a new leader; they will do this."

He left a gap before going on with the more difficult part of his speech.

"The pipeholder of the Forked Lightning Women has asked that her warriors now take their place in our battle line...and I said that I would raise this at our next council fire."

The gasps of astonishment and disbelief from those sitting at the fire were not unexpected and Broken Knife silently gave thanks that he had prepared answers. Two of the elders objected strongly and all listened to their arguments before Bad Elk interrupted and said:

"I suggest they should be given the chance – they are well-armed and well-mounted; they have experience in battle and have proven their loyalty to the Suhtai – even the skinny one from the Lakota!"

There was a ripple of laughter and some nods of agreement. See the Dark and Viajero sat at the back of the council – they were not members of the wise elders but were entitled to listen to what was being said on their behalf. The young Cheyenne nudged the Apache in the ribs when Willow's name was mentioned and grinned; the Traveller sat in stony silence and stared ahead without saying anything. Then Broken Knife added:

"This is just to be for a short time until our two main soldier bands are back up to strength."

The elders remained silent but nodded reluctantly. Bad Elk lit a pipe, murmured some sympathetic words and passed it to the two old warriors who puffed on it vigorously.

One of them, a white-haired old man called Buffalo Walks Lame, blew out a stream of smoke in Broken Knife's direction and said:

"What about the *vehoe*?"

Broken Knife, not understanding the question looked puzzled but said:

"Well, we will do what all Cheyenne will do against the whites – we will fight them..."

Buffalo Walks Lame, sneering slightly, said:

"You know I don't mean *all* white men – I mean the two we have in camp. The widow of Smoke on the Moon has seen them talking to the bluecoats up at the Tallow River; she thinks they are traitors and will bring pony soldiers to attack us."

Broken Knife was about to respond when Bad Elk butted in:

"I know – I saw it myself. I have spoken to Hen-ree and Kah-vuh about it and they say that they were just conversing with their own kind to gather information..."

"Like what?" interrupted Buffalo Walks Lame rudely.

"...information about white forts on the trails up to the Powder River..." added Bad Elk lamely.

The gathering looked unimpressed and talked amongst themselves – what had that to do with the Cheyenne? That was mainly Lakota business, though their northern cousins who lived up in those far lands might be interested.

Without seeking permission to speak, See the Dark butted in:

"My mother is mistaken – Hen-ree and Kah-vuh would never betray this camp. Both men helped save her life some years ago. We should remember that – as my father did!"

Viajero nodded but said nothing as others turned on Dark to condemn him for not supporting his own widowed mother. The young Cheyenne was surprised at the number of voices in the darkness that supported her hatred of the two whites.

Bad Elk sighed as he sized up where the discussions were headed; he knew that Badlands Walking Woman had wasted no time in spreading more rumours about her 'proof' of veho treachery as soon as she'd got back. A sizeable portion of the Suhtai now believed her and even Bad Elk found it difficult to deaden his own suspicions. There was some muttering about the white men being banished but Yellow Bear had a question for Broken Knife:

"Friend," he began, looking directly at the Thunder Bears leader, "...our white guests have their swift firing rifles. Wouldn't they be a useful addition to our weakened battle line – like the Forked Lightning Women?"

Broken Knife thought for a moment or two – he was happier with problems that concerned war:

"Our enemies are now the vehoe – settlers, soldiers and those who lay the iron trail for the smoke wagons. Hen-ree and Kah-vuh did not join us on the revenge trail against whites after Sand Creek – it is hard to know where their loyalties lie. If we have to fight whites in the coming times – what will *they* do?"

"Hah!" said Buffalo Walks Lame, emphatic in agreement. If he couldn't keep the women warriors back, at least the two white strangers could be got rid of.

"It is not a problem I want to deal with when it may be too late to save us all," added Broken Knife.

Yellow Bear looked crestfallen at the nods of approval – in the early days of the whites' arrival in the Suhtai encampment, he had personally helped improve Hen-ree's poor grasp of the Cheyenne tongue and had been pleased to see how his tuition had worked. He liked them both but there was little he could do.

Bad Elk was beaten; Smoke on the Moon had been the main voice in support of the white men living there but now he was gone. The village chief spoke again:

"Very well – Hen-ree may have to go back to his own country across the great lake but Kah-Vuh is almost a Cheyenne man. He is married to a Suhtai woman – I say he stays!"

Bad Elk had just finished speaking when Burnt Hair brought some unexpected food. Her husband stood up and, rudely, said:

"No food – they are just leaving!"

---- 0 0 0 ----

Chapter Thirty Six

There were no tears in Henry Armstrong's eyes as he left the Suhtai village for the last time. Though, as he would admit only to himself, they were just a blink away.

Bad Elk had broken the news but had made it plain that there was no hurry for him to depart; Henry, however, was anxious not to make things more difficult for such a good man by any delays. The longer he stayed increased the time that Bad Elk would have to endure the questionings of Badland's supporters and weaken his position as chief.

He left just after dawn on a sunny day that, he guessed, was maybe in August. It was a sombre moment, even his pony and pack mule could only manage a slow, dejected walk as he rode south from the Saline.

Word of his banishment had been received quietly amongst his friends in the camp; they were unsurprised though, as the influence of Badlands Walking Woman had poisoned many people against him. Still, in defiance of their neighbours, they had sent their children out to him with bundles of cooked food as he'd packed his canvas shelter away. Some of the younger ones clung onto his fingertips, as they'd done in the old days, until he'd sent them back to their parents. His mangling of the Cheyenne tongue had always made them laugh.

He rode past what had been Smoke on the Moon's lodge; outside Badlands Walking Woman and her widow cronies sang an insulting song of triumph about expelling decrepit bull buffaloes from the herd. Burnt Hair, returning from digging wild onions, shrieked fiercely at the swaying group:

"This is not the way of Cheyenne hospitality! You are all treacherous witches!"

The women threw stones at her. Henry caught her eye and nodded his head in thanks. Taking off his hat he doffed it in mock politeness to the singing widows:

"Ladies! You are a joy to behold."

Yellow Bear came out of his lodge as Henry rode past and patted his leg. He hooked a small buckskin bag over the Englishman's pommel:

"A potion to keep you safe – not all of the Suhtai want to see you go."

Henry nodded, leaned down from the saddle and shook his hand:

"Thank you for your friendship – and your teachings in the language of the *Tsis-tsis-tas*!"

Yellow Bear smiled; he was about to say – 'it still needs more work' – but found he couldn't and ducked back inside his lodge as the tears came.

See the Dark and White Rain came out of their lodge, they were about to ride out after some elk that had been seen nearby and were putting their rifles into saddle buckets. Dark handed the reins of his pony to White Rain and ran over:

"Hen-ree! I didn't know you were leaving us so early – may be the talk against you will be just like a passing shower and be gone soon?"

The Englishman shook his head sadly:

"I don't think so, my friend. Your mother may have spoken some true words – why should the Cheyenne trust the whites after Sand Creek?"

"*Those* whites, weren't you… they were bad spirits. You should stay. I'll talk to my mother again…"

When he'd mentioned his mother, the young warrior's face clouded over; she was becoming difficult to talk to. Her craziness seemed to appear in bursts, like dark clouds rushing across the sky. One minute all was well and the next…silence and unknowing looks.

Henry, seeing the sadness, shook his head again and held out his hand:

"No, little brother, your mother has been through enough."

Dark shook his outstretched hand. The young Cheyenne pointed to the medicine bundle on Henry's saddle pommel:

"Maheo is protecting you now – your trails will be safe."

Henry nodded towards White Rain and smiled:

"Look after that woman – at least you look like a prosperous man now!"

He kicked his heels into his pony and walked on.

Sweet Water stood with the rest of the Forked Lightning Women and refused to allow herself to cry as he passed. She merely nodded her head and smiled shyly. Their last night together had only been a few whispered words of affection rather than a torrent of desire; there was no aching void to be filled – if there was love on either side, neither of them had acknowledged it. Henry had brushed her hair back from her face and kissed her on the forehead when she'd left his lodge as the morning star rose. He reckoned that his leaving the camp was probably doing her a favour; he didn't want her tainted any further by Badland's gossip. She would be better off without him.

Despite his protests, Carver had insisted on escorting him back down to the Smoky Hill country where Henry could at least join the expanding number of whites along the rail tracks before he made any plans on what to do next. The two men rode in silence as the sun warmed their backs. It was Henry who spoke first:

"I hope New Grass isn't worried that you'll carry on riding with me; I hope she knows you're going back to her?"

"Yeah, she knows – a few days is all," Carver answered testily. In truth, New Grass had taken some convincing that the two friends weren't leaving together for good. Especially when her husband had taken both his rifles.

"You're packing a lot of kit on that spare pony for just a few days ride," said Henry.

Carver grunted but said nothing; he hadn't yet mentioned to the Englishman that his wife had also become the target of barbed camp gossip because of her marriage to *him* – despite the wolf skinner's affection for the Suhtai, he had now been cast in the same light as Henry. The colour of his skin mattered more than proof of past loyalty. And now he had lied to his friend – he was never going back.

The two men started to ride up a shallow hill, through two stands of live oak. Jackrabbits darted out of their way and a cloud of ravens flew up from a distant hummock. The air whined with insects as the ponies scented water. It was almost noon when the riders eased their mounts alongside a stagnant pool and let them drink; the animals nudged the mossy surface scum aside and slurped noisily.

Henry and Carver stretched out on the sundried grass and held the reins of their ponies. Both tilted their hats over their eyes and feigned sleep – it was better than trying to talk.

The snap of a large twig close by brought both of them back to the present.

Carver's rifle lay across his chest but Henry had to leap to his feet and scrabble for his in the saddle bucket. Both men chambered a round, stood behind their ponies readied for action and looked at where the noise had come from.

A shout in a strange language came next as a small, underfed Indian leading a skinny pony stepped out into the sunlight. His bow was around his pony's neck and he held up the twig he had broken as a warning that he was near. He dropped the twig and signed:

'Peace. I see you.'

"Keep an eye on him Henry – I'll see if he's alone," muttered Carver as he ran up and down the treeline to check. The scrawny Indian was unafraid and seemed defiant, despite the two rifles trained on him. Carver flipped open the man's saddle packs – he had no other weapons and, by the looks of things, no food either.

With the immediate threat gone, Carver and Henry stood in front of the ragged man, though they kept the rifles in their hands.

Lobo looked at the two white men; both seemed well-fed and though both were dressed like others of their race, their clothes were adorned with beadwork and feathers in the Cheyenne style. He'd seen them in the Suhtai camp when he had visited with Hair Stands Up and the Kiowa warriors; he had also watched them leave. He spoke some words in his own tongue but they didn't understand. He reverted to sign:

'You live with Medicine Arrow people?'

Both men shook their heads, Henry surprised, and now suspicious, at Carver's emphatic denial; the wolf skinner was supposed to be going back to his wife. He let it pass for now.

'What do you want?' signed Henry impatiently.

'To warn Cheyenne of attack.'

'Who will attack?' signed Carver, now worried about New Grass.

Lobo brushed back two fingers from his right eye to his right ear in the sign that represented the Kiowa swept back hairstyle as more questions came from the white men's' hand sign. This was going to take a while until Henry had an idea:

"Let's feed this poor peasant first so we don't miss anything."

Lobo understood the next signs for eating and smiled, nodding vigorously. These whites were slow with their hospitality when he had important news to impart as well as his idea to head off trouble. He had eaten the last of his pemmican and jerky two days ago so watched, trying not to salivate, as two former enemies of his people prepared him a meal. It would be a story for his grandchildren.

Dusk was falling when the stilted sign conversation stopped and each party had agreed on what to do. Lobo mounted his horse, thanked Henry and Carver for the food and headed south to tell Big Bow what he wanted to hear about his Cheyenne foes.

---- 0 0 0 ----

Chapter Thirty Seven

Colonel Artemis P. Chase was a happy man. He and his politician brother had raised a lot of money to fund their militia cavalry unit and now here he was out on the plains and ready to kill Indians.

He spat into the dust as the unfamiliar saddle seat dug into his portly backside and made his crotch ache; the money they'd saved on buying surplus, but uncomfortable, McClellan saddles may have been a financial constraint too far. No matter, his boys were in the Indian-hunting business now and seeking a reputation – as well as doing the Army's damn job for them.

Yessir, the US Army had a lot to answer for. His government's lack of interest in the safety of the people of Kansas as murderous Indian attacks continued had angered him. Those hidebound desk rats had provided nary a soldier, rifle nor bullet - but they *had* managed to find time to issue a strict instruction *not* to raise militias that would drain Federal resources. Chase hawked more spittle into the dust with a derogatory "Huh!"

Still, Artemis and his brother were smooth talking men and had persuaded those with deep pockets in many counties of the state to part with enough cash to mount a full company of cavalry. They had played on deeply held fears of Indian atrocities, often reported in over-zealous – and incorrect - detail in local newssheets.

If his militiamen were just temporary and ragged round the edges, so what? They were all Kansans – many veterans of the 'Bleeding Kansas' Jayhawker days and the Civil War who knew what to do with a horse and carbine – some had enlisted for pay but many were just citizens doing their duty. The company had no official regimental number or designation – mainly because, as Colonel Chase reminded himself with a secret smile, the Army was unaware of its existence. But Artemis was proud of the name that the men had come up with themselves; they would be known as Chase's Chargers. Any victory they could chalk up in their ninety-day enlistment would reflect well on him if ever he ever made a run for Congress.

The column rattled its way generally westwards along the north bank of the Arkansas as twilight fell; the moon was hidden by patches of cloud as the troopers halted, unsaddled their mounts, tethered their horses in neat lines and put out sentries. There were no bugle calls or loud orders – just a murmuring of activity and snorting of horses relieved of the weight of their riders.

"You'll be happy now, hoss…" said Carver, "…with all this soldier boy stuff round you."

Henry declined to answer straight away, though Carver had a point – the soldierlike behaviour of the militia going into camp reminded him of his saddle-sore days with the 1st Cavalry when they had swept through Cheyenne country back in '57. The routine was comforting and familiar.

Carver knew what the silence meant and said so:

"Henry, I ain't never goin' back to the Suhtai – New Grass will git over me leavin' her – eventually. She couldn't come with – she's too wrapped up in her family still. That Badlands bitch really did for us both – blame her, not me."

The wolf skinner had made up his mind and he wouldn't change it. He had declared – over-dramatically in Henry's opinion – that the two of them would ride together until their trails parted or they were shot out of the saddle. It was the first time that the Englishman had heard Carver express any feelings about anyone.

Henry sniffed the coffee bubbling in the pot to see if it was ready and stretched out on the ground, leaning back on his saddle. Around him the troopers did the same; the cavalry had settled for the night into a small, rock-ridged depression on a hill top – firelight couldn't be seen and smoking was allowed.

He offered Carver a cheroot as a peace offering between them.

"Did you ever love her? New Grass, I mean," said Henry.

Carver coughed on his glowing cheroot at the unusual question:

"Hell, no. I only moved in there to get away from yer smelly hide and yer goddamn snorin'."

In the darkness, Henry grunted with laughter and knew it wasn't true. He drew on his cheroot and exhaled a column of smoke that momentarily hid the stars. He sat up and faced Carver:

"I hope to God that our little friend keeps his part of the bargain or we'll be laughed out of Kansas."

"Well, it's always a risk trustin' an Injun but if we want head off a Kiowa raid on the Suhtai, we'll need more guns on our side. Just a damn pity that those Regular bluebellies up in the Smoky Hill didn't wanna help'...," said Carver.

Henry nodded; the soldiers they'd spoken to didn't seem to be interested in fighting Indians; they just wanted to stay out of trouble in their forts or escort wagons. Orders were orders.

"We were lucky to find Colonel Chase and his men at Ellsworth..." nodded Henry, knowing that they'd both started to panic when military assistance in putting down a Kiowa raid had begun to seem impossible.

"You mean they were lucky to find *us*," snorted Carver, "these boys were just goin' off on a blind patrol – we gave 'em somethin' real to do. They got real Kansas sass when it comes to takin' on Injuns."

"True, true..." conceded Henry, "...do you feel bad about not warning Bad Elk's people ourselves?"

"Nah…" the wolf skinner replied," …mighta been tempted to stay with New Grass if we'd gone back. If them Kioway do come, we can save the Suhtai usin' our soldier boys here without Bad Elk even knowin'."

Henry shrugged but said:

"I feel slightly awkward in lying to Colonel Chase – you know, about saying the Kiowa were going to come north and attack soldiers…it doesn't sit well with me."

"Hell, Henry – them Kioway just need to be put down like dogs. What they cross the river *for* is neither here nor there – they'll be all painted up and ready to kill anyone who gits in their way. Nah, we're doin' the right thing – if Bad Elk's folk ever knew about this, we'd be heroes again – poisonous squaws or no."

Henry was about to answer when the moon came out and a shadow fell across them both:

"Evenin' gentlemen…" said the Sergeant, "Colonel's compliments, and we'll saddle up at dawn. Rattlesnake Crossing is only a day's ride ahead."

"Thank you, Sergeant," said Henry and hoped that they would see the signal from the skinny Indian. Rain spattered onto his bedroll and he pulled it up around his neck.

"Do you want to hear another poem?" asked Henry mischievously. In reply, Carver farted and pretended to be asleep.

---- o o o ----

Lobo had ridden hard that day to get well ahead of Big Bow and the Kiowa war party; he stayed out of sight off skylines and stuck to valley riding where he could. The Kiowa weren't fools and they would have their own scouts out to clear the trail ahead, though, as this part of the southern grasslands was considered to be theirs alone – it would be a foolish enemy that transgressed on it.

Lobo's news about the Cheyenne village had been well-received by Big Bow and he had thanked the small *Na-ishan-dina* warrior for his dedication with the gift of a pony.

Big Bow had not criticised Hair Stands Up in public but by pointing to Lobo as a good example of completing a task given to him was insult enough. Lobo had smiled, though only when others couldn't see his face; Hair Stands Up had remained impassive but full of fury.

The Kiowa Apache leader hadn't been invited to join the war trail, though some thrill-seeking *Yamparika* Comanches had. They were loud but poorly armed, many still carrying the long, flexible lances that their fathers had used but were now useless against the new guns of the whites.

Usually, it would be the Comanche giving the orders on raids but not today – this was Kiowa revenge business. But no matter who took part, Lobo watched them all make their preparations and timed his departure to avoid them. He had walked around the encampment and counted over seventy warriors who groomed their war ponies in front of their lodges; it would be a strong raid.

Hair Stands Up rode out at the front of the Kiowa warriors, alongside Big Bow. The underchief smiled to himself – Big Bow had made a great play of rewarding the Kiowa Apache tracker but he now knew that the pony gift was flawed. Out of sight of all in the camp he had inspected the animal given to Lobo – it had a cracked rear hoof and couldn't give much service as a saddle horse before it would have to be left behind or eaten.

His father called such gifts 'broken bow' presents – fine as an ornament or for show but they could never work properly. Hair

Stands Up vowed to make Lobo's life miserable when he got back.

---- o o o ----

Chapter Thirty Eight

The piece of notched deerskin was fluttering in the strengthening breeze when Carver saw it and whooped:

"Well, damn me! He made it! That hungry little coyote kept his word."

He reached up in the tree and untied the skin strip as Henry rode up; the Englishman was grinning in delight – just as pleased as the wolf skinner to see the signal.

Henry examined the strip – explaining to the skinny warrior the things they'd need to know before meeting the Kiowa had been hard – so the notches made on it would be important. In truth, Henry hadn't trusted the warrior to keep his end of the bargain and had forgotten what they'd agreed. His face was a blank.

Carver, shaking his head in despair, took the strip from him to decipher its message:

"Well hoss, one V shaped notch means the little guy was one day ahead of the war party. These seven clean slits mean seventy warriors – that's it."

"Yes, I remember now..." lied Henry, "...but they don't tell us *when* the Indian got here."

"No..." said Carver, "but his tracks might do...".

The wolfskinner dismounted and looked carefully around the base of the tree. An unshod Indian pony had been here recently; its hoofprints were on top of the indentations made by the rain shower the previous night. The same tracks had crossed from the south to the north bank.

Carver had to assume that the pony tracks had been made by the hungry little Indian. So, the deerskin signal had only been hoisted some hours ago – the Kiowa were closing on Rattlesnake Crossing.

Carver tutted at the tracks:

"The little guy will need to change his pony – if this is him, it's got a cracked rear hoof."

Both men rode down to the crossing and looked south. There was no sign or dust of any approaching war party – yet.

Carver scoured both banks looking for tracks to see if the Kiowa had crossed before they got there but there was nothing. Some buffalo had crossed earlier, wallowed in the mud and moved on and a couple of faded wagon ruts showed the activity of white men at Rattlesnake Crossing had been light and at least a week ago.

To make sure, Henry rode up and down the north bank for a couple of miles east and west of the crossing – with Carver doing the same on the south shore – to see if there had been any cropping of grazing or fresh horse droppings that could indicate if the war party had crossed the Arkansas anywhere else. Both men met up, not believing their luck:

"Indian village crossed a way up there…" he said, pointing east, "…but there were travois poles marks and not enough horse tracks for a war party. It ain't them. What about you?"

"Well, my tracking skills aren't up to much but even I can tell that the Kiowa haven't got here yet. I think we're in business, my friend!"

They spurred back eastwards along the north bank to tell Colonel Chase their news.

---- o o o ----

Chapter Thirty Nine

Badlands Walking Woman knelt in front of the buffalo hide and scraped off the remaining meat and fat, putting the pieces into a cook pot at her side. She hummed in a contented way as the elk horn scraper, a familiar and comforting shape in her hands, did its work.

A shadow fell across the skin and she looked up; a man was standing in front of her. The man spoke to her and she, irritated at being diverted from her task, sighed and tried to listen, though she didn't stand up.

Whatever this man was saying made no sense to her, as her mind was full of the sound of nesting birds, galloping ponies and the crackling of prairie fires. She even sang the songs that celebrated these things to herself as the man continued to talk.

His words were drowned out by the songs in her head and the rushing wind that she heard often now – even when all the tree branches were still. She couldn't hear what he said and she wasn't interested – she preferred the sound of the wind and the wild neighing of the ponies.

The man now knelt down so he was at eye level to her; this was rude, she thought. He was still talking and put his hand on her shoulder, she slapped it away and put her hand to the hilt of the hunting knife in her belt; the man backed away.

"Who *are* you?" she said. Then, as the man walked away, looked uncomprehendingly at the scraper in her hand.

See the Dark went into the treeline and wept.

---- o o o ----

Chapter Forty

Hair Stands Up lay on his side in the mud at Rattlesnake Crossing, his much loved and ornamented hair being trampled by screaming ponies. Hooves raked lumps of flesh from his cheeks and crushed his face; occasional shots and the panicked yells of his own people added to the chaos on the banks of the Arkansas.

He had no idea where the white pony soldiers had come from but his own scouts hadn't spotted them; the whites must have been hidden deep in a nearby stand of trees. These whites were also well-armed – they must have had a good number of the many-shot rifles and pistols as many of the war party had been shot from the saddle early on.

The Yamparika Comanches had been brave but rapidly lost heart – there had been no-one to charge with their lances and the solid wall of fire and smoke from the treeline had sealed their fate.

Hair Stands Up's own Kiowas hadn't fared much better – few had guns and there had been a panicked swirl of ponies and riders trying to avoid being shot down. He had tried to muster them for a death song charge but, looking around for his chief, saw that Big Bow was riding away, out of danger from a battle already lost.

He had yelled at his chief in contempt for his cowardice but it was too late to reverse the fight and Big Bow probably knew it. It was then that a heavy calibre bullet flung Hair Stands Up out of the saddle, toppling him backwards over the rump of his pony.

The Kiowa man spat out a gobbet of blood and tendrils of reddened spittle drooled from the corner of his mouth and into the earth. Heavier horses pounded by close to his head as the whites, yelling and shooting, chased the remnants of the Kiowa war party south to their homeland.

The trembling earth grew still and Hair Stands Up tried to ease himself onto his elbow to look around; the effort it took told him that he was badly wounded. Though his breathing was shallow and his eyes blurred by pain, his nagging suspicions about the whites' ambush wouldn't go away. The whites had known that they were coming – the crossing place was well known of course, used by many of the southern tribes – but they had also known *when*. Someone who knew of the plan had betrayed them.

The Kiowa warrior made a great effort to sit upright, grunting in pain and coughing up more blood. Then he saw the sign.

Just an arm's length away, but set apart from the churned muddy hoofprints of the main war party, was a set of pony tracks that he recognised. The owner of the pony that made them hadn't ridden with them that day but the split rear hoof was distinctive.

It was while he was pondering how it had got there that Hair Stands Up plunged into the Great Darkness of the next life. The bullet entered his skull on the right side and crashed out of the other, throwing a spray of bone and brain matter for many paces.

"Nice shootin' hoss," said Carver.

---- o o o ----

Chapter Forty One

They had seen the lines of cooking fires from a long way off. Twilight was turning to dusk and the firelight flickered as the shadows of many men and animals settling into a night camp told their story.

"Well, we know it ain't Colonel Fatboy," said Carver, "we left him way behind on the Arkansas."

"That's a terrible description of our erstwhile commander, Mr Carver," said Henry, "though Colonel Chase did have somewhat of a weight problem,"

"Weight problem?" snorted Carver in the darkness, "...the man's horse took one look at him and committed suicide!"

Henry smiled – his friend was back to his usual self after the fight at Rattlesnake Crossing. Colonel Chase had been pleased at the action against the Kiowas and had expressed his gratitude to them both for the information leading up to the ambush – his men had been bloodied but victorious – and his political career was assured. He'd even paid them as employees of the quartermaster – an unexpected but welcome reward as he and Carver now tried to get used to the idea of earning money in their lives away from the Cheyenne. He looked at the array of firelight again:

"Well, it's a military camp alright. A big one too – at least three or four company horse lines and scores of wagons. I wonder where they're going?" mused the Englishman.

"Hell, come on Henry – we all know you just wanna head over there and bore 'em to death with yer soldier boy stories..."

Henry laughed; Carver was right – soldiers were drawn to other soldiers; the profession of arms was a common and uniting factor. Even Carver – who was generally outspoken in his distaste for the incompetence of soldiers and officers – was happy to sit down amongst the younger and more gullible bluecoats and tell tall tales. It was an easy task to scare new recruits.

"Well, soldiers or not, I say we go. We may get a better meal than gnawing on this buffalo jerky all day," said Henry.

He looked around and saw that he needn't have bothered with any excuse – in the darkness Carver had already mounted his horse.

"Let's git over there hoss, before cookie shuts up shop! If they git bored of yer war stories or my fascinatin' stories about wolf skinnin', you can always kill 'em off with those Tombstone tales.'

Henry mounted, farted copiously in contempt and joined his friend as they rode towards the camp fires.

---- o o o ----

Major Joel Elliott of the 7th Cavalry looked up from his tin plate of mess stew when he heard the shot. There was some shouting of instructions from outside the horse lines as his NCOs tried to find out why someone had fired a weapon.

Elliott didn't interrupt his supper and unhurriedly sipped his coffee. His troopers would report soon and he wouldn't seek them out - it was unseemly for an officer to rush around and interfere unless he had to. His men were mainly veterans of the recent war against the South and he thought them steady and reliable. He put down his cup, scraped the remains of the stew into the fire and placed the tinware on the ground for his striker to take away and wash up. He'd just stood up when the Duty Sergeant came in to report:

"Two riders comin' in sir – both white. Saw the campfires and came over to jaw some."

Elliot nodded:

"Bring them over to me Sergeant please...", Elliot put on his service hat and brushed imaginary dust off his epaulettes, "give them some stew if there's any left – but don't plunder the men's rations for it."

The Sergeant saluted and walked off into the darkness, calling for the sentries to bring the two men into the firelight.

Henry and Carver, both carrying plates of food, approached Elliot. Henry touched the brim of his hat in salute and Carver growled:

"Evenin' Boss."

The cavalryman indicated that they should sit and the men sat crosslegged on the ground; he noted that they both did this without pause and at the same time. To him, it was a it was an odd way for white men to sit - most would seek out a box or a saddle to avoid wear and tear on clothing – with these two, it was a small sign that they were used to being in front of many campfires, possibly with Indians. Even their clothing had hints of a native connection but that was a matter for later. He let the men eat – they seemed grateful for a meal that someone else had prepared:

"Gentlemen, Major Joel Elliot, Seventh Cavalry. First, my apologies for the shot my sentry fired – I hope neither of you was hurt? And second, I hope our cook's efforts have met your needs?"

"No need to apologise for an alert picket, Major. We shouted out but weren't sure if we'd been heard." said Henry, "…and my apologies for eating this excellent stew before proper introductions have been made…I am Henry Armstrong, late US Dragoons and First Regiment of Cavalry…"

Carver groaned out loud – but Henry just grinned:

"...and this rude fellow is my friend Mr Carver."

Elliot was intrigued by the polite, parlour-like expressions of the Englishman and the hints of previous service in American units. He was about to reply when the other man spoke in a low growl:

"We're just passin' through Boss – and reckoned we'd try and cadge some real food."

Elliot laughed:

"An honest man, Mr Carver! I would have done exactly the same thing if I'd been in your place."

Carver nodded and seemed mollified but, when the bluecoat major started asking more questions, let Henry do the talking.

They had been scouts for Colonel's Chase's column against the Kiowa, explained Henry – and had prevented a war party's incursion across the Arkansas to attack one of the forts. Now they had been paid off and were looking for work.

"Well Mr Armstrong, sounds like you've had an exciting time but, I regret, work here, for men of your obvious calibre, is almost non-existent – my quartermaster posts are all filled. Right now, I've got around two hundred wagons, most filled with presents for the southern tribes to lure them to attend a meeting with the Peace Commission in a few weeks' time..."

Carver spluttered, spitting out a spray of stew:

"General, I hope to God them gifts ain't for the Kiowa – we've just fought 'em. They didn't look too peaceful to me!"

"Well Mr Carver – and it's just *Major* by the way – I would tend to agree. Free handouts are often a way to stop the fighting, if only for a short time. But the Kiowa, Comanche and some Kiowa Apache say they'll join us on Medicine Lodge Creek..."

Elliot's striker walked into the glow of the firelight and handed a fresh cup of coffee to him. He sipped it, the steam rising into the cold night:

"...then, if all goes well, the Cheyenne will come in later."

Henry and Carver were both surprised when the Cheyenne were mentioned but made great efforts not to show it. To deflect talk in another direction, Henry said:

"Do you command the column sir or should we report our presence to another officer?"

"No, gentlemen – I command it all. My own superior officer – General Custer is back in Washington on other business."

Elliot decided to keep quiet about his boss's reason for being in Washington; no need to blacken the regiment's name with talk of Custer's court martial.

Henry was surprised at the mention of that unusual name again – Custer. The recruiter at Leavenworth had mentioned him commanding a Brigade in the war.

"General Custer? That's an unusual name – I met a cadet called Custer at West Point back in 1857. Would that be the same man?"

Henry remembered the stodgy-faced cadet who'd served him coffee after his lecture. He seemed to be of the wrong type to make a success in the Army.

"That would indeed be the same man, Mr Armstrong! General Custer commanded his Michigan Cavalry Brigade when he was only twenty-three and an entire Division aged twenty-five – a fine and gallant soldier. A great American hero."

"Well, you can see that none of his greatness rubbed off on Henry!" growled Carver.

Elliot laughed dutifully while Henry squirmed.

The Englishman took out a leather case of battered cheroots from his pocket, gave one to Carver and offered one to Elliot who held up the palm of his hand:

"Thank you, sir, but no. My Quaker roots go deep I'm afraid – no drinking or smoking."

Carver plunged in:

"I thought you Quakers were all peaceable like – odd to see one in a soldier boy outfit."

Henry sat bolt upright at his friend's lack of tact but Elliot took it in good part:

"You are right sir – that's why back home in Indiana I'm banned from the meeting house and shunned by my family. Wearing the blue of my country brings hardships other than those inflicted by bullets."

Carver grunted at the disclosure – wishing that, sometimes, he could just keep his mouth shut. It was good to meet a man who stuck by his own principles – even if they were religious. In an odd departure from his normal grumpiness, he growled:

"Sorry Boss – didn't mean anythin' by it."

Henry was amazed and patted his friend on the back.

"Hallelujah! We'll make a human being out of you yet Mr Carver," he said and Elliot smiled.

---- o o o ----

Chapter Forty Two

"Bad Elk says he is tired. The fighting just makes us Suhtai smaller and weaker. He will take the camp south of the *Ar-kan-saw* River..." said See the Dark, as he carefully intoned the strange English word in his speech.

"*Which* river?" asked Viajero, irritated by the alien word.

"*Ar-kan-saw*. It's the veho name for the Flint Arrowpoint – the soldier chiefs used it at the treaty talks."

The Apache just grunted: "Huh!" and was quiet.

"The whites want us to go south of the Flint Arrowpoint to prove that we are peaceful. Then on to a big camp they are setting up for us - there will be food and guns. With ammunition to hunt."

The Apache barked with incredulous laughter:

"I'll believe *that* when I see it!"

Dark just shrugged; he'd just followed his chief's instructions and relayed Bad Elk's message from the council fire to the Traveller. The Apache, like all who lived in Bad Elk's band, was free to make his own mind up whether he went with them or not. Bad Elk had ridden out for the treaty talks with the *vehoe* at Medicine Lodge Creek and, on his return, his uncle had looked relieved that there seemed to be an honourable way to end the fighting.

Bad Elk didn't want any more losses after the long and costly raiding season they'd just had – now was the time for his beloved Suhtai to get out of the vicious cycle of death. He had told Dark that he thought the whites would be victorious after all – they were many in number and very powerful. Perhaps it would be better to accept it and save whatever could be saved of the Cheyenne nation in a safer part of the land.

Dark had been shocked by the note of defeat in his uncle's voice; their wise chief seemed hollowed out. He decided not to tell the Traveller this. He watched his friend gloomily.

Squatting on his haunches, Viajero looked around for Bright Antelope to stoke the cooking fire and start their meal – as seemed to be the case these days, she was nowhere to be seen. He grumpily poked the cooking fire with his hunting knife and threw on another cottonwood branch:

"Are all the Suhtai going south?"

Dark looked at the ground – his own indecision on what to do next weighed heavily:

"No – most are, as well as some Arapaho. The Thunder Bears and their families will go north; some of the Striking Snakes could go with them but they are mainly single men. They will continue to fight the vehoe as long as they have arrows or guns to shoot."

Viajero looked quickly at Dark at the unusual information, his black eyes boring into the younger man's skull:

"So, the warrior societies *and* their families will go north? Normally women and children stay with the main camp. This means the People will split…become two nations?"

Dark nodded:

"Maybe… but not for ever. Many warriors feel that we have unfinished business to keep the whites off our sacred land."

The Cheyenne moved to one side as Bright Antelope stalked silently into the clearing, hung a cookpot of chopped meat on a hooked branch above the fire and walked off without saying a word. Dark said nothing but sensed trouble was in the air. He looked at the Traveller but was met by an impassive stare.

"And what will *you* do?" asked the Apache.

See the Dark squirmed and shrugged but eventually said:

"Go north with the warriors I suppose, though I – we - haven't decided yet."

The Apache nodded – Dark had seemed less keen on the war trail these days. He didn't think the young man was afraid – he had seen him too many times in battle to ever consider that – but since the death of his father, Dark seemed to be more cautious. Perhaps this caution was also because White Rain had moved back into the young Cheyenne's lodge? Dark's clothing was in better repair these days and his inflamed eye socket had healed.

Though See the Dark would never betray his uncle's confidence, Viajero knew that many other people had spoken openly of Bad Elk's growing fear of the whites and what they could do to destroy the Suhtai. Whilst many of their warriors had been active in more summer raiding against the *indaa* up in the Smoky Hill and Saline valleys, Dark had stayed behind. In support of his friend, Viajero had done the same - even though the growing strain between him and Bright Antelope had almost forced him back into the war saddle just to get away from camp. Fighting he could deal with – women, less so.

The meat started to sizzle in the pot and the Apache stared dumbly at it. Dark took up a buffalo gut water pouch and splashed some of the liquid on the browning meat. Viajero said:

"What are the women soldiers going to do? Go north and fight?"

Dark shrugged; White Rain and he had only made tentative plans about where they would go when the camp split. She had her responsibilities as leader of the Forked Lightning Women but she hadn't confided in him yet. However, he had spoken to one of her friends:

"Crow Dress told me that they would go south with the main camp – to protect them on the move while the Thunder Bears were on the war trail."

The Traveller was about to reply when Bright Antelope hurried up, tutted at the burning meat, scraped it from the side of the iron pot and glared at the Apache.

Viajero didn't bother to look up at her; the woman seemed to be all silent fury these days. He sat in a passive but patient huff and waited for her to resume her cooking duties.

Dark broke the uncomfortable silence:

"And what will you do? Go north with the warriors or south with us?"

The Apache, still squatting in front of the flames, cocked his head to one side, looked at Dark from the corner of his eye and said:

"Later, little brother, later…"

---- o o o ----

Yellow Bear, though depressed by the decision of his chief to head south, had brought one piece of good news. Without waiting for a formal request to enter Bad Elk's tipi, he flipped the skin door back and hissed:

"That woman won't be coming with us!"

Bad Elk smiled weakly - 'that woman' only meant one person and he already knew. He gestured to the far side of the lodge. There, contentedly eating his morning meal was Flea, See the

Dark's younger brother. He looked at Yellow Bear, burped and smiled.

"My sister-in-law left him here yesterday. We have to bring him up now so she can go north with our warriors. She will be taking my brother's lodge and her widow friends. She will be going as the Thunder |Bears' healer – she's good at those things."

Yellow Bear nodded though, from what he'd seen of her recently, she seemed unable to remember anything let alone the details she'd need for potions.

Sure, Badlands Walking Woman, in her early life roaming the southern grasslands with her Kiowa Apache family, had honed her skills at finding plants and medicine that cured and healed. He himself had listened to her advice on some simple medicines when he'd made the change from warrior to spirit diviner. He knew that Maheo sent him knowledge in many different forms – sometimes in dreams, sometimes animals spoke to him and, once, the Life Giver had struck him with lightning. But at other times his trail to better knowledge was blazed by a difficult and spiky woman. Who would have thought it? He smiled at his memories.

But there was another, and in his view, a more pressing matter. Her youngest son was about eight summers old and still hadn't been given a proper child name – Flea had just been an affectionate name from his time as a baby. Now his father was dead and his mother appeared to be going mad, the ceremony had been postponed. Despite mentioning this to Badlands Walking Woman several times, she had shouted at him as if her were a stranger and pushed him away. 'That woman' would never be a proper Cheyenne.

Burnt Hair swept into the lodge, beaming a broad smile and took the empty bowl from her nephew. She sat Flea down on a wolfskin bed robe and took out her comb. Bad Elk watched his wife as she ran the serrated bone through the boy's black locks then twisted the long hair into braids and plaited them with otter fur. They had no children – none that had lived anyway - so keeping the boy and bringing him to manhood may have been a solemn duty for Bad Elk but it was a true delight for his wife.

"The boy will need a proper name soon," said Yellow Bear, anxious to take advantage of a better audience for his views. Times were changing quickly for his beloved Suhtai – the sooner Smoke on the Moon's younger boy realised the value of Cheyenne traditions, the better.

Bad Elk nodded in a distracted way and Yellow Bear noticed – the world weighed heavily on his friend's shoulders.

None of the potions he could make nor any of the spells he had woven could lessen the responsibility of those who decided the future of the People. Life was always a balance for the Suhtai – in return for their free roaming ways across the great grasslands, the One God sometimes pressed heavily down with the Iron Sky.

In a few days, his beloved Suhtai would be split asunder – it would be war for some and peace for others. The chances of them joining back together in the future as one group seemed remote. The spirt diviner felt helpless.

---- 0 0 0 ----

Chapter Forty Three

Things were moving quickly – Yellow Bear, during a dry but cold day on the cusp of the Moon of the Falling Leaves, erected his framed buffalo skin outside his lodge and began to arrange his paints and tools. All around him was the blur of change – some minor, some severe but all deserved their place on the great painted spiral of Suhtai life.

Yellow Bear had mused on what shape the symbols should take – he was running out of space on the specially-dressed buffalo hide and hoped that he didn't have to make another one just yet; there was a lot happening.

The previous day, some Arapaho had ridden in to speak to Bad Elk; they had wanted to join the Suhtai in their journey south across the Flint Arrowpoint River and Bad Elk had agreed. The riders had spurred back to their families to tell them the news and the next day a dozen or so families rode in as dusk fell.

The medicine man knew that this was nothing unusual – the Arapaho were long-time allies of the Cheyenne – but in these tumultuous times, everything took on a slightly different meaning. Like the Cheyenne, some of the Arapaho warriors were going north to fight. They too were splitting just like the Suhtai.

But how to paint all this? Cheyenne history needed to be recorded – the events would need to be remembered and passed on to their children and grandchildren. It had to be done.

The usual record of one full Suhtai year could be expressed in one or two symbols of importance – a few hoofprints for successful horse raids, the outline of dead enemy for battles- but Yellow Bear knew that such simple depictions would not be enough in these momentous times. No symbol was powerful enough to portray the division of the tribe.

There was much to record and he'd decided to use the remaining blank part of the skin to capture it all. Unable to sleep for the past few days, he'd groggily arranged events in his own mind and, after some elusive ideas, called it the Year of Splitting Trails. He dipped his sharpened stick into a gourd of water, applied black paint and began…

First, he scratched a line from left to right – this was the main trail in life of the Suhtai. The line didn't need to be straight as life was not like that, it was precarious and unknowable – sometimes there was plenty but sometimes it was full of hunger and hazard. As the People were headed south, he angled the line downwards. To make sure that any future generations would understand the direction of travel, he drew an arrowhead at the southern tip.

The edged pen had to be held steady as stray shreds of skin on the tanned hide threatened to deflect the blade but Yellow Bear was used to this and steadied the frame with his knees.

Staring at the left-hand side of the main ink trail, he decided to portray the first important incident … diverting from the main trail he drew another trail north and, at the end of that line, sketched in a crescent moon with cloud trails across it. After another few lines, the harsh outline of a burial scaffold indicated that this was to remember Smoke on the Moon's death up in the Powder River country. The brother of Bad Elk would always deserve remembrance…

Yellow Bear was working more quickly now as the ideas formed and the design seemed to work. Back on the main trail, he extended another line downwards, towards the south and scratched two broad brimmed hats. *Hen-ree* and Kah-*vuh* had helped the People during hard times. He had liked both men – they seemed like good war companions and laughed a lot, especially at themselves. Of course, Kah-vuh's wife New Grass had been abandoned but Yellow Bear didn't blame the wolf skinner; their banishment had all been the fault of Badlands Walking Woman sowing her seeds of poison amongst the more impressionable members of the tribe. He wished the vehoe well on their journey back to their own country and people.

Even as he dipped his pen back into the ink gourd, Broken Knife's Thunder Bears and their families rode past, heading north to deter the white settlers and track layers for the smoking wagons. Behind them, in an untidy and noisy group, rode what was left of the Striking Snakes.

Yellow Bear just sighed; the young men were already singing boastful songs of victories they hadn't yet earned. He could feel the tension in the air. There were no calls of farewell – those going north or south seemed unable to understand the other group. Those going north thought the others were cowards to shirk the fighting and those heading for peace across the Flint Arrowpoint didn't want any more Cheyenne deaths to further weaken the People. Still, the warriors' departure was easy to mark on his Splitting Trails memorial. There was no separate symbol for Badlands Walking Woman – she had chosen her path in life and Yellow Bear impassively ignored her.

The medicine man now paused. The next trails would be difficult to record as they were recent and unexpected. He had discussed each one with Bad Elk; the chief had started blaming himself for the collapse of his beloved Suhtai and seemed distraught. Yellow Bear had reassured him that it was just the times that they were living through and reminded him of sunnier, calmer times when Maheo had smiled on the People, kept them well-fed and victorious against their enemies. Bad Elk grew calmer, but not by much.

The spirit diviner scratched at the first new, diverging trail. He pointed the trail line upwards, followed by his symbol for the young stone-eyed warrior…

---- o o o ----

See the Dark emerged from his tipi and yawned; he had a busy day ahead to pack all their belongings for the journey north.

Broken Knife, his Thunder Bears and the Striking Snakes had already gone, but he wouldn't be joining them.

He chuckled himself as he thought about 'their' possessions rather than just his own – White Rain's return to the lodge still took some getting used to. She had looked in to see about his reddened eye socket one day and hadn't left. After some consoling words about the death of Smoke on the Moon, she had treated his socket with balm and moss until the swelling had receded. They now spent their nights under the same buffalo robe and revelled in the comfort that it brought. Being together was proving successful so far – but marriage still wasn't mentioned nor was what they would do when both felt the urge to go on the war trail.

He unhitched his war pony outside the lodge and took it to drink in the creek. The animal slurped at the cool water, nosing floating leaves out of the way. Upstream of the animal, he took out his stone eye and washed it in the white water that rushed over the stones.

"Don't put it back in yet – put this on it."

White Rain had come out behind him carrying a small half gourd. She took the stone eye from Dark, dipped her fingers into the greasy ointment and lathered the black stone globe. Before she handed the globe back to him, she squatted down to his level, opened the empty eye socket and looked inside, turning his face to catch the sun for more light.

He tried to twist away, spluttering with the indignity of it - only his mother had ever got this close to the wound to heal him - but she held him firmly by the chin. She gave him a soft piece of calico:

"There are still some insect wings in there – get them out before you put the eye back in. They'll stick to the ointment."

Dark snorted in frustration, the woman never took 'No' for an answer. Still, the swelling had gone down and his stone eye fitted better – the grease helping him to remove and replace it more easily. He did as he was told.

"Are you sure you still want to ride north with me..." he said, combing his hair with his fingers to remove the excess grease, "...won't your Forked Lightning Women want you to lead them south to protect the village?"

White Rain shrugged and wiped out the gourd with a handful of grass:

"No, we met to discuss this yesterday. Crow Dress will probably be the leader and the youngster, Star, will join them. She has healed well since the bear attacked her and her courage then was a good sign of her power. I think Little Snake is sweet on her..."

Though Dark had long since forgiven Little Snake for taking his eye with a poorly shot arrow, the young man always seemed to avoid his gaze. He assumed that if Little Snake was to continue being a Thunder Bears soldier, he would have already left. If he had been sweet on Star, it would have been a hard decision for the boy to make.

---- o o o ----

Yellow Bear completed his symbol for See the Dark then paused again; he knew White Rain would be heading north with the young warrior but he had no symbol for her – nor any other woman. In the end, he scratched a jagged fork of lightning alongside Dark – it would have to do.

Now for the Traveller and his recent decision…

---- o o o ----

Dawn had only just broken, when a polite cough outside Dark's lodge brought him from his bed. White Rain rolled over and peered through the gloom to see who was calling so early.

As Dark drew back the tipi flap, he was surprised to see the Apache standing there. He was holding the reins of his own horse and, already mounted behind him was a grim-faced Bright Antelope, their daughter and, surprisingly, Willow. The Hunkpapa girl looked uneasy though she was erect in the saddle with a sad smile of pride on her lips.

Viajero took Dark by the arm and led him off into the treeline where they could talk:

"What's happening?" hissed the Cheyenne as he waved White Rain to go back inside the lodge; the woman, drew her bear robe around her, looked quizzically at Willow and decided to let the men talk.

"I came to give you this…" the Traveller said and handed Dark a painted armband. It could be tightened around a forearm by rawhide cords through either end.

"…I made it myself."

Dark, still befuddled by sleep, struggled to make sense of the gift. On the armband was a painted image of Viajero's spirit sign, a horned lizard.

"Why are you giving me a gift? And at dawn?"

The Apache gazed steadily at his friend:

"It will keep you safe in battle…"

Dark's throat was dry, he normally drank a gourd of water before getting his day started; his voice croaked and his brain creaked:

"What for?"

The Apache sighed and hesitated:

"Because, little brother, I won't be there with you – our trails will divide today. We are leaving the Suhtai."

The young Cheyenne was dumbfounded – his war brother was leaving? He was about to ask why when he remembered Willow sitting on her pony outside his lodge – surely the Traveller wasn't leaving just because of a woman?

"Is it because of her?" he said and pointed through the tangle of branches inside the treeline.

The Apache didn't answer directly but looked away:

"I'm taking them back down to the Mescalero country and then go on to my own White Mountains. I intend to get married."

Dark noticed that the Apache didn't explain if he was dumping Bright Antelope and the child with the Mescalero and then moving on with Willow. The young Cheyenne shrugged – it wasn't any of his business – but it was as though someone had hit him across his head with a heavy club.

He slumped down and sat with his back against a tree trunk and tried to calm the turmoil in his head. He had lazily assumed that Viajero would always be at his side in battle - and now this!

Dark had always tried to impress the older man – the Apache's very presence made Dark calm but ferocious in a fight. Now, in an instant, the main source of his strength as a warrior was slipping away. He snarled at himself and his foolishness; the arrogance of his own power in battle was just a wisp of smoke in his own head. He had never asked Maheo for spiritual guidance or protection; the Life Giver probably wouldn't know who he was. He had no token that represented him as a man let alone a Cheyenne warrior – only the vainly painted deeds on his war shirt and pony. Dark exhaled loudly and tried to maintain composure.

The Traveller stood silently beside his friend. The boy was taking it badly and the Apache felt ashamed at the suddenness of it all – he should have prepared him more for the break. They had both saved each other's lives – it was a poor decision just to blurt it out.

Dark looked up. Viajero had always consulted his God, Usen, before a fight and asked for strength to make him victorious. The Traveller's veneration of his spirit animal – even an ugly and scaly one like the horned lizard – brought him comfort and certainty in his decisions. Dark had none of those things.

The Traveller squatted beside him:

"Just know this, my friend – if I ever fight again, I'll never find another war brother with courage that will match yours."

This, for the Apache, was a profound speech and Dark's remaining eye moistened, though he was quick to hide it by looking away. He chewed his bottom lip. They had never spoken of what each meant to the other – it was not a warrior's way. But Dark was heartsick and now unsure about how he would fare in later life without the dark-skinned man from the south at his side.

The Cheyenne warrior quickly opened his medicine bundle that hung around his neck and, after pushing various unseen tokens and amulets to one side, pulled out his glass eye that Hen-ree had brought for him from his own country. He pushed it into the hand of the surprised Apache.

"Take this."

The Traveller pushed it firmly into his bandana headband and stood up; Dark did likewise and they stood facing each other – there could be no more words.

The Traveller put a hand on Dark's shoulder and just nodded. He walked back to his pony and remounted. Then, with the headrope of his daughter's pony in his hand, he led the sad little procession away from their home with the Suhtai.

Drained and numb, See the Dark watched them go, their ponies moving through the morning mist on the creek as it swirled up and, at times, made the riders seem to be riding on smoke.

Dark was never one for profound thought but it took only a moment before he realised, he actually *did* have a token for success. It didn't involve prayers to Maheo or spells from Yellow Bear. He smiled as the thought took hold and he put on the armband that the Apache had made.

Dark laughed out loud at his own stupidity - why was he so dumb that he hadn't realised this sooner? He patted the armband affectionately - *his* spirit creature had been Viajero

---- o o o ----

Yellow Bear stared at the completed symbol for the Splitting of Trails; something about it made him uneasy. He got up, walked back inside his lodge and re-emerged carrying his pipe. He lit the pipe and sat down cross-legged again to look at the painted signs. The smoke calmed him and narrowed his thoughts onto the latest symbol; it was more than just a few trails as he might have seen in the dust – but what was it?

A few more puffs of smoke brought it to him as he watched the blue swirls rise up into the cottonwood branches above.

Now he had it - the Splitting of Trails could be seen as *two* things. One was the medicine man's original intent of showing those who had left the Suhtai but the other was sadder and, far more profound than he'd intended.

He cocked his head sideways and looked again. Yes, there it was – the symbol looked like a dead tree fallen onto its side and, like any toppled tree, the life it carried – the moss, leaves, animals and insects - would soon wither and die without its roots to nurture them.

With Smoke on the Moon dead, warriors leaving to fight and other valuable members of the Suhtai going their own way – it seemed to Yellow Bear that, at this time and in this place, a dying tree summed up the Cheyenne perfectly.

---- 0 0 0 ----

BOOK THREE

'I was abducted by Indians in the spring of 1868 from our farm up on the Saline. They violated me several times in front of my husband, then killed him and my children....'

(Statement made by Mrs Sadie Barratt Ackerman, after her rescue from Cheyenne Dog Soldiers in January, 1869)

Chapter Forty Four

"Jesus! These are Cheyenne arrows, hoss!" shouted Carver as another of the familiar banded shafts thudded into the rail sleepers that he was hiding behind. About forty Cheyenne and Lakota warriors swirled around the trackside embankments, yelling and blowing piercing shrieks on their bone whistles.

"So, I notice…" remarked the Englishman as he peered through the gun smoke to see if they knew any of the attackers.

"…can't see any Suhtai war bonnets though…"

"Don't matter…" shouted Carver as chambered a fresh bullet into the breech and fired back, "…none of these boys will be recallin' happy times in front of the ol' campfire – just shoot 'em down!"

The Indian attack hadn't been unexpected – it was the second one that week – but there was a persistence about it that Carver had noticed.

Usually, when a war party came upon any organised resistance, they would back off to avoid needless casualties – hitting isolated civilian settlements meant easier pickings with more loot and captives.

This time though they seemed determined to stop the railroad going any further. He had watched as a young cook's assistant had been caught out in the open when the riders came charging into the cut. One Indian looped a rawhide lariat around the boy's neck and, despite the hail of bullets, dragged him up and down in front of the whites. Yelling and disdainful of the gunfire, the warrior had pulled the boy to a nearby ridge and cut his throat in full sight of his friends. All the railroad men fell silent. But the pause lasted only a moment as the warriors resumed their charge.

Henry took careful aim at an oncoming rider - the quillwork of his breastplate made a good aiming mark - and shot him in the chest. The man toppled sideways from the saddle and, with the momentum of his fall, the dead man ploughed through the soil, ripping away a stuffed bird that he'd attached to his head and came to a rest by Henry's rifle muzzle:

"This one's Sioux!" the Englishman shouted and ducked as a lead ball from another brave whistled off the timber and whined off into the distance.

He reloaded and looked up across the newly laid trackbed. Firing was easing off as the war party rode out of range of the rail workers' guns.

"Stay low, hoss," warned the wolf skinner, "them Injuns ain't beat."

The Indians rode to a ridge and milled around, talking loudly and pointing to the work site where their dead and wounded lay. Carver watched and listened as best he could.

"They'll be wantin' to git their bodies back – don't go out in the open yet," he warned again.

One Indian who'd been lying inert on the ground, raised himself onto an elbow and weakly signalled to the warriors. He was bleeding heavily from his face – the lower part of his jaw had been shot away and a dark sheet of blood poured from the gaping space.

The war party tentatively heeled their ponies back down the hill to pick him up, firing volleys of arrows and bullets to keep the white men back.

Henry and Carver aimed their weapons as the targets got closer. Then, before they could pull their triggers, a heavy burst of firing broke out from a group of men taking cover under a railroad wagon. As the sound of the gunshots faded away, another sound took its place – it was men singing:

"That's those goddamn Irish – what the hell are they doin'?" shouted Carver.

The war party halted, then rode in circles to raise dust to cover the recovery of the fallen warrior. The singing increased in volume and it seemed to unnerve the warriors who hesitated to dismount and collect the injured man.

"The singing is quite good!" shouted Henry, "A Minstrel Boy to the wars has gone', I think – a good tenor section over there."

Carver just muttered curses under his breath; only a dumb Englishman could praise the quality of singing when arrows were flying.

But if the warriors wanted to save their man, they were too late. One beefy track layer, carrying an axe in one hand and a revolver in the other, got to the wounded warrior first. Tucking the Colt into his waistbelt he smacked the prone brave with the blunt side of the axe head, laying him out. Then, to anguished cries from the watching Indians, hacked off the man's head – holding it aloft by the hair. He screamed insults at the war party until they rode off amidst more firing from the whites.

"Hmm…" mused Henry, "… full marks for bravery Mr McGuinn but just one out of ten for diplomacy."

---- o o o ----

Chapter Forty Five

It was early afternoon; Henry Armstrong and Pythagoras Carver were tired – long hours of hunting for game to feed the railroad men had diminished their strength as well as ammunition supplies. Having to fight off Indian raids didn't help either.

The trail back to Fort Hays was a long way from the advancing railhead but their horses needed oats and rest. They hoped too that their extra boxes of ammunition had arrived from the east. Owning the quick-firing Henry rifles was ideal for hunting but the metal-cased cartridges were chambered just to that weapon – firing them was an expensive business and resupply was uncertain.

Carver knew that even the hunting would just get harder as time went on; game, including buffalo, was getting scarcer as the animals learned to stay away from the smoking wagons and swarming men. The need to range further out meant that their horses were run down, ribs showed through their hides like bars on a cage and saddle leather was cracked and dry. But work was work and the pay - when the resupply trains brought it - was good. He and Henry had stayed in the scattered tent townships at rail side over the winter, saving their cash to buy forage and cartridges.

But, try as they might to keep their cash for practical things, they weren't monks – Carver had been surprised at the amount of whisky and the number of whores available within the sound of the train whistle and had, on several occasion, been grateful for them. Even Henry, usually fastidious about these things, had also sought comfort there. 'Bad whisky is the author of poor judgements', Henry had slurred poetically, as they hung on to each other outside some nameless canvas tavern and roared bawdy songs into the night. It seemed a long way from the order and calm of Bad Elk's camp.

Now, as they followed the beaten track to the fort, late summer rain drummed off their hat brims, splashed into their faces and revived them slightly:

"Y'know…" said Henry, "I've never worked for a wage before. First time."

Carver snorted with friendly contempt:

"That's 'cos yer Daddy gave you an allowance to fritter away to your heart's content - and when you'd spent it, there was always more. Unlike the rest of us down-trodden workin' folk."

"Bollocks," said Henry smiling. "It's actually quite liberating earning a crust – it was a good tip from Major Elliot to work for the Union Pacific. Especially boosting our income with our performances at the theatre."

Despite himself, Carver laughed at the memory:

"Performances! Is that what you call 'em? Yeah, the ol' Tombstone Tragedies went down well – especially the one about the guy who watered his drinks. Pity about the shootings."

As Henry had predicted, Carver had been busy in his off-duty time, laboriously drafting lines of verse to add to the growing volume of frontier poetry – often sitting next to a lantern until the late hours.

The Englishman knew his friend well – they'd had a similar competitive race when they tried to outdo each other with back-country sayings from their grandmothers some years back. At that time Carver had claimed victory and Henry had accepted it - but only after noting that Carver was much closer to the peasantry and folklore than him. They'd been in Bad Elk's camp at the time and neither of them had the language skills to explain the reason for their raucous laughter to the Cheyenne.

With Carver's efforts, their choice of 'frontier poetry' grew.

They had drunkenly started to recite extracts of this to customers in the Dead Centre Saloon one night and demand grew. Carver had gone round with a hat at the end of the evening and was astonished at how much the railroaders paid to relieve their boredom. He had been pleased at the reaction and the reward - it beat the hell out of gutting white-tailed deer.

Not everyone had admired their work though, one Irish tracklayer had shot at Henry in the middle of a poem; he'd been disarmed and thrown into the mud outside the bar.

"Well, there'll always be critics," said the Englishman, still in a good mood.

He now flung his arms out wide, face tilted up to the slanting rain and declaimed his latest work - based on the one-legged recruiter at Leavenworth:

Surprised by death
Poor Captain Smee
With just one limb
Below the knee
Caught on the hop
For eter-nit-ee.

Carver laughed dutifully but was quick to criticise the poem's failings:

"Hmmm...only fair to middlin', hoss. There's no mention of a gun and I thought you said his name was Driscoll?"

"It was..." said Henry, "...but it didn't rhyme."

Both men were laughing loud and long at their own foolish rivalry as they rode into Fort Hays - a drab clutch of small buildings that served as a railroad supply point. Their horses stepped carefully, raising nervous hooves, over the shimmering iron rails that ran directly through the fort. Hays may not have had the air of a brisk military installation but Henry for one was glad of it and pleased to be out of the Hell on Wheels township. Though the bellowing of dumb doggerel to drunks had paid well, they both needed serious work.

---- o o o ----

Major George Forsyth was on a mission. He stood outside the Headquarters building of Fort Hays and checked the content of the handwritten notice he was carrying – he would put it up in on the HQ noticeboard and see if he got any volunteers to join him on his quest. Forsyth, though, was a realist – he knew that the type of men he wanted for his mission may not be able to read so he would personally visit and speak to any likely candidate that he came across.

Today, though, he was not seeking soldiers – at least not any in uniform. His instructions from General Sheridan had been clear. He was to recruit fifty 'first class, hardy frontiersmen' to pursue and attack Indians who had been busy killing and plundering the railroad, ranches and mail coaches, almost stopping commerce on the surrounding trails. The Indians needed to be caught off-guard and taught a harsh lesson just when they were busy congratulating their murderous selves on another successful raid.

Standing just inside a shallow lean-to to read the flyer, he was shielding the paper with his hat from the easing rain when he heard the laughter.

Two mounted men had ridden through the fort entrance, both dressed in worn but serviceable buckskin and had, at first glance, some excellent rifles in their saddle buckets. Thinking that these may be suitable candidates, Forsyth hurried forward, noting the Indian beadwork and quilling as ornamental touches on their clothes. Still, no harm there – many squaw men wore the same. Their horses were worn-out; though both riders *and* mounts needed feeding up.

"Gentlemen! Welcome to Fort Hays – Forsyth's the name – Major George Forsyth. When you've rested some, have a read of this; it's work that may interest you."

"No thanks General – we've bin workin'. We just need food and a bath. Our horses are tuckered out…," said Carver.

Undeterred, the man gave the leaflet to Henry:

"I can see that sir – you have some days to decide yet. But I'm raising a company of frontiersmen. I've already signed up several at Fort Harker. You gentlemen are well armed, your clothing and tack hints at a hard life in the open you so you may fit the bill. Think it over. Read this at leisure."

"What's the work?" asked Henry, ignoring Carver's groan of dissent.

"Those goddamn Sioux and Cheyenne Dog Soldiers have been on a killing spree recently – seventy-nine of our citizens have been killed over the past few weeks," said Forsyth, "troops are never quick enough to track and punish them so Little Phil reckons that the best way is to play 'em at their own game with men like yourself."

"Just who the Hell is Little Phil?" growled Carver, annoyed at being kept from his bath.

"Why, General Philip Sheridan, sir! He's in charge of this whole military department – I'm his aide."

"Well go and give your aid someplace else, mister…" snapped Carver, "…my pony needs feedin'."

The officer stepped back at the insult but he kept quiet – he was here to recruit, not piss off the locals.

Carver pushed his pony past the officer and headed for the livery.

Henry took off his hat and shook the raindrops from it:

"On a practical note, sir – we are almost out of ammunition for our rifles. So, we may not be much use to you…"

"That's not a problem my friend…" said Forsyth, "…we will issue you the latest Spencer carbines and a Colt revolver – both with all the ammunition you'll need and …"

Henry, suddenly surprised at himself for being so forward on financial matters, was about to ask how much Forsyth was going to pay when the Major beat him to it:

"…fifty dollars a month; seventy-five if you bring your own horse. There'll be rations for you and your mounts."

Henry nodded – it wasn't a bad wage, if a bit less than the railroad paid – and the costs of food and forage would be covered as well. He would need to speak to Carver though.

"We'll let you know, Major," said Henry.

He was as bone weary as the wolf skinner but, he reasoned, fighting the Sioux would make a welcome additional chapter to his book and probably be a more exciting read than the boredom of feeding bloody Irishmen on the Union Pacific.

Of course, persuading Carver to go with him may be a tad more difficult – the wages could swing it or, a more indirect approach may work. Like investing in a bottle of the sutler's finest whisky.

"May I take your names sir?" shouted Forsyth as Henry rode off.

Without looking back – and aware of his own rudeness – Henry just said:

"No."

---- 0 0 0 ----

Chapter Forty Six

See the Dark and White Rain halted on a small ridge some distance from the large encampment. Both stood up in their stirrups and used the height of their ponies to get a better view.

"Well, most of those lodges are Cheyenne but there are some Lakota and Arapaho, I think," said Dark and sat back down on the saddle seat.

White Rain murmured her agreement, then:

"We've been seen – there are riders coming across."

Both took out their rifles, rested the butts on their thighs and watched the approaching fingers of dust get nearer. As the distance closed, they could hear the approaching warriors yelling:

"Why are they shouting?" said White Rain.

"Maybe they're scared," suggested Dark with a grin.

"They should only be scared *after* they meet me," said the Forked Lightning woman. Dark looked across at her, she was smiling but she meant what she'd said.

Dark laughed and nodded but further conversation was cut off by the arrival of the sentinel riders. He watched as the six men, still shouting, galloped round them in a diminishing circle, coating the two Cheyenne in dust. None of the men had guns.

See the Dark made great play of brushing the white powder from his rifle barrel and White Rain did the same. He also cleared Viajero's armband of the dirt and smiled as he imagined what the Apache would do next.

The riders stopped and faced them in a half circle. One, who seemed to be in charge, yelled some words that Dark didn't understand. The young Cheyenne just shrugged his shoulders and said in his own tongue:

"Does anyone speak the language of the Medicine Arrow People?"

Two men shouldered their ponies forward and said that they did. Dark eyed them with contempt - both were young Dog Soldiers with not a trace of battle honours on their shirts or ponies. Viajero would have had a good time now…Dark smirked and said:

"Well, it's good to see that such a big camp is guarded by pony minders and children…"

The two Dog Soldiers look insulted but seemed uncertain what to do next; the other four looked at each other, unaware of what was being said. One struggled for something to say and eventually blurted out:

"Why does that woman have guns and those war deeds painted on her shirt?"

Dark smiled – the Traveller would have loved *this*:

"Oh, it's because she captured the guns from the Comanches and she's actually earned those war honours – though I see you two have none."

"Not yet..." spluttered one of the Dog Men, "...but we will soon!"

"Well, I hope so," said Dark, "because we bring news – some well-armed white men are heading this way…they're about a day off …"

Dark, dramatic as ever, sat back in the saddle and looked at the group smugly.

In truth, he knew he and White Rain had been lucky to spot the vehoe; the men had been moving cautiously and silently along the trail of the large camp. They didn't look like soldiers, though two of the men wore the bluecoat shirts under their buckskin jackets. All the white riders had been heavily armed and were closing in on the Cheyenne and Sioux camp. Dark knew that the warriors in this camp would have no fear of the men – their war strength far outnumbered the handful of whites – but the vehoe looked to have purpose and seemed undeterred by the width and depth of the trail they were following. Perhaps they were just scouts for a larger force and would report the location of the village…

Dark's short reverie was interrupted by one of the Dog Men:

"Don't you think we don't know about the whites coming? We've been watching them for days – do you think we're stupid?!" he shouted in White Rain's face.

The Forked Lightning Woman looked at him coolly as she reined her horse towards the village:

"I don't know. Are you?" she said.

---- o o o ----

Chapter Forty Seven

White Rain and Dark, amongst the mass of advancing Cheyenne, Lakota and Arapaho warriors, had stopped a short distance away from the camp of the white scouts, hidden in a series of hollows behind a hill.

They watched as many of the warriors dismounted and made their spiritual preparations, painting themselves according to their beliefs – some sang low songs and danced a little. Medicine men from the various tribal bands walked amongst the men and purified them with smoke or rubbed earth from their homeland onto the bodies of their kinsmen. If they fell in the coming battle, the One God would know who they were and where their spirits should rest.

Dark and White Rain had no such rituals and ate some food instead – Dark spat out the pemmican:

"We've been in the saddle too long – that food is bad."

"Well, we're not going to get anything fresher here – too many mouths in that big camp and too little game," replied the Forked Lightning Woman.

Dark nodded but kept silent; his dislike of fighting amongst a bunch of strangers weighed heavily on him – despite the many Cheyenne in camp, they knew no-one. He'd hoped that Broken Knife's warriors would be there - even Little Snake would be a relief – but no.

They'd spoken to one man from the northern Suhtai, a survivor of Sand Creek who knew Broken Knife. He told them that the pipe holder of the Thunder Bears had ridden up to the Saline for easier plunder and pickings from white settlers. That seemed sensible – so White Rain and Dark decided that, after this battle, they would head there too.

White Rain loaded her rifle, checking each paper cartridge as she put it in the chamber. The bullets were a weakness - she could never keep them completely dry in her buckskin pouch and they leaked powder. She too was assailed by doubts – whilst she was pleased for the chance to fight alongside the men, she was uneasy. None of her Forked Lightning Women were here and she had long since realised that her confidence and power came from fighting alongside *them* – Dark was strong and brave of course but she missed the friendship and laughter of her own kind. Those women were important to her – like the men, she wanted to show her courage to *her* war companions.

Like Dark, she also knew that the chance of collecting war honours with so many attacking warriors would be slim, it didn't seem to be worth the risk and finally, as if the poor food wasn't enough of a burden, her supply of bullets and powder was getting low. She kept this from Dark – she hoped that this would be solved when they raided the white settlers down on the Saline.

The hum of the incantations stopped and warriors climbed into their saddles. Dark and White Rain had only just mounted up to spread out for the attack when they heard the volley of shots; many of the others gathering to attack the white scouts were taken by surprise too:

"Well, the vehoe can't be taken by surprise now! Those young Cheyenne have spoiled it!" yelled one warrior near the front of the massed horsemen. Dark agreed:

"We thought we'd catch them as they sat and drank their coffee," Dark grumbled, cranking a bullet into the chamber of his rifle, "…now they'll be ready for us coming."

"Hah! It's exactly what you would have done when you were younger," said White Rain. "Those boys need to prove themselves before we all get there."

"Perhaps it was those two that you insulted yesterday! They'll be keen to make a good impression on a handsome woman," said Dark as White Rain smiled shyly.

Dark looked around and rested his rifle across the saddle. He and White Rain were in a large group of yelling and chanting Cheyenne Dog soldiers as they moved towards the sounds of the guns. As usual, he rode in front of the Forked Lightning Woman but after a moment's thought, pulled back on his reins so he could talk to her:

"Save your bullets for the vehoe on the Saline. Stay at the back for the charge." It wasn't an instruction, Dark wouldn't have dared, but White Rain nodded with relief:

"You too," she said, spurring her pony up the slope.

Cresting the rise, it was hard to spot the veho camp. Though it was some distance off, Dark eventually spotted a small sandy island in the middle of a shallow riverbed where dismounted saddle horses and white men plunged through the scrub to get into cover; it didn't seem much of a place to defend. Orderly puffs of rifle smoke issued from the bushes as volleys of bullets tore into the warrior ranks and toppled a few from their saddles before the charge had even started. This wasn't a good way to win a battle.

Dark, with White Rain following, reined his pony round to another ridge to try and get closer but the massed body of warriors, both Lakota and Cheyenne, prevented it. Both the Suhtai warriors hissed with frustration and tried a different route where the attackers seemed less numerous.

The charges against the white scouts now began to build up and Dark watched as the disciplined fire of the whites blunted the momentum that threatened to overwhelm them. Driven wild by shrieking whistles and the cries of their riders, war ponies splashed into the shallow river, flung up clods of wet sand and pushed towards the deadly shrubs where the whites were coolly gunning down any who came close.

Bodies, shields, lances and guns lay in the water, some warriors were wounded but still alive – comrades tried to recover those who had fallen only to be shot down themselves. The warriors were too numerous to let the whites win but, right now, staying out of the range of their bullets seemed to be a good idea.

---- 0 0 0 ----

Major George Forsyth cut into his leg wound with a cut throat razor and used the surgeon's own spatula to open the wound and probe for the bullet. The two men holding his leg in position, grimaced and looked away. The surgeon had no further use for his implements as his skull lay split open from a heavy calibre bullet – he had died that morning and lay nearby in a shallow scrape. Now Sheridan's aide cursed his bad luck, wounded in each leg, food gone and his horses all dead.

Forsyth ducked instinctively as bullets thudded into the earthworks bordering hastily-built trenches in the sand. Arrows occasionally arched into the sky above them and plummeted to earth, sometimes pinning an unfortunate scout from above. Gunfire from the Indians ploughed into the small island in the middle of the north fork of the Republican River as his small command dug in deeper for the fight. The heavy willow and alder brush on the shallow mound hid most of them from open view but the Indians still shot at them through it, hoping for a lucky hit.

Tying off his wound, Forsyth mused on whether he should have listened to the experienced scouts who warned him about the heavy trail they were following. Their food rations were almost gone by the time they had even found the village and an early attack by some young Cheyenne had lost the command two of their supply mules and several horses. He had been lucky to spot the island earlier and mentally mark it as a good defensive position should they ever need it; it had been a wise move.

Now, as the hordes of warriors appeared out of the ravines and cutbanks, survival - not taking the fight to the Indians as Sheridan had wanted – was his main priority.

---- o o o ----

There was little for Dark and White Rain to do except await an opportunity to attack; they pushed their ponies around the rear ranks of the warriors. They soon found themselves in a small gully, alone except for a tall Dog Soldier warrior and a few of his companions. The tall one, holding a magnificent war bonnet in his hand, seemed calm but strong:

"My brothers, I have already explained, my medicine was broken last night – I cannot fight today – I will be killed."

One of the warriors next to him, grabbed his arm – though to Dark, that seemed like a dangerous thing to do – the tall warrior didn't seem to be the type that any sensible man would want to manhandle in that way:

"Surely, the great Hooked Nose – one of our finest war leaders – will not be deterred from battle just because a metal spoon touched his meal last night? Our attacks need your magic to enter the hearts of our men. With you in the lead we will win!"

Hooked Nose looked at him and brushed away his hand; he looked across at Dark and White Rain;

"You young Suhtai! What do you think?"

Dark reined his pony across to Hooked Nose and the Dog Men as White Rain followed warily. See the Dark knew he was in the presence of a great man and tried to think of something serious to say:

"All we Cheyenne warriors carry our medicine bundles…" Dark said, holding his up from his neck, "…and it is for each man to know his own heart and power of his medicine. If you say your medicine is diminished – then don't fight." It seemed to set the tone.

The Dog Men shrieked their disapproval but Hooked Nose ignored them and looked at Dark:

"Did you fight today?" he asked.

Both Dark and White Rain hung their heads:

"Not yet – too many men pushed in ahead of me!" said White Rain, jutting her chin defiantly.

Hooked Nose smiled patiently – she was just a woman and her war deeds were not important - he turned his gaze back to Dark.

"Has your medicine ever failed you?"

Dark looked troubled but was honest:

"I have no true medicine or warrior rituals – sometimes I pray to Maheo to keep me safe – but only when I remember."

"What did the Life Giver say to you when you prayed last?" asked the tall one.

Dark's serious side, ever thin and superficial, had faded – encouraged by the great man's smile. He put on a sombre face and said:

"When I last prayed, Maheo said – 'And who might *you* be?'"

Hooked Nose laughed out loud and put on his war bonnet:

"Come! If a godless youth and his woman is unafraid to fight – I will have nothing to fear!"

Now mounted, the small party surged up the rise and charged down at the whites. Dark and White Rain followed, eager to fight alongside such a man. Other warriors, hanging back out of range of the whites' rifles, cheered as Hooked Nose rode by and joined in the tumult waving shields and lances as they pressed forward.

Riding down, Dark and White Rain were again shouldered aside by men now encouraged by the presence of such a great warrior amongst them. The Forked Lightning woman lashed out with her rifle to clear her path to glory but all she saw were the backs of Dog Soldiers as they charged across the river; even the volley of gunfire smoke was hidden from her as the bullets raked their ranks.

Both at least managed to get close enough to fire bullets at the white scouts – they were difficult to spot now as they'd spent time digging earthworks in the sand – but neither seemed to hit anything.

White Rain wheeled her pony away and back up the hill – she would need to reload. Dark noticed that all veho horses had been shot down and, as he turned back to get out of range of the gunfire, saw the body of Hooked Nose lying still in the water.

The young Suhtai shook his head and was still for a moment – the power of good medicine was either with you or it wasn't – no man could guarantee it to extend his ride along life's trail. Here he was, godless and upright in the saddle while a true follower of the Great Spirit lay face down in the wet sand. Life could be strange and short.

The two young Cheyenne had developed a call - an eagle's screech – that meant they should join up. Dark gave the call and White Rain answered, reining her pony down the slope towards him. The whites could have their small island – these two Suhtai were off to the Saline.

---- o o o ----

George Forsyth reloaded his pistol and gathered his breath. The repeating Spencer carbines had proved their worth, initially at least. Massed charges by the Cheyenne and Sioux had been halted by the rate of fire and the Indians had been reluctant to try that tactic again any time soon. In one of the early charges, a tall warrior with a large and colourful war bonnet crashed into the shallow water, stone dead from a Spencer bullet:

"That's ol' Roman Nose Major! We killed an important man!"

Despite suffering from his wounds at the time, Forsyth, trying to remain cool, had replied:

"Thank you, Mr Alderdice, – introductions are not necessary!"

Now, as he squinted along his pistol barrel, Forsyth knew he should have argued with General Sheridan about raising more scouts to pursue Indians. Either that or he should have abandoned the trail earlier as their food was running out. The two squaw men with the Henry repeaters that he'd met at Fort Hays would have been useful about now.

---- 0 0 0 ----

Chapter Forty Eight

The baby had been hung upside down, suspended from a live oak with a warrior's bowstring; ravens had already pecked the child's eyes out though the body was not more than a day or two old.

"Jesus, Henry! Have you seen this?" called Carver as he gagged at the sight – dismembered warriors or scalped white men were one thing, but a child...?

Henry didn't answer directly put came from around the back of the crude cabin carrying another child – a girl of about four years old. He laid her carefully on the ground, straightening her apron and skirt. The child's neck and back had been slashed and blood caked her linen dress.

"She's been lanced to death – they left her in the potato patch..." he said; "...the Cheyenne did this, y'know."

Carver nodded carefully – he too had seen the distinctive moccasin prints in the soft soil. They spoke in low tones now, trying to keep their knowledge from Klas Lindstrom, their Swedish companion. He knew these cabin owners and was now anxious about his own family, only a few miles away.

Carver cut the baby down and put it into an empty flour sack. He lay the child next to the dead girl. At a loss for a moment, he and Henry stood over the children and took off their hats.

Klas Lindstrom staggered out from the cabin and onto the stoop, retching and wailing:

"My friend Jakob is inside – scalped and killed next to his own kitchen stove ...Goddamn those savages!"

Henry nodded and, followed by Carver, went inside. Jakob Ackerman lay on his back, arms akimbo – a tell-tale, circular cut on the top of his head had removed his scalp. Henry counted twelve arrows – striped in the Cheyenne way - in him. It was a lot of arrows to waste on a prone man. Ackerman may have put up some sort of a fight as his face had been disfigured by many blows from a hatchet, possibly as he'd lain dying. Grey embers, probably taken from the iron stove next to him when they were hot, had been heaped on his chest. Jakob Ackerman had not died quickly or easily.

Carver checked the food boxes – flour, coffee, salt and sugar were gone but the rest – oats, molasses, eggs and pickled vegetables had been strewn over the floor where Ackerman lay. Feathers from a ripped bedding mattress were mixed in and handfuls of goose fat from a wooden tub had been thrown at the walls. The place stank.

The wolf skinner squatted on his haunches and looked more closely. There was another outline in the pooled mess – another adult had lain there but was now gone. Henry joined him and stared at the signs – from the absence of any of the food waste around the lower part of the outline, he knew he was looking at the place where a woman's skirts had been spread. The scuff marks from several pairs of moccasins showed where more than one warrior had violated her.

"No wonder ol' Major Forsyth and his boys went after the Injuns – them Cheyenne's got some anwerin' to do," said Carver. Henry looked at his friend but said nothing – the wolf skinner had already distanced himself from the Suhtai. They were the enemy now.

Outside the sound of a shovel being repeatedly plunged into the earth brought them back to reality and they walked outside.

Lindstrom was savagely thumping a spade into the softer ground near the vegetable patch and throwing the spoil into a growing heap. Tears fell from his eyes in an almost constant stream as he dug the graves:

"Jakob was my friend. His wife Sadie was a good neighbour to my family – always cooking the best pies when we worked out in the fields. We ate here often…"

Henry walked over to him and patted him on the shoulder – knowing as he did it that it was a useless gesture – a sign of someone who didn't have anything comforting to say.

Lindstrom was digging like a man possessed; he was in a hurry:

"Gotta get back to my own kin and make sure they're alright…"

"Of course, Mr Lindstrom we understand…" said Henry, "…why don't you let us finish the graves and we'll catch you up later?"

The Swede took off his hat, wiped his hand across his forehead and then down over his face, dragging the tears away. He nodded gratefully and climbed back aboard his wagon.

"My place is just a small soddy – three, four miles from here maybe – it's hard to spot from the road. I just hope to God that the Indians haven't found it."

Carver came over with another shovel he'd found:

"Let's hope so too, Swede. We'll be along soon to meet your Mr Shen…Shin…somethin'"

"Schengenhorn" said Lindstrom over his shoulder as he flipped the traces of his team and lurched out of the devastated yard.

"Yeah, him," said Carver and started on the final resting places for the Ackerman children as Henry dragged Jakob, already stiff in death, out of the cabin door and across the yard.

Carver walked over to the two small bodies and gently lifted each one into the communal hole he'd dug. Flies crowded onto the blood stains and he brushed them away. He left the baby in the gunny sack without looking at it. He was surprised when a tear fell from the end of his nose onto the young girl's dress.

Covering the bodies only took a moment but he collected some sawn timber planks and put these on top of the grave, held down by the heaviest rocks he could find. Coyotes would have to work hard to get at this carrion.

A lone hawk wheeled in the sky and mewed its song. A breeze blew the scent of the dead back into the long grass bordering the small farm where two prairie wolves edged on their bellies and watched where their next meal was being buried.

---- o o o ----

Chapter Forty Nine

Mathilde Hoffmann kept her gun trained on the Indian woman and watched her eat the bread and milk from a tin bowl. The woman looked thin and hungry but she smiled occasionally as her dirt-encrusted fingers scooped out the white mush; she huddled into a rancid deerskin cloak though Mathilde had thought that the day wasn't too cold.

The arrival of the squaw had taken Mathilde by surprise as she sat out on the stoop plucking a game hen but, as she'd been warned by her husband, she'd kept the old musket to hand and soon waved the barrel under the Indian's nose. There had been too many Indian attacks this year along the Saline and the Solomon to be careless. Redskins or no, while her husband was away in town, she knew she could manage the farm for a day or two.

She'd swung the musket muzzle at the woman and made her move away from the house as she checked her pasture and behind the cabin to make sure the woman was alone; she seemed to be. Her two mules, a milk cow and a spare wagon horse cropped at the rich grass and showed no sign of unease. The Indian had arrived by pony and it too had wandered off to pull at the grass beneath the rail fence.

The gun was heavy and cumbersome, Mathilde sighed and shifted her forearm under the wooden stock.

She realised that she was sighing a great deal these days, though she was careful never to do this when her husband was near. They had been used to a comfortable life back in her native Bremerhaven – her husband had made a good living from his work with a shipping company and she liked the smell of the sea – she had never wanted to come here but Manfred had wanted more; America seemed to be the place to get it. Manfred had once worked in city clothes and smelt of nice hair oil but now seemed happy in rough work gear as he ploughed his own patch of new earth. Out here, the hair oil just attracted flies.

She checked herself back into watchfulness as the Indian woman was draining the last of the milk from the bowl, the tin edge clacking against her teeth. She then held it out, as if for a refill:

"*Nein, nein!*" Mathilde brandished the musket and indicated that the squaw should remount and ride off.

The Indian woman shrugged but smiled and came towards her with an outstretched hand – as if to thank her. Mathilde was puzzled – a handshake was the gesture of civilised whites not savage Indians – but she was still wary. She held the gun across her chest with the barrel in the air. It was a mistake...

The squaw rushed across the open ground between them, grabbed the musket barrel with her right hand and, with her left, pulled a hunting knife from under the deerhide cloak and stabbed the white woman in the throat. As Mathilde went down with the shock of the iron blade puncturing her neck, the Indian woman shrieked in her face.

Mathilde Hoffmann, sliding into unconsciousness, was aware of several more riders galloping into the pasture. From the terrified mooing of the cow and nervous braying of the mules, she could tell the riders were running off her stock. She tried to speak but her larynx had been shattered by the knife blow.

Now, with blood gushing over the dirty linen collar of her blue work blouse, she knew that the child inside her was lost; its eyes would never see the sun rise nor smile at the faces of its parents. Manfred had wanted their first child to be born in America – to root them all into this new country and to keep them there. She sobbed into the uncaring dust and drew her final breath.

---- 0 0 0 ----

Broken Knife jerked the hair of the white woman in the blue shirt and looked at her face and gashed throat. He bared his teeth in frustration and shouted at White Rain:

"It was a mistake to kill her – she would have been worth more alive as a captive! We could have traded her for food or guns later on…"

White Rain just glared at him:

"There will be food in the house, we have her gun and animals – and don't shout at me, I'm not one of your novices!"

Broken Knife stopped and breathed deeply; he was not used to back talk from anyone, let alone a woman:

"Well, it's good to discuss these things with *such* an experienced warrior …"; he let the sarcasm lie heavily, then remounting his pony, said:

"…killing is not the only thing of value. If the vehoe ever come looking for us, we can stop them attacking when they know we have a white woman in camp…"

White Rain snorted in disbelief:

"No! Once the white soldiers *know* we'd taken her, they'd just keep tracking us down until we were found; killing her removed that problem."

See the Dark heard the raised voices and rode in between the quarrelling pair. Both fell silent. He looked at White Rain; she had never liked Broken Knife.

The pipe holder of the Thunder Bears had been aloof and taciturn back in the Suhtai camp, but out here was proving to be a disagreeable war companion. Neither he nor White Rain owed Broken Knife any loyalty other than tribal kinship but they'd found him and his few followers during a raid on a white settler's cabin further west. Then, it had seemed to be a wonderful reunion between two parts of the Suhtai band, now they weren't so sure.

Dark reined his pony towards the woman warrior and held out the bridle of her own horse tied to his saddle. She didn't look up but plunged her bloody knife blade into the soil to clean it.

"Do something useful – go into the house and gather as much food as we can carry. The white woman had an old gun – I'll look for powder and ball; we can trim the bullets down to fit yours…"

Whooping and yelling emerged from the house as the few Thunder Bears resupplied themselves with whatever came to hand first. Incensed, the Forked Lightning Woman ignored the proffered bridle and raced into the cabin, bundling three of the youngsters out into the yard:

"Stay back! I was closest to the enemy and made the raid succeed – I get first choice!"

Dark watched and listened. Broken Knife rode up with the long musket across his saddle and waved the three dejected youths away from the cabin. Dark thought he was probably trying to mollify the snarling woman, even though White Rain hadn't seen the gesture.

His pony reared slightly when a storm of feathers issued from the open cabin door as the Cheyenne woman ripped open a striped blue and grey cloth covering from a mattress and dumped the contents onto the porch. She went back inside and eventually re-emerged with the bulging cloth used as a sack, over her shoulder:

"There's enough food for two of us here – I couldn't see any powder or ball," she said and threw the heavy bundle across her saddle, the pony sidestepping as the unaccustomed weight fell on it. White Rain mounted up and Dark followed her.

Broken Knife watched impassively from his saddle and summoned Little Snake:

"Take this gun – it is yours…" he swung the heavy weapon into the youth's eager hands. Little Snake was too delighted to thank him or to notice that his leader seemed to be relieved to be rid of its weight.

"… now, go back inside and collect our food. And you two…" he pointed to the other young men, "…get the horse and mules – we don't need the cow, it will only slow us down."

The two young Thunder Bears smiled at being given something definite to do, raced back to their ponies and drove the complaining animals into the yard. Laughing and chattering, they nocked arrows onto their bowstrings and fired them into the sleek belly of the milk cow. The animal stumbled, groaning and roaring in pain and fell to its front knees, rump in the air. A stream of bloody faeces spurted into the dust as the animal lay panting but not dead.

The young men dismounted and stabbed the cow in the neck – more blood flowed but the animal seemed too stubborn to die until Little Snake rode up, pointed the gun at the cow's head and pulled the trigger. He'd found more powder and ball in a horn and bag under the wooden flooring– so he could afford to be generous as well as show off the fact that their leader had given *him* the gun and not them.

Broken Knife smiled, noting Little Snake's leadership using the gun, and called them all back into the saddle. The raiding party moved off at a casual pace. He would need to think of how to deal with See the Dark and his woman; there was no place for dissent on the war trail. Some food might be welcome and help him consider the problem – they would make an early camp. He spurred his pony forward.

Behind him, mules brayed and his warriors sang songs of victory as the blood from a white woman and a brown cow merged and seeped into the earth.

---- 0 0 0 ----

Chapter Fifty

"I've always liked the name 'Albert'," said Carver. The comment came out of thin air and made Henry splutter into his whisky, gagging as the fiery liquid fought its way down his throat:

"What! Where the Hell did that come from? Is it a middle name that you haven't told me about?"

"Nah. I just like the sound of it – 'Albert Carver' – I sound like a man of means. Solid like. It'll save you calling me 'Mister'."

"Well, Queen Victoria's husband goes by that name – but of course, he's a bloody German – my apologies, he *was* a bloody German. He died a few years ago. Anyway, we get by with 'Mister Carver' very well – so you can forget 'Albert'"

They shuffled uneasily in their seats, neither had sat on an upholstered chair in a long time – sitting on rickety biscuit boxes waiting for whores in the Hell on Wheels camp probably didn't count.

The Englishman looked at his friend – he looked glum and ill-at-ease. Their surroundings didn't help – carpets, chandeliers and polished wood in the grand Schengenhorn house were an odd backdrop for their buckskins. Their host had gone upstairs to change clothes after pouring them a drink. Henry tried to cheer Carver up:

"What about 'George'? That's a solid name. I'd be happy to call you that."

"Nah. Too common. That shit-shoveller at the railroad was called George."

"How about 'Patrick'?"

"Too Irish." Carver folded his arms grumpily.

Henry smiled, then braced himself as he offered:

"How about 'Mirabelle'?"

Now it was Carver's turn to choke:

"Mirabelle? Makes me sound like head honcho in a whorehouse! Goddamn you Henry!"

"Mirabelle was good enough for the second President of Texas – Mirabelle Bonaparte La Marr. Very classy, Mr Carver," said Henry, laughing out loud. A Texan track-layer had told him the name.

Carver was about to reply when their host appeared on the staircase:

"'Mirabeau' gentlemen. I think you'll find that President La Marr's name was Mira*beau* – not Mira*belle*."

"Bow or Bell – makes no never mind to me. It's a goddamn stupid name," grumbled Carver, glaring at Henry. The Englishman sat with a fatuous grin on his face – only slightly put out at being corrected.

August Schengenhorn walked slowly down the stairs; both Henry and Carver had been surprised to see a two storey, stone and timber house in the wilds of Kansas, so a staircase was even more unusual. The businessman was dressed in a padded silk smoking jacket, a tasselled cap on his head and embroidered slippers on his feet; the only odd note was the Colt Dragoon in a tooled holster on his hip.

"More drinks, gentlemen?" he said and sat down across from them. He rang a small bell with an ivory handle. A black servant noiselessly emerged from a door at the bottom of the stairs, took the decanter from its polished stand and poured more amber liquid into their outstretched glasses.

Carver looked at the black man, then at Schengenhorn:

"Thought slaves were illegal now?"

Schengenhorn smiled indulgently and said:

"Oh, Nathan isn't a slave – he's a free man who chooses to work for me. Isn't that right Nathan?"

The black man nodded and smiled at the two rough guests sprawled in the damask-covered chairs – he'd need to put the chairs out in the yard tomorrow to get the fleas off.

"That is correct, sir…" his voice spoke of some education back east," …in these uncertain times it's good to have a roof and food provided. Mister and Missus Schengenhorn have been very kind." He refrained from saying that if the 'Boss' ever let him close to that Colt Dragoon, social change would come a lot sooner.

"*Missus* Schengenhorn? You have a wife here too?"

"I do Mister Armstrong – she's upstairs taking a nap before dinner."

"Will these -er, - gentlemen be staying for dinner sir?" asked Nathan.

At the mention of food both Henry and Carver sat up in their chairs only to be reminded of their place in this grand house:

"No…" said their host, "…we have some business to discuss first then they can make their lodgings in the barn with the others…"

"Others?" asked Henry.

"Yes, indeed Mr Armstrong. I'd asked Lindstrom to be on the lookout for likely candidates for our, er, work when he was at the fort…"

He stood up and walked over to a board draped in yellow silk. Dramatically, he swept the silk from the board to reveal a map – he gestured Henry and Carver to come closer and then pointed to the ink lines on it:

"This, gentlemen, is a map of the Smoky Hill, Saline and Solomon valleys – see here is the route of the railroad – now with these damn Cheyenne and Sioux creating havoc and destruction, this is rapidly becoming Indian country. And we Kansans won't have it!"

Carver peered at the map – one of the few he'd seen; he'd seen the Cheyenne version of maps of course but they were just childlike, rough guides compared to this. He had never used a white man's map – landmarks – rivers, mountains, valleys were all in his head. But he was impressed with the detail.

Their host had taken his seat again and refilled their glasses himself:

"Boys, I've been here near a decade now – one of the first to settle, back along the Solomon. Got along pretty well with the Cheyenne in those days – gave 'em a beef or two when buffalo weren't too plenty, that sorta thing…"

The floor creaked above them and all looked up. A tall, bronze-skinned woman in a red dress had come out of one of the upstairs rooms and looked over the rail at them. Now Carver and Henry could see why the Indians had left the Schengenhorns alone – the woman looked as though she could be Cheyenne herself.

"…Darlin' – Mister Carver and Mister Armstrong…just concludin' our business, my dear."

Unbidden, Henry and Carver stood up and nodded to the woman. Mrs Schengenhorn merely inclined her chin slightly upwards at Carver but her gaze stayed on Henry. Carver grunted in surprise; the woman's gesture had reminded him of New Grass. Henry was unable to say anything – the brown eyes locked on his rendered him speechless. Suddenly, the woman broke the spell and went back into her room.

Schengenhorn sat down again and refilled their glasses, holding up the nearly-empty decanter to Nathan who took it and refilled it.:

"Where was I? Oh yes…the folks in these valleys look to me to set an example. I have a good business – two stores in Junction City, one in Salina and this ranch. We have a lumber mill out back and the forts along the Arkansas and our new railroad buy just about all we can produce. Those damn Indians are not going to drive me or the other settlers off – no sir!"

Schengenhorn pulled out the Colt and waved it around; surprised, Henry and Carver both put their hands on their gun belts but relaxed as their host walked to the map again, tapping the inked lines with the muzzle of the pistol:

"Patrols, gentlemen – that's what we need – patrols. Those Indians are killing families, burning houses and stopping trade and settlement stone dead in these valleys. Some of the weaker brethren are going back east. But I can't pay for enough men to protect all the scattered homesteads - so we need to find those savages *before* they attack and then hit them hard."

Nodding with satisfaction at his speech, Schengenhorn stuffed the revolver back into its holster.

Henry and Carver looked at each other – it sounded a bit like the job that Major Forsyth had tried to get them to do back at Fort Hays. Still, at the time, they - and their horses - had been worn out then and both had declined his fifty dollars a month.

Now, they were rested, their ponies were sleeker and, as Henry admitted to himself, they were at a loose end and almost broke.

"How much?" asked Carver gruffly. Henry sighed at Carver's usual bluntness but agreed with his direct approach. Winter was coming, they needed some sort of base and a job. This might do it.

Schengenhorn smiled affably, unabashed by Carver's demand:

"Seventy dollars a month - but for that, I'll expect you out in all weathers. Those savages will be settling down under their buffalo robes when the snow comes. You'll be able to track them easier and find their camps. Then hightail it back here and we'll tell the Army to go get 'em."

Carver stood up and stretched, draining his whisky. He looked at Henry who shrugged and nodded:

"Fine Mr Schengenhorn, we'll go the barn and meet the others."

The cold air hit them both hard when they walked out of the house; both reeled a little from the effects of the whisky:

"That Mrs Schengenhorn is a fine-looking woman," slurred Henry. Carver tutted:

"Henry, she'd eat you up, spit you out then probably scalp ye!"

---- o 0 o ----

Chapter Fifty One

The arrival of Viajero and his family in the Mescalero country had caused a great stir. A Mescalero sentry had seen them first and Viajero heard him - yelping like a coyote – a warning to their small encampment in the mountains.

Bright Antelope called to the man in his own tongue to reassure him but he didn't hear her. Whilst she belonged to this part of the *N'De* family, she couldn't yet be sure that she'd found anyone who would remember her – her family were long dead.

The secretive band of Mescaleros had moved much higher up the slopes than Viajero remembered and the horses in his small group had a hard time scrabbling up the steep and rocky trail. It was a hot day for so late in the year – turkey vultures, alerted by the commotion, soared above them as they kept a hungry eye on the stumbling ponies.

A pack of rangy wolves, spotting the vultures, trotted along the opposite mesa to rush in and grab a quick meal if the opportunity arose. Viajero saw them and smiled – if this wasn't quite the White Mountain country of his own people, the birds and wolves made it seem familiar enough.

He glanced back over his shoulder as Bright Antelope, their daughter and Willow slowly guided their animals up to the Mescalero camp. The three females were silent – concentrating on staying on the trail without crippling their horses. The Traveller adjusted the load of deer meat across his saddle – it would make a useful present to the Mescalero and hopefully take away any suspicions that they might have about their sudden arrival.

He remembered the last time he'd gone into a Mescalero camp, now many summers back. Back then he remembered the Mescalero band had been well-fed, successful in battle and with plenty of stolen stock to trade and eat. Though his sudden presence had alarmed them, the Mescalero had merely shouted insults but made no move to harm him.

Now as he rode through the broken-down *wickiups* of the Mescalero village on a small, dust-swept plateau, things had changed. Warriors and women, close to starvation, bundled frightened children into shelter and brought out their weapons – mainly bows and arrows, a few short spears and old guns. He was surprised at the consternation amongst them as they milled about, pointing at him and his family – he thought at least one of them may have remembered a famous warrior of the White Mountain people.

This time, to show he came in peace, he'd left his rifle in the saddle bucket but, without warning, some of the underfed warriors leapt on him and pulled him from the saddle.

He hit the ground hard, his bandana wrenched from around his head as he shook the dust out of his eyes. Oddly, the scrawny warriors were now standing in a circle looking, not at him, but an object on the ground. They looked afraid and yelled in fear.

Viajero now spotted what had caused them to back off – Dark's glass eye lay staring up at them from the dust. The young Cheyenne would have made the most of the incident, so the Apache thought he might try it too. Pulling his headband back into place and tucking his loose hair under it, he picked up the eye and held it out to them; all shrank away:

"See this! Usen gives me the power of an extra eye to spot treachery amongst my enemies – do not test me again!"

It was quite a speech for the taciturn warrior and they probably didn't understand the words but the Mescalero seemed to respect the image. The Apache nodded in satisfaction; See the Dark would have been proud.

One man, less impressed than the others, went to take the Henry rifle out of the saddle bucket but Viajero pulled his hunting knife from his long moccasins, wrenched him away by his hair and held the blade threateningly across his throat. The atmosphere got calmer.

Bright Antelope spurred her pony forward and barged the skinny ones aside. She spoke out – haltingly, as she'd not used her own language in a long while:

"I am of your people – we bring you food as a sign of our good faith…" she gestured towards the drying cuts of meat that hung from Viajero's saddle. Some of the women made moves to get it but Viajero waved them off with his knife – he was still smarting at being pulled from the saddle by weaklings.

"…some of you may remember my grandfather, Wolf in the Water…?"

She looked around to see if there were any familiar faces but starvation had taken its toll on the small band – they looked hungry and haunted – she recognised no-one. As she was about to continue, one old man, with two deep scars on his face, spoke out:

"I remember Wolf in the Water – he was my friend; he died some winters back. You went off to follow a *Coyotero*."

Bright Antelope nodded but without emotion – her grandfather was already old when she'd slipped out of his camp to follow Viajero, so his death was no surprise. She'd called Viajero her *Coyotero* then – back when her affections were strong.

"Thank you… "she said, "…we are just passing through to my husband's White Mountain country. If you consent, we will camp with you for a couple of days to rest our horses. We have brought our daughter and this other…person." She pointed at Willow.

She had used the word 'husband' only in the Mescalero tongue, knowing Viajero wouldn't understand.

The Mescalero now stared at the silent, lanky girl – she obviously wasn't of the N'De. Perhaps she was a slave? Odd that she carried guns and seemed to have war deeds painted on her shirt. It didn't really matter though, getting their hands on the deer meat was more important. They watched as the White Mountain warrior threw the cuts to the women. The hunks of meat were heavy and some of the women dropped them into the dust. Bright Antelope tutted.

The Traveller signalled to his daughter and Willow to dismount and help Bright Antelope erect their lodge; Willow did as she was told but only with gritted teeth. She was bored with the domestic chores – she was a warrior and she'd hoped that Viajero would treat her differently. But this seemed now to be just a wisp of dreams that had disappeared.

The Hunkpapa girl was tired, but not from hardships or occasional hunger on the trail; her war quest with the Forked Lightning Women to take the guns from the Comanche and Comancheros had been much more dangerous and exhausting but, at least, it had been exciting. This marriage quest was dull. The Traveller had not even lain with her on the journey south, though Willow thought that was probably because Bright Antelope may have killed them both in their sleep.

With a bitter "Hah!", Willow untied the pack saddle and deliberately dumped the tipi covers into the red mesa dust.

In a wordless fury, Bright Antelope picked them up and heaved them over to a camping place pointed out by the Mescalero.

Willow sighed in resignation. Their many days of riding down from Bad Elk's Suhtai camp had been full of hostile silences as Bright Antelope struggled to accept her as Viajero's next wife.

During the long trail southwards, Willow failed to get Bright Antelope to speak to her; worse, the Mescalero woman barely spoke to Viajero either. Only the daughter of the warring pair – Deer Running – was any sort of ally. She and Willow spoke in whispered words when out of sight of her parents, sometimes giggling about the difference in height between her father and the Lakota girl.

Willow snorted to herself in despair. If silences were bad, the quarrels between the Traveller and his wife were worse. Even Deer Running's very *name* had been the start of more trouble; Viajero only called her 'daughter' when speaking to her and Bright Antelope had once challenged him - during a flood of bitter tears and shrill recriminations one night at the campfire - to say his daughter's name. The hapless Apache couldn't remember what it was – proof to the Mescalero woman, that his heart was not in being a part of any family.

Viajero, true to his nature as a warrior, had not considered this to be important and stalked off into the mesquite bushes and spent the night alone. Willow had felt a worm of doubt wriggle into her head.

Across the encampment, Bright Antelope arranged the tipi poles on the ground, laid the buffalo skins over them and stood up, rubbing a twinge in her back. She glared at Willow and Viajero. The scarred man came up behind her:

"Is that the man you followed on his quest?" asked the scarred man, pointing with his chin at Viajero. Bright Antelope nodded.

"Was he worth it?"

The Mescalero woman looked at him bleakly, then turned away.

---- 0 0 0 ----

Chapter Fifty Two

Crow Dress Woman and her scouts had seen the file of moving black dots first.

The thin black line was some distance away and wound down a far-off hill heading towards them. The dots hadn't raised that much dust as the ground was hardening with the oncoming winter. Clouds behind the distant hill were dark and threatening, snowflakes already whirled in the breeze.

As the Forked Lightning Women had been given the duty of protective screen in advance of Bad Elk's moving village, Crow Dress told them to find out if the approaching dots were any kind of threat. So, they'd ridden closer and watched it for a while. They decided that it was too slow to be a column of white soldiers or an advancing enemy so they rode out to meet it. Now, they spurred back to their chief to report:

"They are Arapaho. Their leader, Red Raven says he knows you and sends his greetings …"

Crow Dress had to shout her report as their chief was sitting on a high rock so he could get a better view of the country ahead. His deafness was getting worse, she hoped he'd heard her.

Bad Elk nodded – he and Red Raven had met during a ceremony to rededicate the Medicine Arrows; there was always a couple of Arapaho lodges around when all the Cheyenne met for the sacred rites. It seemed like a lifetime ago; he shouted back down to her:

"That's true – where are they going?"

Crow Dress, knowing that this was no way to conduct a conversation, dismounted, handed her bridle to Sweet Water and climbed up to join him.

Beyond the grey buttress, the village column paused as horses were rested and children allowed to run and play. She sat down next to her chief:

"They are going to the land that we agreed to live on – after the treaty with the whites…"

"Did you tell them that we'd already been there and didn't like it?" said Bad Elk; his voice as loud as ever, though the woman now just sat an arm's length from him.

"Yes. I told them that there were no buffalo, the water was poisoned and we couldn't find any game."

"What did their chief say?"

"They didn't seem to have a chief – Red Raven spoke for them. He asked to share our campfire tonight to discuss what to do next."

Bad Elk nodded his agreement:

"Send Bear Killer back to tell them to join us…"

"Her real name is Star..." interrupted the Forked Lightning woman.

"I *know* what her name is – I'm your chief and I don't have too many names to remember these days – 'Bear Killer' is better suited to one of my warriors!"

Crow Dress grinned in satisfaction – it was rare that any Cheyenne man, even a wise one like Bad Elk, ever acknowledged them as warriors. She would tell Sweet Water and Star later. Perhaps she would call her youngest fighter 'Bear Killer' from now on – the girl would be delighted, though her parents may not be.

Bad Elk scrambled back down the slope after her; he'd instruct the village to pitch camp and receive guests. His eyes weren't as sharp as the young Forked Lightning Women but even he could make out that Red Raven didn't seem to have too many people with him.

Snow fell more heavily now. Bad Elk watched and shouted encouragement as the Suhtai lodges were unfurled swiftly; better to get them up quickly than wait and then camp on damp ground.

Bad Elk mounted his pony and went out to bring in Red Raven and his followers.

His plan for the immediate future of the Suhtai was not his best and he knew it. They would head north of the Flint Arrowpoint River and hunt buffalo – the terms of the treaty with the whites allowed this so he hoped they would be in no danger from soldiers – but at this time of year, getting food supplies to last them the many days through the Hard-Faced Moon would be tricky. He prayed to Maheo to help him.

As if in reply, the gunmetal clouds closed in above him and a heavy snow fell – at times like this, he often wished that someone else was chief.

---- 0 0 0 ----

The Arapaho circle of lodges was erected quickly – there were only a dozen families with Red Raven – and when all had been fed, Bad Elk lit his pipe. Yellow Bear muttered some prayers to help the leaders of both bands to seek wisdom and find a way to survive the winter.

Red Raven accepted the pipe from Bad Elk and, after pointing the redstone bowl in all four directions of the winds, spoke out; as allies of the Medicine Arrow People, he knew the Cheyenne language well. Folk from both bands had gathered round to hear what had been decided. Some of the people were illuminated by the red and yellow glow of the campfire, others just unknown shapes in the darkness:

"I thank our Suhtai friends for their food and hospitality…"

There were murmurs of agreement in the growing gloom.

"I respect Bad Elk's decision to leave the poisoned grounds of the white man's place – so we Arapaho will not go there! No-one can ever entrust a part of our sacred land to another man…"

There were howls of agreement at this; Bad Elk thought that Red Raven had become a better speaker since they'd last met.

"…but I would advise against going north of the Flint Arrowpoint River as the Suhtai intend to do. The treaty at Medicine Lodge Creek offered us many things – good land, guns and bullets to hunt and, above all, peace. None of this has been true. Hah!"

Red Raven paused to draw in the smoke from the pipe; he looked at Bad Elk – the Suhtai chief encouraged him to continue.

"Though the soldier chiefs say that they won't attack us if we are north of the river just to hunt, who is to say they will keep their word? Sand Creek was a great lesson here – don't believe them!"

Bad Elk took the pipe and explained:

"The Arapaho leader told me on our way in, that many other bands of our people – as well as Kiowa, Comanche and *his* own people – are making their winter camps along the Lodgepole River. I think we should do the same…"

There was some puzzlement amongst the Suhtai. Crow Dress found the courage to speak out of the blackness; she spoke loudly so her chief would know who it was even if he couldn't see her face:

"Is there food there? We've hardly seen any buffalo down here – getting north of the Flint Arrowpoint River at least gives us a chance to hunt."

"True, sister but on the Lodgepole we will have timber for fires, water for us and our horses and we'll be surrounded by friends…"

Red Raven looked around, irritated by the fact that a woman had questioned his argument but he needn't have worried, Bad Elk had already been persuaded:

"We will go tomorrow" he said and dashed the ashes out of his pipe.

---- o o o ----

The snowstorm blinded both men and horses, a thick wet swirl of white hid the entire landscape; troopers were forced to stay close in formation just to see the blurred outlines of their comrades and keep the direction of travel. Horses slithered in the mush on the trail and silver plumes of winter breath rose from the column, only to be whipped away by the wind. Coffee and a campfire would have been a welcome break for his men but George Custer would have none of it.

The commander of the 7th Cavalry pulled his buffalo hat down to his eyebrows and pulled the caped collar of his overcoat up to keep the snow off; lack of action or information made him agitated. Where the deuce was Major Elliot and his scouting troop? Why didn't he report back? While the snow fell as fast and thick as this, even a recent trail could be covered within minutes. It had been three days since his second-in-command had gone off with the Osage scouts to find some sign that would lead him to a target. They must push on south and find an

Indian trail to a village that they could attack – without it the entire winter campaign against the Cheyenne would be deemed a failure.

Impatience welled up inside him again as he nudged his horse into the freezing waters of the Canadian River and, after some floundering, stepped safely up on the far bank. As he patted his horse's neck, a welcome cry came from the troopers on point:

"One of Major Elliot's scouts comin' in General!"

Hard Rope, Chief of the Osage scouts, rode forward; it had been a long and tiring ride back to the main column but he managed his own version of a military salute to the fair-haired soldier chief who, despite the snow, pushed back his hood and returned the salute. Amid the swirling snow flakes, Hard Rope could see he was smiling and eager for news. One of the white scouts rode up and joined the soldier chief – Hard Rope was glad, as his English was poor.

He explained using hand sign what he and Major Elliot had found – the white scout, interpreting, asked him some questions then delivered the message to the General:

"Gen'l, the boys have found a good trail – mebbe a hundred or so warriors and hoofprints from some shod horses. They're in a valley alongside the Lodgepole River, headin' east…"

Custer lifted his chin:

"Which river?"

"The Lodgepole, Gen'l – it's what the Indians call it. But they mean the Washita."

"Very well – get this scout a fresh horse. Tell the troop officers to keep the men in the saddle. We need to join up with Major Elliot tonight and see where that trail leads."

"Yes sir! Seems we were right all along about the Washita – big times comin' Gen'l… big times comin'."

---- o o o ----

Chapter Fifty Three

Broken Knife and his small war party had seen the big stone cabin before but, in those past times, had ridden in a wide circle to avoid it when they'd seen soldiers' tents pitched across the pasturelands. The house owner was obviously an important man if soldiers came to stay.

Now, many days had passed and the horse soldiers had moved off elsewhere, probably chasing Cheyenne shadows along the Saline or the Smoky Hill. The leader of the Thunder Bears smiled to himself and waited for Little Snake to complete his scouting task and report back.

The Thunder Bears leader looked down the slope where the rest of his warriors were resting; they'd dismounted and loosened the cinches on their saddles to rest their ponies. Because they were close to the white man's house, they only spoke in low tones. See the Dark and his woman were sitting slightly apart from the rest, eating something from a buckskin bag. He had not disciplined them since the last raid when the white woman had been needlessly killed – not that he sympathised over her death; she was just a good bargaining piece if things went wrong in the future. In truth, he had no authority over either of them but he *would* make sure that it didn't happen again.

Down in the barn of the wealthy white man, Little Snake crept along the lines of prime horses and could hardly believe his eyes – at least six tall, sleek mounts; all fit for a chief - moved restlessly in their stalls and snorted at the alien scent. Broken Knife would be as excited as him at the prizes here; it wasn't just the horses but steel axes, leather harness, iron hammers and nails – all useful to the warrior band as they kept constantly on the move – there may even be guns in the house. Best of all, there were no menfolk here – he had watched a squat white man ride out early in the morning in his small, polished wagon and no others were left behind. He'd checked the horse tracks out of the barn and the white men belonging to the owner had ridden out at least two days ago. The black-skinned man he'd seen outside the door of the house was probably just their slave; there was also a woman in the house – he had seen her shape as she passed between rooms. It was an easy target with rich pickings.

He looked up at the sun – it was almost noon – time to report back. He circled wide of the house, keeping well into cover of grass and trees and reached the hill where the others were. As arranged, Little Snake made the call of a wild turkey as a signal before coming in. He crouched behind sage bushes as he made his way up the hill.

But even before he could give his good news, he was criticised:

"Little brother, your bird calls are poor – you need to practice more!" said Broken Knife.

Little Snake sighed and sat down dejectedly; would his war chief ever relent in finding fault with all they did? His ego bruised, he gave his report in a dead voice – if Broken Knife noticed the change in tone, he didn't mention it.

Still, Little Snake's spirits were revived slightly when the austere warrior nodded in satisfaction at the news of the horses and lack of opposition. Instructions came quickly:

"You sister – ride down and beg for food – like before. But this time, the white woman is to be a prize as well. Coming from a rich house like this she'll be worth much."

White Rain nodded and gave her rifle and pistol to Dark; he would bring them down to her when the raid started. She tucked her long knife into the rope belt around her waist and arranged the skin cloak over her shoulders to hide it and mounted up.

"The rest of you…" continued the war chief, "…mount up and stay on this side of the hill until you hear my shot, then attack. Dark and I will ride round and get those horses."

All nodded eagerly – even Dark; with the prospect of action, he became his usual animated self and smiled. Little Snake raised his long rifle above his head, his thin arm shaking with the weight, and wished them all well.

White Rain rode out from the shelter of the hill towards the high stone and timber house.

---- o o o ----

Claudia Schengenhorn adjusted her broad brimmed hat, knocked some dust off her riding breeches and shiny leather boots then mounted her horse outside the front porch of her grand home. There were Indians around, she could smell them.

She had never let the black man saddle her horse - he was from the east and didn't know much about horses - and had gone into the barn to do it herself. There, the smell of woodsmoke-filled hair, bear grease and sweat had been strong; the prints of moccasins along the entire length of the dust floor confirmed it.

She saddled her nervous roan and walked it outside, noting the same moccasin tracks leading away from the house. Whoever had left the tracks had been young, inexperienced or stupid.

Swinging into the saddle, she took her Henry rifle from Nathan and put it into the long leather bucket alongside her left knee:

"Indians about. Get the shotgun and stay inside – lock the door. I'm going to ride around the hill and see what I can see. Kill anyone who breaks in."

As she was speaking, her horse snorted and brought its head up; there, walking calmly down the trailway towards the house was an Indian woman on a pony:

"Get the shotgun now!"

Claudia let the woman come closer, then pulled out the rifle. The woman stopped her pony and made signs that she wanted to eat. Claudia raised her rifle into the aim.

The wife of August Schengenhorn then did something that she hadn't done in many years; she spoke in Cheyenne:

"That's far enough little sister or you'll die in the saddle!"

White Rain Woman, amazed by very little these days, reined her pony in suddenly, dumbstruck by the change in fortunes. Where was the white woman who was to be such an easy target? Perhaps this Cheyenne woman was a slave, though she sat astride a fine horse and had a gun like Dark's. She kept silent, but again tried the signs for being hungry. The woman in the veho hat just kept the rifle trained on her; the black man that Little Snake had reported on now came out of the house with a long, double-barrelled scattergun and stood beside his employer.

White Rain gathered enough composure to speak calmly:

"I see you speak my tongue…yet you live in a veho house!" Claudia nodded but didn't put the rifle down:

"I speak *my* tongue, you crone! I am Eagle Heart Woman of the Wutapiu band of our people. That is all you need to know."

Despite her nervousness and resentment at being called a crone, White Rain laughed out loud:

"Then why are you dressed like a white man?"

Claudia lowered the rifle but kept the muzzle towards the scruffy Cheyenne woman:

"And why are *you* dressed like a pauper? You sound like a Suhtai – have you been cast out of your band?"

"Of course not! I just seek something to eat."

"There's nothing here for you, you Suhtai wretch – just an early grave. Remember, I know about your tricks."

Claudia cranked the lever on the Henry and put a round into the chamber.

Only a second after the metallic crunch of the bullet loading had faded, White Rain was aware of the drumbeat of a single horse galloping behind her. Little Snake, impatient with women talking, had decided to act alone.

Nathan raised his shotgun and fired but the mounted warrior was too far away; the Indian woman now screamed a shrill cry, thumped her horse with her heels and charged Mrs Schengenhorn. She leant well over the horse's neck to avoid the bullet from his employer's rifle but Mrs Schengenhorn shot the woman's pony in the chest. It pitched forward and rolled head over tail, flinging its rider off to one side, before sliding to a stop on its back, screaming and kicking in its death throes.

Claudia Schengenhorn, discounting the fallen Suhtai woman, now sought her targets elsewhere. The young warrior was struggling with the long musket he was carrying; he'd tried to shoot her as he charged past but the empty snap of a poorly-loaded black powder gun was plain to hear.

The young man leapt from his pony and ran across the flat ground towards her, yelling and pulling out his war hatchet. Claudia cranked another round into the rifle and shot the boy down. She whirled round in the saddle looking for the Suhtai woman but she was long gone.

"She limped off Mrs Schengenhorn..," said Nathan, "…away behind that hill…"

"Then you should have chased her and shot her!" replied the woman, still mounted, her horse whickering nervously at the gunfire.

Nathan still had one round left in the shotgun and – for a fleeting moment – considered using it on her. But his boss was a vindictive man and he knew he'd be hunted down for the rest of his life. He would choose another time to go – when there was both money *and* freedom to be had. He would wait.

There was little time to spare for thought…the remainder of the young Thunder Bears had charged out from behind the hill and bore down on the woman with the rifle, screaming insults and yelling war songs.

Claudia dismounted quickly but lined up the rifle across the cantle of the saddle and waited for the approaching warriors to get close enough. She sniffed the air and looked round, the barn was burning and her husband's prize racehorses were being run off by two other Indians; the horses were panic-stricken by the smoke and the rough whipping from their captors.

But Eagle Heart Woman was able to prioritise over life and death – the horses didn't really matter, only surviving the raid did.

She turned back to the three poorly-armed youths and shot two of them out of the saddle. The third saw the fall of his comrades, reined his pony round in a flurry of dirt and fled.

Nathan was walking across to the sprawled young warriors when Claudia shouted out to him:

"Leave them! There may be more Indians about…"; she smiled at using the word 'Indians' as enemies but that's what they were now. She now was also an enemy of the Suhtai – she shrugged, that's what marrying a white man did to you.

"…we just have my horse left – take it into the house and reload your gun…"

Nathan was appalled – a horse in the house! God Almighty it could shit on the carpets or…

"Do it now!"

The black man took the reins of the twitching roan and led it up onto the porch, its hooves sliding on the smooth surface of the planking, and, after some pulling managed to get it into the house through the front door.

Claudia now strode over to the prostrate warriors, only one of whom was dead.

Turtle breathed heavily and tried to get up, the bullet in his belly hurt; his insides seemed to be churned up and his sight was blurred. The tall woman approaching was carrying one of the new rifles that See the Dark had – no wonder she'd managed to shoot so quickly. He didn't have the energy to call out or sing his death song. The woman stood over him and to his surprise spoke in his own language:

"The whites believe that the image of the enemy that kills you remains on your globe of your eye after death. Do you believe that?"

Turtle coughed up blood; he had no answer - he was still surprised at being addressed in the tongue of the *Tsis-tsis-tas*.

He didn't need to reply – the woman said it for him:

"Well, I'm not sure either - but I don't want to chance it," she said and shot the boy through both eyeballs.

---- 0 0 0 ----

Chapter Fifty Four

"What month d'ye think it is?" asked Carver as he shook the snow from his hat.

"God knows – November, December?" said Henry.

"We must've missed Thanksgiving and Christmas somehow," said the wolf skinner.

"That's because we're taking Mr Schengenhorn's money to track down Indians; we are merely mercenaries now, Mr Carver. Riding out as our master dictates..."

Carver grunted in disgust at the word 'master'.

"...at least it keeps the wolf from the door!" grinned Henry, aware of the poor joke.

"How come you're so damn cheerful in this weather, hoss?"

"Because back at home, it rains a lot – anything that's *not* rain is always welcome. The only way we can tell when summer has arrived is that the rain is warmer."

Carver smiled – his first this morning – Henry always tried to raise spirits:

"Still, snow helps us do our job – tracks are easier to find and we don't raise any dust..."

The wolf skinner paused for a moment:

"What did you make of the scalps around the front door of the Schengenhorn house?"

"That woman is a force to be reckoned with – I wouldn't want to get on her wrong side. She is handsome though..."

Carver groaned in mock dismay:

"Fer God's sake Henry – git yer brain outta yer pants!"

The Englishman smiled; Carver's humour seemed to have returned.

"What did you think of Mrs Schengenhorn's story about the raid?" he asked.

"Well, one of the dead was that new kid – Little Snake or somethin'. I saw him a coupla times when he got back from the Crows…"

"So the Suhtai were on the raid?" asked Henry.

"Nah, it's hard to tell, hoss. Warriors can go off and fight anywhere if they want to. That boy was hangin' around the Thunder Bears when we left but it don't mean that a Suhtai soldier band is up here – the boy could've just gone off on his own hook."

"What about the woman? The one that escaped? One of White Rain's people d'ye think," said Henry.

"Too hard to call, Henry – the wife of the boss man mentioned a 'pauper' – don't sound like any of those Forked Lightning gals that we know."

"True…" said Henry, as he dismounted and walked ahead of his horse, keeping hold of the reins – eyes on the ground;

"…perhaps it doesn't really matter – we seem to have lost the bloody trail!" he said.

"Those Dyson boys had the best idea – sneakin' off before the weather got too bad…" said Carver as he too swung out of the saddle.

Henry nodded – neither he nor Carver had liked the men when they'd gone out to the barn at the Schengenhorn place. They were the 'others' that the Boss had mentioned. The Dyson brothers had just been simple gun hands – anxious to kill Indians but less keen to stay out in bitter weather to do it. They had promised to help, taken their advance of one third of their pay and then headed for Salina and safety. The wolf skinner had called them by some colourful names.

Carver joined his friend - both men searching for any sign that would mark the passage of the Indian raiders. The trail had been good at first, even though the ground was hard. Disturbed leaves inside the treeline and ashes from cooking fires, though buried for concealment, had melted the snow that fell on them; broken twigs at the height of a mounted man showed the raiding party had grown careless and had ridden through low hanging branches; dung from a mule or two showed they had stock with them. Most obvious of all were the hoofprints of a large draft or wagon horse and the smaller, almost dainty, hoofprints of the Schengenhorn's stable of prime racers.

Now – out in the open - they had all disappeared – the falling snow had hidden them.

Almost.

Carver suddenly straightened up, sniffed twice and pointed to a nearby ridgeline:

"Woodsmoke!" he whispered.

---- 0 0 0 ----

Chapter Fifty Five

The screaming woman had been hard to understand. She had galloped into the village of Old Whirlwind as people were just finishing their first meal of the day.

Bad Elk, carrying his rifle, ran out to see what was happening. His Suhtai had been one of many bands to make a winter camp along the Lodgepole River – they had been pleased to make their circle with Whirlwind's people. Safety in numbers seemed sensible.

Burnt Hair had been by the river and closer to the frightened woman as she same skidding in on her pony, the snow and slush almost bringing the horse down. She had managed to calm the girl down and get the news; a gathering of Cheyenne from many kindred bands quickly clustered round her to hear what had happened. Burnt Hair spoke loudly and clearly so her husband would get a clear picture of what had been said:

"White pony soldiers have attacked Black Kettle's village..."

The Cheyennes were perplexed; questions poured forth – Black Kettle's camp had been the one to suffer in the massacre at Sand Creek as well – he was known as a peace chief. Why was *he* being attacked? The murmuring grew louder.

"Listen! Listen!" Burnt Hair raised her voice again:

"...the vehoe came with the morning star and surrounded them. They are killing everybody!"

The men in the group needed no more urging – they scattered to saddle their war ponies picketed outside lodges, gathered weapons and rode off in the direction of the fighting. Some rode in the other direction to warn all the other villages along the northern loop of the Lodgepole – no-one could tell where the bluecoats would attack next. An aura of panic rose into the cold air.

Crow Dress, Sweet Water and Star, already in the saddle, rode up to Bad Elk, the hooves of their ponies slipping on the hard ground. They were ready to fight but loyalty and respect made them seek out their chief.

Bad Elk looked at them – those girls had proved their worth already, keeping the Suhtai village safe on its journey south:

"You don't need permission…" he yelled, "…just go!"

The Forked Lightning Women smiled, waved their rifles and yelled their war cries as they galloped out of the camp circle, headed west towards the rising columns of smoke and the soft pattering sound of distant gunfire.

The Suhtai leader watched them with sadness, his breath slowing to wisps of silver issuing from his mouth. Is this what his band had come to? Now down to a score of lodges inhabited by old men, women and children?

Burnt Hair had seen him still standing in the open; her husband was shivering with the cold. She went back to their lodge and brought his favourite buffalo robe and wrapped it round him. Bad Elk shrugged it up around his neck and sat down, leaning against a tree:

"I need to think," he said and dismissed her with a lift of his chin.

There was much to ponder for the Suhtai chief. His people were short of food, bullets, powder and fighting men. The vehoe had lied to them about the southern allocation of land for them to live on in peace; no-one could survive there. The whites had also lied about not attacking them when they were south of the Flint Arrowpoint River – Black Kettle was now finding this out for the second time.

There seemed to be no end to their treachery – Bad Elk had tried the peace trail to preserve his people and it didn't seem to work.

The Suhtai chief hefted his rifle and laid it across his thighs; he stroked the cold metal barrel – it had been a while since he'd used it for anything but hunting but he was skilled in its use. Peace may have to be abandoned and the gun used to kill more than just game.

---- o 0 o ----

Chapter Fifty Six

Sadie Ackerman had decided to just stay quiet and stay alive - sooner or later the Army or her neighbours would discover that she was gone; someone would be looking for her…that's what Kansans did.

When she'd first been pinned down in her own kitchen by the Indians and made to watch as her husband and children were slaughtered, she'd wanted to die herself. The many rapes by the warriors only confirmed that she was just a piece of flesh to be used or discarded at the whim of others - of little worth now to anyone.

But, in captivity, the Scotswoman's spirit had since hardened, like the ground beneath her, with the onset of ice and snow. The seemingly-powerful Indians, once arrogant and cruel, were now hungry and desperate. She was no expert on Indians, had no idea which tribe they came from and, frankly, didn't care. But she was observant. She knew that the Indians had been scouting near the Schengenhorn place – she, Jakob and the Lindstroms had once picnicked by the river there a couple of summers ago – and, though she was kept strictly guarded in camp when the small war party rode out, she could see when they returned that they were a few warriors less. Maybe the raid on the handsome stone house hadn't gone well – she hoped so.

She bundled the kindling she was collecting in the woods, tied it tight with a rawhide rope and balanced it on her head, as she had seen the Indian women do.

Even now, doing menial chores, she was guarded – a short, fierce woman with a dark bronze skin kept a close watch and thrashed her with a willow switch if she slackened off. This woman wasn't as tall or loose-limbed like the others – though there were precious few other Indian women in the camp to compare her to – but she seemed to have some sort of say or power in the circle of lodges. Perhaps she was a chief's wife or a witch. Whatever she was, she was no lover of white women and Sadie felt the sting of the switch many times each day.

The Scotswoman dumped the pile of kindling near the guttering cook fire and selected some of the drier sticks to make it flare and catch the split boughs. Smoke billowed from the pile as flames caught on green wood and, as ever, her dark tormentor was on hand to beat her for her stupidity, ranting away in a high yip of complaint.

The short one was smothered in a plume of smoke and wandered off, coughing, towards the circle of lodges. Sadie sat on her haunches by the fire and coaxed it into life. She watched the woman go and, in a sentiment far removed from her upbringing in a Lanarkshire parsonage, vowed that she would kill the Indian woman if she ever got the chance.

She was still smiling at this image – and how shocked her prim father would be – when she leant across the fire to grab more sticks. It was then she saw the two white men.

---- o o o ----

See the Dark and White Rain packed up their lodge at dawn and prepared to head off on their own raid. They had discussed it the previous night and had decided to journey south towards the Flint Arrowpoint. If there were no pickings from poorly-defended settlers, they would continue south to Medicine Lodge Creek and try to find Bad Elk in the spring. It wasn't much of a plan but it would get them out of the tense atmosphere of the war camp.

The Suhtai warriors were in the minority in the camp – even more so since Broken Knife's losses at the stone house raid. The majority of fighters were Dog Soldiers and some Arapaho – making Dark uneasy about what they were achieving on their war trail. All warriors fought their own battles without a plan –

courage and nerve in action were the most admired qualities; they could be sung about at campfires and war deeds could be painted on shirts, lodges and ponies. But, out here, away from the close Suhtai group of families led by Bad Elk, none of that seemed to matter.

He admitted to himself that plunder was occasionally good – the fine horses from the stone house had been much admired by all, as were the few guns and barrels of powder and lead that they had taken from the whites. But he could see that these things did not really stop the whites coming into sacred Cheyenne country. Whites always seemed to have plenty of everything and, however many of them the Cheyenne killed, it just seemed to make space for more vehoe to come. And this time, agreeing with White Rain, he felt they had made a grave mistake by taking the white woman with them. If they hadn't been pursued by bluecoat pony soldiers before – they would be now.

Living with Broken Knife and his dwindling band of followers was irksome. Even though his mother was in the camp as a Suhtai healer, she was now a woman that he didn't recognise nor who recognised him. He had seen her beat the white captive woman for little other than spilling water out of a skin pouch – there was nothing he could do about it. He had watched as Broken Knife had given her as a slave to his mother once all the other warriors in camp had used her. The veho woman now belonged to Badlands Walking Woman – she could do as she wished with her.

These days, Dark had noticed a strange anger in his mother. Rather than be grateful for her gift she had rounded on Broken Knife for not stripping the woman of her veho clothes and shoes before they had rejoined the main camp. Things - she had shrieked to anyone passing - that pursuing white soldiers could recognise when tracking them.

Broken Knife – aggrieved at being torn into by yet another woman – had lashed Badlands across the face with his whip. Shaking his head, Dark knew that it was time to leave.

With their lodge firmly packed on a travois behind a spare pony and each leading one of the rich white man's prime horses – their share in the spoils of the raid - Dark and White Rain set out for better times in the south.

He had not said farewell to his mother nor the leader of the Thunder Bears; Broken Knife would probably be pleased at his departure and certainly relieved of the burden of the dissenting White Rain Woman.

Though the couple were happy at their decision to leave, the young stone-eyed Cheyenne rode in sad silence – his mother now didn't even recognise him during her many outbursts of fury.

Even when at rest, her eyes seemed to be non-knowing; Yellow Bear had mentioned to him about meeting an old Lakota man many moons ago in his youth. The old man had what the Sioux called the forgetting-time disease. Perhaps it was that? Whatever her illness was, watching her spitting with rage and lashing out at anyone passing, few of the sick ever went anywhere near her for healing. And now Dark avoided her too.

The jovial, chubby woman that comforted and protected him as a child was now missing; he didn't recognise the angry demon nor the unseeing stranger that she'd turned into. Her spirit was elsewhere; he doubted that he would ever see her again.

---- o o o ----

Henry Armstrong and Carver made rapid signs to the white woman when they saw that they had been spotted. Vertical fingers on lips, they melted back into the undergrowth and withdrew out of casual hearing range to talk in furtive, soft tones:

"That must be the Ackerman woman – we'll need to get back to the Boss man to bring the Army out here, "said Carver.

"Only one of us need go…" said Henry, "…the other should keep watch on the camp, track it if it moves and lay a trail for the others to follow."

At the mention of the 'others', Carver smiled:

"Those Dyson boys woulda been useful right about now…"

Henry, though, stayed serious:

"You're the best at both sides of this job, my friend – at tracking, concealment and laying trails – I'll go back to the Schengenhorn place and get him to put the word out and bring the troops. Just mark an easy trail for me to follow when I get back…"

Carver rubbed his beard:

"An easy trail for an Englishman to follow, eh? That'll be a goddamn bonfire every twenty yards then!"

"Bollocks," said Henry amiably and took his spare food and ammunition out of his possibles bag, handing it to the wolfskinner.

"Just stay low and silent, Mr Carver…" said Henry earnestly, "…just like you do when you have to pay for a drink!"

Carver grinned and patted his friend on the shoulder; he would keep himself and his pony well back from the war camp. Both he and the Englishman had seen Badlands Walking Woman beat the white captive – neither of them would feel any remorse in killing *her* but the woman's presence may mean more friendly Suhtai around.

He shook his head to dispel the thought – there probably weren't any *friendly* Suhtai anymore. Pulling the trigger on the right people would just come down to his own survival first – no matter who got in the way.

---- o 0 o ----

Chapter Fifty Seven

"Bloody Hell!" said Henry out loud; his breath parting the few falling snowflakes, "It must be Christmas…"

There - but better than any wrapped presents in the family hearth - was a sight for sore eyes; soldiers, at least a company's worth of them, all camped in the Schengenhorn pasture.

Henry rode down, smiling with relief – their presence in the Boss's fields would save him a longer, onward journey to alert the forts. He could get back on the trail to the Indian camp with the troops in a much quicker time.

Though he would never admit it to Carver – mainly because his friend knew him well enough already - Henry was strangely comforted by military order and neatness. Off-white tents, some of the larger ones with smoking chimneys in amongst the smaller shared shelters of the troopers, stood in neat rows. Men in buffalo overcoats tramped around on some military errand or other, horse lines stood a few hundred yards off and a queue was forming at the cook tent while a bugle sounded mess call. He had known this sort of life since he was eighteen years old, then a skinny subaltern in his English regiment of Light Dragoons. No matter, cavalry life in the field was much the same in any country - and he liked it.

Now, looking at the busy camp of bluecoats, if he could get them moving by mid-morning, they could be closing with the Cheyenne within a two-day ride.

A sentry challenged him as he rode up the trailway to the house. He was about to answer when a Sergeant ducked out of the small shelter that served as a guardpost:

"Jesus! Mr Armstrong, sir – good to see you. Mr Schengenhorn said you were out scouting for them redskins."

Henry stared at the man – he seemed familiar. The Sergeant saw the look of puzzlement on Henry's face and explained:

"Sergeant O'Neill sir – of Chase's Chargers at Rattlesnake Crossing. We sure gave them Kiowa somethin' to think about!"

Again, before he could reply, a tubby officer in a large hat hurried up. He had a sabre on a leather belt – the tip of the scabbard etched a line in the snow as he bustled forward.

"Mister Armstrong, d'ye bring good news?" he asked without introduction. Henry grinned and saluted in the English style:

"Colonel Chase – good to see you sir! I thought you'd disbanded after the fight on the Arkansas? I was expecting you to be President about now!"

Chase laughed, his face red with the effort of hurrying. Henry dismounted and shook the officer's outstretched hand:

"You flatter me Mister Armstrong – I fear my political popularity stands in the shade of General Grant. But protecting Kansas is my main priority now!"

An orderly summoned by the Sergeant took Henry's bridle and walked his horse to the tether lines and forage dump. Steam rose from its flanks in the cold air.

Once settled with a cup of coffee from the Colonel's striker, Henry gave his report - strength of the enemy, their food supply and possible intentions. The questions came thick and fast – in truth, just watching an encampment couldn't answer all Colonel Chase's concerns but the mention of the captured white woman saw Chase suck his teeth and become focused.

Henry emphasised the need to get back on the trail quickly. Even for an experienced frontiersman like the wolf skinner, the weather was treacherous but it could mean possible death for Mrs Ackerman. He reported that the woman had looked defiant but that wouldn't keep her warm or well fed. The Colonel stuck his head outside the tent and issued orders. There was some shouting to repeat them down the lines and a bugle blared to break camp and saddle up.

"Well, Mr Armstrong, we'll get you a fresh horse and some rations; you can lead us back up to that redskin camp."

He shrugged into a hairy buffalo robe coat and rammed his hat hard on his head:

"Most of my boys that you saw at Rattlesnake Crossing ain't with us today – they joined up with the 19th Volunteers and have ridden off to help General Custer somewhere south of the Canadian – they'll do well, I'm sure."

A Corporal arrived outside the tent with Henry's fresh horse, saddled and supplied. Colonel Chase mounted his pony by standing on a biscuit box placed next to the stirrup. Henry swung into the saddle and checked his rifle in the bucket; someone had wiped the caked snow off it and rubbed oil on the metal work. It was a nice touch.

Around Henry, all was activity. Tents were left in place; extra food would be a priority instead of shelter; boxes of ammunition and medical supplies were hoisted on the backs of protesting mules. Harnesses jangled, men shouted and, slowly, a living column formed in the scuffed snow, eager to be off.

Before they moved out, Augustus and Claudia Schengenhorn hurried out of the house; the black servant running behind the tall woman. He was leading two saddled horses. Her husband was saying something to her but she ignored him and stood by Henry's horse looking up at him, her hand resting casually on his foot in the stirrup:

"Mr Armstrong. You are back sooner than we'd expected – the enemy must be close…"

Henry said:

"Well, a day or so ride, Ma'am but…"

She cut him off and gave him an unnerving direct stare: "I'll be coming with you."

Henry looked round, bewildered. Both her husband and Colonel Chase shrugged their shoulders:

"Claudia is a strong-willed woman, Mr Armstrong. She'll have her revenge on those who attacked her house," said Chase.

"Not without me she won't," puffed Schengenhorn clambering onto his horse and shoving a gleaming hunting rifle into his saddle bucket.

Claudia reached back into her saddle bag and handed two tin boxes of bullets to the Englishman:

"I noticed that you and you friend, Mr..er?.."

"Carver," said Henry.

"Yes… Carver. I see we all favour the same gun – there's fifty bullets in each tin – one tin is for him."

Henry thanked her – much of the extra ammunition that he and Carver had ordered at Fort Hays had been used up in the Indian raids. The ammunition was a welcome bonus – three extra full loads for the rifle wouldn't go amiss.

An officer in a blue military cloak rode up to Chase and reported that the column was complete and stood in its traditional columns of four.

"Very well," responded Chase, "…get the column into double file; the trail will be too narrow for anything more than that.

Keep the supply mules well up to the main body – no tellin' what'll happen when we reach that Indian camp."

Henry turned his head to watch the troopers sort themselves out and then looked back ahead. He was disturbed to see Mrs Schengenhorn, head slightly to one side, looking quizzically at him; she had a smile on her face.

He shifted uncomfortably in the saddle as the column moved out. It hadn't *looked* like an amorous smile – though Henry's experience in deciphering the emotions of strong women was limited; the attentions of money-hungry bar girls in the tented brothels of Hell on Wheels probably didn't count. The Englishman hoped that it was the smile of anticipated vengeance for Mrs Schengenhorn – otherwise it could become a distraction in the coming fight. And worse – Carver would never forgive him.

Under shouted orders from officers commanding the sections of the soldiers, the column moved off – back along Henry's trail. The Englishman, alongside Colonel Case at the head of the lines of cavalrymen, turned and said:

"Which month is this, Colonel?"

Chase paused – he had to calculate it for himself:

"Why, it's January Mr Armstrong – about the fourth or fifth of the month I think."

Henry nodded his thanks. He and Carver, though well-paid for their tracking of Indians, had missed Thanksgiving, Christmas *and* New Year celebrations.

The Englishman grinned to himself; Carver was a sociable man who still liked to indulge in a few drinks at the drop of a hat - any excuse would do. Now they had missed the three main social events of the year. Henry couldn't wait to break the bad news to the wolf skinner – just to watch the expression on his face.

---- o o o ----

Chapter Fifty Eight

It had been a rash decision but Carver didn't regret it. The more he thought about leaving Mrs Ackerman in camp until Henry brought the soldiers, the less were her chances of survival.

Henry could be days away and it was getting difficult to keep an eye on the camp without leaving tell-tale tracks – though it was winter, hunters rode in and out of camp; a few children played and the older ones came into the trees to strip bark for forage for the pony herd. He was also sure that, at the first sign of trouble, the vindictive Badlands Walking Woman would kill the white woman. Now he had a chance to get the jump on the Cheyenne.

He had heard the singing first – a series of barking yips that formed a sort of tune; it came from up the trail, towards the Cheyenne camp which lay about a mile away. He had heard the same thing before, but in a different place.

Though hitched to undergrowth deeper in the trees, his horse smelled the strange scents as they approached and began to whinny and shuffle restlessly in the brush. The wolfskinner knew that he would be discovered if he didn't act. He cranked a round into his rifle and stepped out, firing…

Badlands, astride an unsaddled pony, fell first and writhed on the ground. Carver, still in the aim, swept the rifle round his targets and shot any who seemed to pose a threat, almost shooting Sadie Ackerman in the process – her light brown hair had been blackened with soot and she was dressed in a deerskin shift like the others. He hurried forward, made her grab the dangling bridle and told her to mount the Indian pony and head downhill, away from the camp.

Mrs Ackerman seemed to be unused to horseback and jolted around on the sway backed piebald, trying to pull the horse's head round to the right direction. Yelling and shouting were now coming from up the trail – the camp had been alerted by the shooting, easily heard in the cold, crisp air.

Carver wrenched the scared pony's head round and whacked it on the rump as it slithered downwards on the icy trail.

Even though the shouting and shrieking of eagle bone whistles were getting nearer, Carver walked across to where Badlands lay, still alive:

"*Kah-vuh,* you treacherous snake!" she hissed, blood staining her buckskin shift – she looked to be gutshot. She began a staccato series of words that Carver couldn't understand, she was pointing an accusing finger at him – probably a curse from her own Kiowa Apache people.

The wolf skinner shrugged to show he didn't care and looked at her gravely:

"Woman, you poisoned the Suhtai against me an' Henry; you said we were traitors and in league with the whites. Now you'll never know if you were right…"

The noise of the approaching warriors got louder – it was time to go.

Carver considered leaving her – dying of a serious wound in the gut would be painful and well-deserved for this cruel crone. But she might survive long enough to talk, so he took out his pistol – the ammunition for the rifle was too expensive to waste on a witch – cocked the hammer and shot her in the middle of the forehead with a cheap lead ball instead.

Crashing through the underbrush to get back to his pony, he mounted quickly and set off to find Sadie Ackerman. It was only when he'd put a safe distance between himself and the camp that he stopped to reload his rifle.

As he slid five replacement bullets down into the tube magazine, he realised that his cool and efficient shooting had not eliminated any real Cheyenne threat – he'd merely shot down five women who were just out gathering firewood.

---- o 0 o ----

Chapter Fifty Nine

Viajero was up early; it was time to leave the Mescalero camp - a break in the weather meant that travelling towards the land of his own people would be easier but they needed to hurry.

He roused Willow:

"Saddle your pony and pack your things for the journey. I want to leave soon."

He walked outside the tipi – Bright Antelope and Deer Running were crouching in the open, blowing life into the cooking fire. The Mescalero camp was already awake, despite the sun's early rays being just a glow off to the east. He urinated into a cholla cactus, stroked his picketed pony then went back inside his lodge and sat down, leaning against his backrest.

Viajero brooded a little; he felt odd in the pit of his stomach and was slightly nervous - a feeling alien to him. His own White Mountain people hadn't seen him for many summers, his parents were dead and he had no other relatives; he hoped someone would recognise him. But he knew that, even when he *had* lived amongst them – he had been an outsider.

His small band of raiders had been deadly and successful – they had enjoyed looting stock, food and guns from Mexicans and whites, killing anyone who got in their way. But some tribal elders had chided him and wanted him to be quiet, grow corn and leave the war trail – they didn't want their people to live looking over their shoulders in fear of revenge attacks.

The Apache had been scornful of their peaceful ways – raiding was the only time *he* felt alive; returning to camp in the aftermath of the killing and looting had always been a frustrating burden. He had no desire for the smells of old men, women and children - just the heady scent of burning powder, running ponies and freshly-spilled blood.

His first wife had agreed with the elders. At first, she had been happy with the wealth he brought - in ponies, sheep, calico and iron pans but she wanted a safer life for her and their son – but she had become uneasy at the growing numbers of marked, stolen stock that was certain proof of her husband's guilt. She had argued with him once or twice but, as he thought back to those times, he knew he had been cold and indifferent to her pleading. For him, it was the war trail or nothing. In those days, it was easier to ride off and avoid her than explain or talk.

Typically, he had been out of camp when the Mexicans attacked the a*pacheria,* killing all his family. It had even provided the perfect excuse that lit his vengeance trail of blood and slaughter for the next few summers. But Usen, the Apache One God, had made him suffer – not with grief or pain but with guilt. During his talks with his Maker, Viajero had been shocked to explore the depths of his own black soul – that he saw the death of his family, not as an unbearable loss of loved ones, merely as a release from the burdens of camp life. Warriors like him couldn't live with it – better to die in the saddle than rot away in peace. His true nature was that of a hollow man – like a rotted cactus, prickly on the outside but just dust inside. He wondered what Usen thought of him now…

Bright Antelope eventually ducked inside followed by their daughter, both carrying food. They offered it to Viajero who took it without comment or thanks. All of them ate in silence.

Willow finished first, lay down her wooden bowl and started to gather her things together – stuffing smaller items into a parfleche saddle bag decorated with her own Lakota designs.

Bright Antelope, lip curled, watched her, she had heard the conversation inside the lodge – today must be the day that her husband and the Hunkpapa girl would leave to find his White Mountain country and get married. She ground her teeth in frustration. Deer Running, sensing the familiar, rising tension, said nothing.

Eventually, Viajero finished his food, burped and stood up:

"Come! We need to be gone before mid-morning – that snow won't hold off for ever…"

He turned to Bright Antelope, adding:

"Make sure the lodge is secured well on the packhorse – it was loose when we got here…"

Bright Antelope stood up, pale with anxiety:

"The lodge? You're taking the lodge?"

Viajero looked at her, puzzled by such a stupid question:

"Of course! Where would we shelter otherwise?"

"But you are taking the lodge - our lodge - down to your own country to marry this girl…"

"Yes, you know that, "snapped the warrior.

"If you take the tipi, where will your daughter and I live when you are gone?"

The Traveller sighed – what was wrong with this woman? He tried simpler terms:

"You are coming *with* me. We are *all* going to my country… so we'll need the lodge." He shook his head – how hard could it be to understand what he wanted.

His Mescalero wife brightened slightly:

"So, we will come to your wedding?"

Viajero, exasperated, said:

"No, you will be going to your own wedding – I intend to marry you *both* in the country of my people. What is so difficult to understand?"

Willow laughed out loud, Bright Antelope screamed in relief – she had forgotten that only the Suhtai considered them man and wife when they had arrived to live with them; they had never married under Cheyenne custom. Deer Running bravely slapped her father's arm:

"You have three women in your family – we cannot see your thoughts; you'll need to be better at telling us what you want!"

Viajero, still puzzled but glad to see that all three were now hugging each other, shrugged and went outside to saddle his horse. Suddenly, in a rare moment of understanding women and sensing a smile on his face, he felt less hollow.

---- 0 0 0 ----

Chapter Sixty

Colonel Artemis Chase was a happy man – tubby or not, he had proven himself to be no slouch in the killing department; the charge of his volunteers through the Cheyenne village had been a great success and he had personally shot and sabred his way through tipis and Indians in a riot of excitement and war fervour.

His imagination ran wild. My God! If he linked this raid, his outstanding rescue of Mrs Ackerman *and* the Rattlesnake Crossing attack in his political speeches, he could be in the White House in four years' time. The American people loved heroes. Ulysses S. Grant would be a washed-out relic of the Civil War by then and Artemis P. Chase – Indian fighter, Protector of the People of Kansas – would be proud to serve his country...

There was a polite cough to catch his attention.

"Er...Colonel..."

He snapped out of his reverie to see his troop sergeant salute and point to the far end of the small encampment:

"Injun bodies laid out there, sir – ready for countin'."

Chase returned the salute:

"Thank you, Sergeant. Report our casualties please."

The sergeant took a crumpled piece of paper out from under his campaign hat:

"Just the one dead sir – Lieutenant Booth..."

Chase nodded; he was close friends with the Booth family and had tried to hold the boy back from joining the unit, to no avail. It would be a difficult conversation with his folks even though

Chase could honestly say that the young man had died bravely in action, leading his troop from the front.

"…and three wounded – all just slight, the doc says."

Chase nodded – surprise had been on their side; they were lucky to get off so lightly.

He trotted his horse across the small circle of smouldering lodges. Some of the warriors had stayed behind when the attack began to protect the families – this is where the fighting had been most severe. The ground was churned from iron shod cavalry horses riding down the defenders – broken bows and lances were strewn about and blood trails in the remaining snow, where the troopers had dragged the bodies for display, stood out as gashes of unsettling colour. Some women, children and men had escaped before the Kansans got there, spooked by the shooting of the women collecting wood. Their trail was easy to follow – Chase would reckon with them later.

The colonel dismounted and walked over to the line of corpses, already beginning to stiffen in death, helped by the freezing air:

"Well, Mr Armstrong – what d'ye think?"

Henry bent over and looked at the corpses; though he recognised the bodies of Broken Knife and Badlands Walking Woman something stopped him saying so. He kept to generalities:

"Just Cheyennes, Colonel – some Dog Soldiers and a mix of other bands. They're just the ones who wanted to keep fighting after the treaty at Medicine Lodge…"

"Some women and children as well, I see…," said Chase.

Henry remained silent but Carver, who'd walked over from a different part of the village, interrupted:

"Some of those women had weapons and tried to kill yer soldier boys, General – they knew what would happen…"

Chase stood up nodding, wiping the mud and blood from a beaded pouch that he'd taken as a souvenir from one of the dead women; the beading was prettily done and had probably taken hours of work. This, though, was not just a personal memento of a battle fought and won but such an arteface would be important reminders for the public of his past daring and courage when he got onto the campaign trail. Some of the grimmer types of pork barrel politicians carried dried Indian scalps and waved these in the face of their electors – but Chase would have none of that, no sir - fainting ladies and prissy preachers were not great bringers of votes.

He looked at the small crowd gathering around the bodies:

"Good to see you made it back in time for the charge Mister Carver…what happened to Mrs Ackerman?"

Carver stood up, keeping a wary eye on Badlands Walking Woman – just in case she was mean enough to come back from the dead:

"I left her with your escort, General – they should be able to find their way back to the Schengenhorn place …"

As if on cue, Augustus and Claudia Schengenhorn walked across to the bodies, leading their ponies; Mrs Schengenhorn wiped a scalping knife on her saddle blanket and threw a bloody hank of hair across the pommel. Augustus Schengenhorn saw the look of disgust on the faces of the troopers:

"My wife follows her own ways in these things boys…"

Claudia, however, would not have her husband explain her actions for her:

"That Suhtai wretch who rode up to my house, isn't here – pity…"

She pointed to the fresh scalp:

"That's from the young warrior who rode off in fear when the fight started – his scalp won't be worth much but it will decorate my porch nicely."

She stared directly at Henry – even Carver saw it; neither of them knew if it was a challenge or an invitation.

Chase broke the spell and remounted – his troop sergeant giving his foot a lift into the stirrup – and looked at the Englishman and the wolf skinner:

"Any more details for your report gentlemen?"

Henry and Carver kept looking at the slowly stiffening evidence of Suhtai involvement in the recent Cheyenne raids. But to mention the name of a specific band would be to condemn them to a lifetime of being hounded and hunted – they owed Bad Elk more than that:

"No," they lied in unison.

---- 0 0 0 ----

Chapter Sixty One

It was Flea who'd noticed the lone tipi, almost hidden in a stand of high alders by Medicine Lodge Creek; the boy was on the flank of the moving village, digging for wild turnips as he'd been told by his aunt, Burnt Hair. He knew instantly who owned the lodge. He left the small straggling column of Bad Elk's hungry Suhtai, threading through the forward scouting line of the Forked Lightning Women and ran across the burgeoning spring grass, shouting joyfully.

See the Dark ran out from the thicket, rifle in hand to confront the noise maker. It took him a while to recognise the skinny boy as his own brother.

White Rain, returning from the river with an armful of soaked deerskins, yelled a welcome as the familiar ponies of the column came in sight; she threw the skins down and ran, stopping only to pat Flea on the head, to greet her war sisters in an ecstasy of excitement.

Bad Elk spurred his pony towards his nephew, dismounted in a flurry of dirt and green grass shoots and hugged the stone eyed warrior; Dark laughed out loud – his own father had never shown such affection. Burnt Hair, looking for the missing Flea, cantered up to the front of the column, swung down from the saddle with a graceful ease that Dark hadn't seen before and, squealing with joy – the stone-eyed warrior had always been one of her favourites - joined in the celebrations.

Yellow Bear cantered up behind his chief but when he saw who they'd encountered, swung his pony round and galloped along the line of Cheyenne families, calling out the joyous news.

There were yips of excitement and the old songs about Suhtai greatness were sung - surely the return of two of their warriors was a sign of healing? Ponies were led to drink as the camp slowly came together and pitched their lodges.

Red Raven and his Arapahos were some way back but heading in the same direction; he and Bad Elk had decided to combine camps as they made their way into the more dangerous territory north of the Flint Arrowpoint River. Both leaders knew that there was a better chance of finding buffalo in that country but it would put them on the death list of any marauding pony soldiers. The fate of both bands was now in the hands of their gods. He was pleased that the Suhtai leader now seemed more amenable to attacking whites – by combining warrior numbers they could take to the war trail and gather many prizes. He was tired of running and tired of being the prey – they would make the whites pay for their invasion of sacred lands.

Once all lodges were erected, Bad Elk himself strode around the Suhtai circle:

"Brothers and sisters! It is a joyful time to be reunited with our relatives and we will celebrate with a feast – but not tonight. There is little food in camp so, at daybreak we *all* hunt and tomorrow night we will sit and eat together…"

When Bad Elk had reached the Arapaho circle, he looked at Red Raven who nodded in agreement. Though he had never met the Suhtai chief's stone-eyed nephew nor encountered any women warriors before, he would keep his own counsel for now but make sure that the needs and wishes of his Arapaho were met. Both tribes had been instinctive allies for a long time but working together hadn't made them one people – collaboration seemed sensible at this stage.

He drew the arrows from his quiver one by one and straightened them in his hands – damp weather made them bend slightly and he needed them to fly straight when they joined the Suhtai at hunting. His band would not become a burden on the Cheyenne, they would provide their fair share of food.

But he was already planning ahead; afterwards, when all had eaten their fill, he would try to persuade the Suhtai to take an early war trail to plunder the food stocks and spring plenty of the white farmers.

If the Suhtai wouldn't join them, his Arapaho would do it themselves; he smiled at his own confidence – the weather was warming the ground, grass shoots were pushing through and they would soon find buffalo.

Their scuttling retreat from the Lodgepole attack of the pony soldiers in the depths of last winter would soon be avenged on white farmers. Red Raven adjusted the quiver on his belt and smiled. It promised to be a good raiding season.

---- o o o ----

Chapter Sixty Two

Henry Armstrong awoke to a herd of wild horses thundering through his brain and the smell of stale vomit caking his shirt.

He opened his eyes. As the blurring partially cleared, the world seemed strangely tilted - then he realised he was lying on the floor. His cheek rested on a carpet, so he wasn't in the Schengenhorn barn, he must be in the main house. He lifted his head to look for Carver and the carpet stuck to it – a mixture of dried stomach contents and spittle clamped it to his skin. His skull seemed to be much heavier than yesterday and it hurt to keep it up there. He flopped back, wrenched his cheek off the rug and looked at the ceiling – there was no sign of the elaborate chandelier that hung in the main ante-room – where the hell was he?

He groaned a little and remembered there had been some sort of party to celebrate the successful rout of the Cheyenne. Fragments of memory - of he and Carver yelling out their frontier poetry, spilling brandy onto his clothes and trying to light each other's farts - much to the delight of Colonel Chase and Augustus Schengenhorn, then came back to him. God knows where the wolf skinner was.

A door creaked open nearby – the lower part of the wood knocked against his head as he struggled to see who had come in. His eyes eventually focused on the Schengenhorn's servant; the black man offered him a cup of coffee in a ridiculously small porcelain cup but Henry took it anyway, slurping the hot liquid down and burning his tongue.

Nathan looked contemptuously at the prostrate white man but, smirking, he brought important news:

"The Boss Lady says you were too drunk to do anything useful last night…she was disappointed."

So that's where he was – in Claudia Schengenhorn's bedroom. The words took a while to sink in – but when they did, Henry suddenly felt much, much worse.

---- o o o ----

"Mr..er..Carver is it?" The woman's voice was soft with a Scottish burr.

The wolf skinner looked up blearily from the column of cold water splashing onto his head at the yard pump. The woman's face swam into view but Carver's mouth couldn't form a single intelligible word. He grunted instead.

"It's Sadie Ackerman, Mr Carver – just come to say Thank You for rescuing me from those redskins. Colonel Chase and his soldiers will be taking me back to Fort Hays…"

A massed of blurred blue behind Mrs Ackerman, sharpened into images of mounted cavalrymen. Carver grunted again but this time tried some words:

"Yer welcome, lady. Pleased to do it…"

"I didn't see Mr Armstrong, so please thank him for me – the soldiers need to be off right away 'to catch the daylight' as they say…"

"Yaargh," said Carver and held back his puking.

Sadie Ackerman looked at her saviour; he may look like a wild man of the woods but he had been the one that had shot all the Cheyenne wood gatherers that allowed her to escape. She touched his shoulder with a laced glove on her hand – Mrs Schengenhorn had dressed her from her own fine wardrobe though Sadie was a good six inches shorter than her and her skirts scuffed along in the dirt. Odd that after the slaughter of her family, she had never been so well-dressed in her life.

Carver looked at her and tried to bring her green eyes into focus.

She saw his eyes were red and blotchy though it was probably with the drink - and she smiled. She had been in one of the guestrooms as the party had progressed – she reckoned that a man who shot down half a dozen Indian women and had then caroused until the early hours was not one to be overcome by teary-eyed emotion in a farewell.

"Colonel Chase will take me to the railroad – I have family in Canada…I think."

She leant across and pecked Carver on his cheek; his beard was rough and he smelled of the wilds that were his home, but she recognised when a good man was in front of her. Lord knows what she would do now – a dead family, no home just an abandoned cabin that she couldn't go back to and the howling nightmares of all the wrongs that those damn Indians had visited upon her. She could marry again but the memory of the repeated rapes couldn't be held in – her father's strict code of honesty would ensure she would have to confess these to any future suitor. No-one would want *that* in a wife – soiled and violated, she would be alone for ever. If Mr Carver had handed her his pistol, she would have shot herself there and then.

A young officer brought Mrs Ackerman's horse to her and helped her into the uncomfortable Army saddle as Claudia Schengenhorn walked out to say goodbye. They had exchanged some stilted words beforehand and now merely nodded at each other as the blue-coated column rode out of the pastureland.

Sadie Ackerman was in tears, Carver was puking and Claudia Schengenhorn, who had long lost interest in her sudden guest, went to find the Englishman. There was another celebration to be had at the Lindstroms' barn-raising party in a week or so and she would make sure that Henry was in a fit state to enjoy it – and her.

---- o o o ----

Chapter Sixty Three

The good news of Sadie Ackerman's rescue had spread quickly but Klas Lindstrom was surprised to see her at Fort Hays so quickly. The badly abused wife of his murdered friend sat staring blankly into space at the depot. She had no-one with her. He called out to her but, amid the bustle of people hurrying about and wagons rolling by, she didn't hear him.

The Swede finished unloading the rail flatbed wagon that had carried in the planking and shingles for his new barn, roped it down tight onto his own cart and walked across to her:

"*Hej*, Sadie, *min kära*. What are you doing here?"

Sadie Ackerman looked up – it was the first time she'd seen Jakob's friend since her release; she burst into tears but shook her head determinedly to stop the flow. However much she told herself that she would not live her life looking back, emotions still crept in at unexpected moments:

"Hello Klas. I'm leaving Kansas; just waiting for a train to go east – there'll be one along in a day or so, I guess."

The Swede sat down next to her; though he said nothing to her directly, he was surprised that the strong-willed Scot would leave. Instead, he put a comforting arm around her shoulders, and they reminisced about the strong link of friendship, often brought on by hardships, between their families. The sharing of food, tools and farmwork – Jakob often lent Klas his plough horse until the Swede could afford one of his own and the Swede had repaid it by long hours of scything and planting at the Ackerman place. These things, Klas reminded her, were the bedrock - not just of being friends and neighbours in a remote part of Kansas - but of their newly adopted country.

Sadie managed a smile as Klas recalled how Jakob, who'd never left Holland before he came to America, used to joke that Sweden was just one big forest with a few tracks through it.

Klas would counter that his countrymen had launched an expedition to Holland once to climb mountains but had to be content with standing atop a molehill outside Amsterdam…

"Agnethe and I always had to take the whisky jug from you at that point – otherwise you'd both be useless for the chores in the morning" said the Scotswoman, wiping her eyes.

"I know – that's why you have to think again about leaving…"

Sadie looked at him, puzzled.

"The weaker ones fled with the first Indian raids; you are not one of *those* …" Klas almost spat out the last word. And though he had never consulted Agnethe, his wife, on his next offer, he made it anyway:

"If *you* leave, those *förbannat* redskins win. The blood of your family is mixed in the soil you own – that you and Jakob worked hard for. Don't let some savages tell their version of your American story – you belong *here* and deserve to tell it yourself…"

He stood up and squashed his broad-brimmed hat back on his head:

"Your home from now on will be the Lindstrom house - until we can clean up your cabin and you have laid your ghosts to rest…"

Smiling, he held out his hand to help her down from the raised planks of the walkway:

"…and Agnethe will be pleased to have reinforcements to keep me out in the fields day and night!"

---- o o o ----

Chapter Sixty Four

"Father said you were never good with a bow," said Flea as he dumped four dead rabbits on Burnt Hair's cutting block.

"Did he now?" said Dark, sitting against his uncle's willow backrest, and slapping at the boy's calf for his brazenness.

"I may only have one eye – but even I can see the huge piles of buffalo meat lying dead outside my lodge. Do you think the animal surrendered or did I – a poor bowshot – actually kill it?"

The boy laughed:

"You have your rifle! Perhaps your wife killed it – she is good with a bow and arrows; I saw her bring down an elk this morning…"

Dark didn't react to the word 'wife' coming out of Fleas's mouth – he was too young to understand that White Rain and he never gone through the marriage ceremony, despite occasional mutterings from Bad Elk and Yellow Bear. And indeed, White Rain had again been using her bow to conserve the powder and lead bullets for her rifle – her heart was set on one like Dark's though even his metal-cased bullets were getting scarcer. Still, when they took to the raiding trail once more, they would both hope to return better armed.

Dark stood up as Bad Elk approached; Flea walked up to him and boasted of his rabbit kills, pointing to the furry lumps on the wooden block. His uncle smiled and patted him on the shoulder but told him to go and get water from the creek, the men needed to talk. The Suhtai chief motioned for Dark to sit again:

"Does the boy know his mother was – unwell – that you'd seen her?"

"Yes. He knew something was wrong before she left him behind. He saw what I saw – her eyes only saw us as strangers and her anger frightened him."

"Me too," said Bad Elk. "Your mother was always a formidable woman, even on her good days. My brother would often come to my lodge until her temper had cooled…"

Dark smiled at the memory of his father – a fearsome warrior in his own right – Smoke on the Moon often just kept out of the way during disputes.

Flea came back with the water in a buffalo gut pouch and set it on the ground; he'd just had a thought and had questions for his relatives:

"When will I get my adult name? 'Flea' is a name for a child… and when can I go off on my vision quest?"

"All in due course," said Bad Elk, realising that it had been many moons, under pressure from many enemies, since *any* young Suhtai man had enough peaceable time to go off on a vision quest to find his spirit and discover his trail in life as a Cheyenne. The boy looked crushed.

The Suhtai chief nodded thoughtfully:

"These things can't be rushed – our people need to have a settled time before your aunt and I allow you to go off into the hills; while we fight the whites it is too dangerous for you to be out alone. I'll consult Yellow Bear," he said.

"I never completed any vision quest…" said Dark conversationally to his brother, "…because of my eye injury. But our father named me without one – he was wise."

Flea nodded sagely:

"Your friend did his vision quest though – I think you told me of him…Horse, something?"

"Yes, Shining Horse – he was killed when the Pawnee attacked our village, a long time before you were born."

"Shining Horse, yes – that is a good name – I would like a name like that…" mused the boy.

"Oh, I have several that would suit you…" replied Dark, "…let me see – ah, yes - there's Skinny Legs, Big Nose or Badger's Backside. Any of those would suit a fearsome warrior like yourself!"

Flea threw the water pouch at his brother and ran off howling with laughter as it burst open on his chest. The stone-eyed warrior, soaked to the waist, grinned with a pleasure that had been lacking on the war trail with Broken Knife.

Bad Elk walked off chuckling to himself; at last, some small semblance of the old Suhtai family ways. He would remember it – such memories are precious and could not be traded for all the ponies on the great grasslands. He was looking forward to the feast tonight – then there was work to do with his rifle.

---- 0 0 0 ----

Chapter Sixty Five

Viajero was bored but said nothing – Escapa, one of the tribal leaders, was droning on about his recent talks with the white soldiers. He seemed excited that the soldier chief – Green – had accepted that his White Mountain band didn't want to fight and Escapa would help them select a location for their fort; they would grow crops under the protection of the bluecoat camp and never have to raid again. The Traveller fumed at the peace leader – how could his people survive merely as farmers? It was work for women; only raiding brought wealth and status to the men

He was though, partially content - his two prospective wives seemed to like the beautiful White River country with all its game and plenty but he hadn't seen them for a day or so – they'd built the marriage shelter some way from camp as instructed by the elders and were now being chaperoned by the crones of the camp; he couldn't visit them for a while yet.

Viajero tried to relax and not kick against the strictures and time that traditions took – but a new life seemed to be calling and he wanted to be on the trail. At least the women in his life were speaking to one another. He just wished the ceremony givers would hurry up.

He switched his attention back to Escapa. It was a novel experience for the Traveller to take part in conversations in his own language and he often drifted into the Cheyenne tongue out of habit. His old raiding companion, Cruz, sat next to him and corrected him when needed. Viajero snorted in derision at this – Cruz had been abducted as a child from a Mexican family and had spent his life slaughtering his own kind in Sonora. It was odd to be tutored by the spawn of a former enemy. Still, Cruz spoke Apache and Spanish so shared inside information with Viajero:

"I heard from the bluecoat scouts that Colonel *Verde...*", Cruz used the Spanish translation of Green's name, "...wanted to attack and kill us all. He'd found all the corn we'd planted along the rivers. Escapa heard about the plan and we put out white flags to stop it. He's been sucking up to the *indaa* ever since."

Squatting on his haunches, Cruz paused and lit a cheroot that a visiting soldier had given him. He nodded towards Escapa, who was still talking:

"The *indaa* call him 'Miguel' – it is a dog's name." He spat into the dust.

"Are you all going to be corn-planters now?" asked Viajero.

Cruz whirled his head round, hacking and coughing as the smoke caught in his lungs – he rattled off curses in Spanish. The Traveller took it to mean 'no' and watched as Cruz hacked the brown juice from his failing lungs into the earth.

Viajero just shrugged; he didn't care what his people did now:

"I'm only here to get married," he said.

---- o o o ----

There were shouts of joy in the White Mountain camp as Bright Antelope and Willow led Viajero's horse down to the creek to drink. Deer Running sat in the saddle and enjoyed the attention of her father's folk. The crones followed in single file and sang the wedding song.

Cruz and Viajero came out of the council lodge and watched:

"They are taking your horse to drink – both women have accepted you…," said Cruz.

"Just as well, as I have a child by one of them – see, she's in the saddle there…" But he grimaced as he saw that his daughter was carrying a corn doll given to her by one of the old women. He would have been happier if the girl had been carrying a hatchet or knife.

"No son then?" challenged Cruz though he knew that Viajero's other son had been killed when the Mexicans had attacked the camp many years ago.

Previously, during his many clashes with Cruz and his insolence on the war trail, Viajero had been close to killing him just to stop the annoyance. Now, even though he bristled at the tactless mention of a son, he was confronted by an ageing man with bad breathing – he would die soon anyway.

"Maybe with the taller one," Viajero countered and shuddered at his calmness and good humour. Perhaps *he* was getting old.

Whatever his change of behaviour meant, he vowed never to spend any more days than he was forced to, here amongst the defeated corn-planters.

---- 0 0 0 ----

Chapter Sixty Six

"Y'know hoss…" the wolf skinner said conversationally, "…you look different without yer beard – ten years younger maybe…"

Henry looked across at his friend as he paused, hammer raised, nailing shingles to the Lindstrom barn:

"Well, you just look even more weird without yours – at least your beard hid half your face. And now ladies wince, babies cry and horses stampede…"

Carver chuckled at the insult but wouldn't be outdone:

"And what does the Boss Lady think of her smooth-skinned veho?"

Henry blushed and looked around guiltily, though the bustling activity of neighbours erecting the Lindstrom barn drowned out all but the loudest noise. Carver cackled at the nervous reaction of the Englishman and raised his voice a notch:

"We heard you creep out at night when the Boss was in town orderin' his new racers – me and the black guy both. And that Claudia is lookin' a lot more peaceable and content these days…you must be doin' somethin' right!"

Henry finished putting up his shingles, swore at the wolf skinner and walked to the water cask. He drank from the tin dipper and took his hat off, wiping the sweat from the inner hatband. He *had* thought of asking how Sadie Ackerman like Carver's fresh-shaved look – it had been a surprise to both men to find her living with the Lindstroms –the Scotswoman and the wolf skinner seemed pleased to see each other. Perhaps something there to bait Carver with later?

Henry looked around at the busyness of the Lindstrom barn – over a dozen people had travelled, mostly in shared wagons, to help put it up. Some had brought food, some brought tools and some arrived just willing to work for their neighbours. It was an act of defiance in the teeth of continued Indian raids. A handful of draught horses and saddle mounts grazed in the swaying green pasture while ducks clattered onto the smooth surface of the Saline River. Oddly, it reminded the Englishman of home.

He watched as men shouted, sawed or hammered and threw timber onto piles while women clinked pots and pans preparing the midday meal. Several children ran round the workers, playing tag. The day was warm and seemed set fair to get the barn up in a day or two...

"*Hen-ree...*"

The Englishman whirled round; Claudia Schengenhorn had come up behind him and pronounced his name with exactly the same inflections that Sweet Water had used. It was unnerving.

But the Cheyenne woman was disciplined; she stood over arm's length away from Henry and didn't make any gesture of affection as she spoke:

"...the women tell me that there will be a feast tonight and dancing..."

Henry tried to look interested and put his hat back on.

"...I like the white man's way of holding women close when they dance. Will we do that?"

"Claudia – your husband is here...I can't ..."

Henry sighed as the woman jerked her head to one side, cutting the conversation; the woman overrode any objections as always. Their couplings in the stable, apple cellar and even the ice house had set the scene over the past few days – she wouldn't be denied:

"Oh, he'll be drunk by nine and won't notice…"

"No, but other people might!"

She took the tin dipper from him and stared at him knowingly.

Possibly for the first time in his life, Henry Armstrong wasn't looking forward to drunken jollities followed by guaranteed fornication.

---- o o o ----

Chapter Sixty Seven

Bad Elk stroked his wife's forehead as he prepared to leave camp. He put his rifle into its decorated rawhide sleeve, beaded in patterns designed by Burnt Hair and hung his bow and quiver across the saddle. The Suhtai leader checked his possibles bag – powder, ball and caps – all there, though like many of his people, supplies of these were dwindling or had run out. He was nervous, though couldn't show this to anyone - it had been many moons since he had been out on a raiding party. Being responsible for men's lives in war was to ride a trail under a much more dangerous iron sky.

Burnt Hair spoke through tears as Bad Elk mounted his pony:

"Husband – you are the leader of our people. Just let the young warriors go out, you are needed here…

"I've tried the peace trail and it didn't work," said the Suhtai leader settling into the saddle. He looked down at her and patted the hand that rested on his knee:

"Yellow Bear will lead the village to our next camp in the shelter of the mountain timber – we will join you there in a few days. All will be well."

Nodding to a disconsolate Flea, he reined his horse to the north. The boy had wanted to go along as a novice and cut brush for shelters or look after the horses but Bad Elk had forbidden it, making a poor excuse about him being too young.

Kicking his heels into his pony's flanks, Bad Elk trotted off, catching up to Dark and White Rain. Crow Dress Woman and Sweet Water rode out of the Forked Lightning part of the circle of lodges to join their war sister on the raid.

Star looked glumly on; her new warrior's name of Bear Killer hadn't persuaded the rest of the Forked Lightning Women to take her along. She had been asked to stay behind to guard the dwindling Suhtai. A small group of chattering Arapahos, led by Red Raven, trotted past her and brought up the rear of the small column of raiders.

Bad Elk hoisted the rifle across the saddle cantle and rested it in a more comfortable position; he wondered why the gun suddenly felt heavier and why did his back ache so much? The sooner the raid was over, the better.

Though he'd never been a war leader or a member of the Suhtai soldier societies, Bad Elk's battle instinct was to be cautious – get there, attack and get back without losses. In his talks with Red Raven, they'd decided to ride for a full day, just to exercise their sleek ponies, now filling out on spring grass. He also knew war parties needed to settle to their new routine outside of camp but Red Raven's younger warriors seemed impatient with such rules, excited by approaching battles that could win them great glory and prestige back in camp. He needed to make sure that their youthful energies didn't get the rest of them killed. So, he'd instructed Dark and White Rain to take a couple of the Arapaho young warriors as forward scouts as they moved into enemy country. He hoped his nephew's wise head and fighting prowess would be a lesson in discipline for their talkative allies.

Avoiding skylines and using the cover of familiar valleys and forests, See the Dark and White Rain rode in companionable silence, relaxed to be back in the service of their own people. Irritatingly however, the Arapaho youths riding alongside seemed unable to shut up. Dark hissed through his teeth in frustration but said nothing. White Rain snorted with laughter:

"You are getting grumpy as you get older – they are just boys!"

The Cheyenne warrior just sighed. He winced, blinked and then probed at his stone eye:

"There's insects or dust on this – I'm going to clean it," he said and reined his pony off into a clump of underbrush where no-one could see his eye removal ritual. And apart from his mother and White Rain, he'd kept it that way. It was a small conceit that even Viajero used to respect – he idly wondered where the Apache was now.

Unslinging his water bottle – a tin one he'd plundered from a dead white settler – he squeezed his eye muscles to pop out the stone globe and wiped it with a soft piece of deerskin, rolling it round in his hand until he saw what he was seeking. The engraved gazelle or antelope on the black shiny surface was still there – it was the handiwork of Bright Antelope when she'd given the globe to Viajero as a love token. The Apache's present of the round stone to Dark had sealed their friendship.

Dark liked the gazelle to face outwards when he wore it; closing with an enemy, that was sometimes the last thing they saw in this life. He took out a small pouch of grease made from bear fat and rubbed it over the globe – he pushed it back into his head and, satisfied with the weight and balance that it gave him, trotted off to follow White Rain.

White Rain beckoned the two young Arapahos to follow her; she'd seen a stand of alder and ash ahead. She would let the boys choose the next landmark and safest route to cross the flattening country as it opened out. They could look for smoke, soldiers or settlers. She looked on the boys' inexperience just as a shortcoming in their normal warrior training – the Arapaho had lost a lot of warriors recently. There were few men around to pass on their skills. So, she would pass on hers.

Bad Elk's small column picked its way carefully over rocky outcrops and shale slopes – no need to raise dust if they didn't have to. Suddenly, there was some excited yipping at the rear of the column and a couple of young Arapaho galloped forward:

"Buffalo, Buffalo!"

Bad Elk stood up in his stirrups and gazed ahead; sure enough, a small, wandering group of the sacred animals had appeared on the skyline – just black dots some distance off. He was about to speak when he heard Red Raven ordering the young ones back into line. The Suhtai leader sighed – his brother's Striking Snakes or Broken Knife's Thunder Bears would never have been so foolish. He hoped it wasn't an omen.

Shrugging, the Suhtai pipe holder decided that it was a problem for another day and rubbed his aching back. The sky darkened for a while as a dense cloud of pigeons flew across the sun.

Ahead, as White Rain and one of the Arapaho boys rode back to the column to guide them all to the first campsite, the north star shone into the darkening sky. At dawn, they would head for the white mens' cabins along the Cedar River.

---- 0 0 0 ----

Chapter Sixty Eight

Klas Lindstrom danced a jig outside his cabin in the dusk; one hand on hip, he held a tin cup of whisky and slurped at it as he heeled and toed in front of his smiling, clapping friends.

George Essler, who'd arrived a day late from his distant timber yard on the Smoky Hill, played a reasonable fiddle tune; his wife Edith strummed an ornate banjo to keep time.

"Dess upp! Dess upp! Ladan är klar!"

"What's he saying?" said Augustus Schengenhorn, standing next to Agnethe Lindstrom, both shaking their heads in affectionate amusement at the antics of the Swede.

"He's saying the barn is up – he's very pleased!"

"So he should be…though the rear wall still needs finishing off and the door hung," replied Schengenhorn; but he too was content. The new barn was the sign that the Lindstroms were staying and such permanent settlements along the Saline would soon bring peace and prosperity to this part of Kansas.

Pythagoras Carver looked on, passing a jug of whisky between himself and Sadie Ackerman; the Scotswoman hooked her finger through the loop near the jug neck and rotated the earthenware vessel onto her right shoulder in true frontier fashion to take a long drink:

"Whoa, Ma'am – I thought you were a preacher's daughter!"

"I am, Mister Carver - but life can be hard…"

The wolf skinner nodded uncomfortably – they both knew he'd buried her husband and children just a few miles away last fall. The woman drank from the jug again before handing it back to Carver. There was a pause as she looked at him:

"I wish you'd call me Sadie…" she said.

Nodding, as he felt the warm glow of the alcohol, he blurted out:

"Sure – if you'll call me Pythagoras," and waited for the expected laughter.

Sadie Ackerman though, just nodded calmly and said:

"That's a fine name."

Carver, happy but stunned by her positive reaction, howled like a wolf…

Even Henry heard it as he stood up amongst the long grass, some hundred yards away on the banks of the Saline. Claudia Schengenhorn adjusted her skirts and stood up too – the Englishman hoped that they hadn't been missed yet at the party. He walked up the slight sandy slope and looked back at the silver ribbon of water – the rising moon dappled pale yellow on its surface. The woman was pulling on her moccasins, so he paused:

"Do the Cheyenne have a name for this river?" he asked conversationally, even though he knew it well as Bad Elk's people had often camped near here. Henry, always cautious in admitting his links to the *Tsis-tsis-tas,* had decided not to let Claudia know that he spoke her language.

Across from the barn, there was the sound of cartwheels squeaking and rattling as wagons were pushed under the newly constructed roof, even though there was no sign of rain. The fiddle bow squeaked again alongside the mosquito sing-song of a banjo being tuned; lamps were being lit and Henry could see food being laid out on long planks resting on sawhorses.

The tall woman joined him, brushing the grass from her skirt and fixing her hair back into place:

"Yes, we call it the *Shistotoiyohe* – it means the Cedar River," she said.

---- 0 0 0 ----

Chapter Sixty Nine

For once, even though he'd had a chance to drink himself into oblivion at the party, Carver had restrained himself. He grinned at the unfamiliarity of being so abstemious, Henry would never let him forget it - the influence of Sadie Ackerman was obviously stronger than those jugs of the Kansas Krippler that the fiddler had brought in.

Taunted by the Englishman, he remembered admitting that he found the Scotswoman to be a lady worth spending time with – and, yes, even had growing affection for - even though her recent loss made Carver cautious about declaring any intentions towards her. Still, he liked the way she pronounced his name – large oaks from small acorns, he told himself.

In a good mood, he hummed and whistled one of the fiddle tunes from the previous night as he scooped water into a bucket at the riverbank and looked back over his shoulder to see Sadie's outline at the cabin window. Smoke curled from the black stovepipe chimney; the women were making breakfast and there were many mouths to feed.

He was still smiling when the arrow struck him in the chest.

---- o o o ----

There had been much to do in the aftermath of the Lindstrom cabin fight - not just disposing of the dead and dousing the blaze in the new barn but rounding up enough mules, horses and serviceable wagons to carry their owners back home once they were sure that the Indians had gone.

Augustus Schengenhorn had written a despatch to Fort Harker to summon help and Henry- one of the few to stop the Indians running off his saddle horse – rode out to take it.

The absence of Carver by his side on the trail – normally regaling him with tales of women or drink in their common past – was palpable. It was an odd feeling - like a limb was missing or riding with a ghost.

At noon, he dismounted to let his horse drink at a creek that led down to the Smoky Hill and Fort Harker; he was making good time and didn't want to tire the animal. He patted it on the neck and looked at the holes where two arrows had gone in during the fight. Flies clustered round each one but the axle grease that he'd applied would keep them at bay for a while. The pony trembled as his fingers touched the wounds.

A light rain pattered onto the brim of his hat and Henry moved to check his saddlebags were shut. He opened the one with Schengenhorn's letter in it, waterproof inside a canvas pouch, and pushed it to one side as he sought some food. Instead, his fingers then closed on a familiar shape – it was his old leather journal.

He took it out smiling – given to record his adventures on the Plains by his mother decades ago and since used as a sketch pad to impress the Suhtai – it had remained unopened for some time. As if in anticipation of opening it, the rain eased off.

A jumbled collection of thoughts crowded in as he sat down in the damp grass and leafed through it… a poor sketch of Sweet Water and one of New Grass, both of them looking exactly alike; some lines of frontier poetry – some his, some Carver's; a rough sketch map of the location of Kansas forts along the Smoky Hill and Arkansas Rivers and some musings on friendship that he and the wolf skinner had argued about, probably whilst drunk.

He tipped back his hat and looked at the result of his scribblings after being in America for fifteen years or so and snorted at his own idleness. Following your own trail in life was fine but there was no legacy to it. He assumed he'd get married one day and have children – what would he tell *them* about his wanderings on the Great Plains? About Carver or them both living with the Suhtai? At this rate – probably nothing.

He got up, fed his pony a handful of oats and remounted. Ramming his hat back down on his head, Henry trotted off towards Fort Harker determined to record all the events he had experienced – starting with the Lindstrom fight…

---- o o o ----

Henry had been awakened by a scream – he looked up from the wagon bed that he, Carver and Manfred Hoffmann had been sharing in the barn. Carver was nowhere to be seen but Sadie Ackerman was yelling the alarm, running out of the cabin towards the river, shotgun in hand:

"Indians! Indians!"

Henry grabbed his rifle and ran out of the barn; others, also weary and roused from a drunken sleep, fumbled into their clothes and boots. Running towards the river, Henry saw Carver – motionless on his back with an arrow in him. A young warrior was splashing across the river to get to Carver.

Henry fired but missed and the warrior reached the bank, falling slightly as his moccasins filled with water. Sadie Ackerman, trying to pull Carver out of danger by his collar with one hand, let the Indian get closer then blasted him in the face with the scattergun; the boy went down screaming in a red mist of his own flesh and blood.

Mounted warriors now came galloping towards the same riverbank and it was clear that others had surrounded the cabin…

White Rain was angry at the Arapaho youth – he had just alerted the whites with an arrow shot too early. The boy, Porcupine, hadn't listened to any advice she or Dark had given.

None of the Arapaho, nor even some of the less-experienced Suhtai, had bothered to count the horses in the pasture nor the wagons in the wooden veho crop store.

As she galloped across the river, she could see far more white men coming out from there than they had expected – they may pay for Porcupine's mistake in blood.

There was no time to warn anyone – the attack was under way. She cocked her rifle, yelled her war song and charged down on the white woman pulling the dead white man...

Henry saw an attacking rider splash across the river in a welter of stones and spray and stepped between the warrior and Carver. He raised his rifle, lined up the foresight and rear sight, held his breath and squeezed the trigger. Even as the warrior toppled out of the saddle – he knew the yell he'd heard was oddly familiar – it was a woman's voice. Now, as the warrior's body was dragged past him, slewing from side to side across the ground with one foot still in the stirrup, he could see that he'd killed White Rain...

Bad Elk had been startled by the unexpected start to the attack but, taking Red Raven and two of his warriors, had galloped to the rear of the cabin to force their way in; three more followed up behind and one young boy had managed to climb onto the roof and was busy throwing a deerskin over the chimney to fill the house with smoke. Bad Elk saw it – the Arapaho may be foolhardy but they were brave.

He reined in his horse, shouting to Red Raven to torch the barn - it could help lessen the deadly fire coming from the vehoe in there. Even as he looked through the unfinished wooden walls of the barn there seemed to be far more white men than the scouts had counted – gunfire now blazed out in a steady roll and smoke filled the air. The whites in the cabin – who all seemed to be women – had closed the wooden shutters and the occasional shot rang out from there.

A white man's horse was tethered to an iron ring by the water trough at the side of the cabin – it looked to be a good animal in decent condition; he would take it – a good prize to show to Burnt Hair and boast that he wasn't too old to go to war…

Henry knelt by a pile of timber and shot coolly – shocked by the knowledge that he was facing the Suhtai in battle – always his and Carver's worst fears. But friends - even close ones - can become enemies and, for now, that was all that mattered.

Steady shooting now came from the stoop of the cabin as Claudia Schengenhorn, still in her nightdress but joining the battle, cranked round after round into her repeating rifle.

More warriors rode up; only a few had guns but even the weight of fire from the barn didn't seem to deter them as arrows thudded into the wood work and war shrieks split the air. Lindstrom had dismantled his soddy walls over the past few months and replaced them with timber; the piled earthen blocks now formed a useful barricade at the front of the house. Ducking below the edge of the pile to reload, Claudia breathed deeply – her husband was now on the stoop firing his expensive hunting rifle.

The dead woman warrior, her horse now shot down and kicking in its death throes, lay close by. Claudia recognised her as the tattered beggar that had approached her house asking for food. She was pleased that Henry had killed her but she put another bullet into her anyway to make sure she didn't get up and run away again.

The fire from the attackers slackened slightly as they drew off to regroup.

Henry now heard his horse whinny in terror around the corner. Keeping low, he ran round to the side of the house to see an Indian on foot untethering his pony. Instinctively he shot at the man, though his aim was rushed – the warrior staggered back and with one hand held out his rifle and fired back. Henry recognised the rifle as the well-kept Hawken gun owned by Bad Elk, though the man himself was less easy to recognise as the Englishman had never seen him in battle paint. Another warrior rode up, helping Bad Elk into the saddle as Henry raised his rifle again:

"Hen-ree, I see you!" shouted the Suhtai leader as the other mounted warrior, probably puzzled by this conversation with an enemy, tried to wrench the bridle of Bad Elk's horse around to let him escape. Henry shot the other warrior who slumped over his saddle cantle as his horse, terrified by the noise and smoke cantered off towards the river.

"I see you too!" yelled Henry, "But go before I have to kill you!"

Bad Elk kicked his pony's flanks and rode off, almost falling out of the saddle but recovering and ducking across his horse's neck as other whites shot at him. Red Raven had tried to save him and was probably dead because of that - but he knew that the only reason that he was still alive had been the final grain of friendship between him and Hen-ree.

He galloped past the wooden shell of the barn, now alight with tall flames and much black smoke, thanks to those Arapaho boys. White men and some women staggered out into the sunlight, some slumping into the dust as arrows now found easier targets. But he knew the raid was over – he yelled out to his few remaining warriors to withdraw – none of them had enough bullets or arrows to keep on attacking:

"Use the smoke to hide us and escape!"

The ones that heard him obeyed. All except two...

Henry now ran to the cabin stoop and bent over Carver; the wolf skinner was still alive; his face was being stroked by Sadie Ackerman. Henry felt a surge of relief as his friend came back to life:

"Bloody Hell, Pythagoras – I thought I'd lost you! And you still owing me twelve dollars for that whisky…" Carver wouldn't expect any unmanly emotion from him.

"Hoss, that name still don't sound right comin' outta yer mouth!" croaked Carver. Sadie Ackerman told him to hush and save his strength.

Claudia Schengenhorn stood up as Augustus struggled to prise out a damaged copper cased bullet from his own rifle:

"Damn, these people don't know when to give up!" she yelled as she clawed at her bandolier for more bullets.

Henry shot to his feet and whirled round with his rifle. There charging on their ponies and leaning out of the saddle to recover the body of White Rain were two riders…

Crow Dress, in tears at seeing their war leader on the ground couldn't reach over far enough to grab her, so she dismounted and hauled on the dead weight; the whites standing by the cabin seemed content to just watch – good! Sweet Water had now skidded to a halt beside her though Crow Dress could see her pony was badly hit and was breathing heavily, blood pouring out of its belly.

A bullet cracked over their heads as a plump white man with a shiny gun fired at them. Though Crow Dress was calling her to help get White Rain over her saddle, Sweet Water saw the threat from the whites at the cabin and ran towards them.

Pulling her revolver from her holster she shot all six bullets at them. A woman in a white shift was hit and staggered back but the man next to her seemed calmer. He raised his rifle but, oddly, paused and didn't shoot. Good – it was time for the hatchet!

Time and motion seemed to slow down for the young Forked Lightning Woman as she threw her pistol to one side and drew her axe. She pounded across the dirt clearing towards the shocked vehoe – now they would see the power of a Cheyenne woman. But – someone was calling her name – and it wasn't Crow Dress...

"No - Sweet Water! Stop! It's Henry!" the Englishman shouted as he'd lowered his rifle. Unfortunately, he'd shouted this in English and he cursed his stupidity. He shouted the words again in Cheyenne...

Sweet Water stopped and stared as she'd heard the familiar poor accent of Tsis-tsis-tas. She couldn't recognise him without the whiskers – but it was Hen-ree!

Henry sighed with relief and smiled. The Forked Lightning warrior smiled back.

But Henry jumped as an explosion of a gunshot, close to his ear, threw Sweet Water to the ground. He ran to her side and knelt down – the girl was wincing with the pain but she chose to smile again even though the bullet had gone through her heart. He held her small, slim hand as her spirit departed this life.

Claudia Schengenhorn cranked another round into the rifle and fired another round at the remaining Cheyenne girl who'd given up trying to hoist the other dead woman across her saddle. The woman shouted in defiance but galloped off. Claudia yelled something back but Henry couldn't make out what it was and didn't care; it was as much as he could do to stop himself killing Claudia Schengenhorn.

---- 0 0 0 ----

Chapter Seventy

Deer Running had woken suddenly; she'd had a bad dream. Willow and Bright Antelope held the girl until she stopped shaking:

"Our people are gone!" she shouted.

Viajero now awake, crawled on hands and knees to his daughter's bed on the other side of the lodge.

"No – our White Mountain people are still here. See we are all safe…" he said, looking out into the pink dawn light through the door flap.

"Not those ones…" said the girl," …*our* people – the ones we left behind – the Suhtai. They are gone now."

Her mother hushed her and Viajero stared at his daughter; living with three women was difficult.

Willow though kept her own counsel; she too had felt a prickling of danger in her heart – not from any danger to her husband's family but to her war sisters. Perhaps her daughter - and she now thought of Deer Running as that - had powers that she didn't know yet.

At the morning meal, Viajero joined his family at the cookfire – all the women noted that this was unusual as he'd normally check his ponies before he ate. He squatted down on his haunches in front of them and told them the news:

"We will leave in two days. Cruz has told me of a great warrior who is still fighting Mexicans and whites. We will join him – he lives in the mountains."

Willow said:

"Good, better a warrior than a farmer!"

Bright Antelope nodded her approval:

"We will be safer in the mountains. Who is this war leader? Is he one of your people?"

"No…" said the Apache tearing at a piece of meat and stale flat bread," …he is Chiricahua and known as *Goyathla*. The Mexicans call him Geronimo."

Viajero was happy. That morning Usen, the Life Giver, had sent him a sign. The Apache's spirit creature, a small, horned lizard had appeared at his feet as he'd saddled his pony. It had been many years since an animal had spoken to him but this one, like the one when he'd found the Cheyenne, gave him instructions:

"Ride north," it said and scuttled away.

Two days later with four pack horses – one behind each rider – the White Mountain Apache, his family strung out behind him, headed off to find the Sierra Madre Mountains to make their future with a man they had never met.

---- 0 0 0 ----

Sadie Ackerman tutted affectionately as Carver staggered out onto the stoop of her cabin; following Klas Lindstrom's advice she had moved back in, despite the memories, and Carver had decided to stay with her. The Lindstroms and their other neighbours had again gathered round to rescue the small shack from dereliction as the prairies had overtaken their crops and pastures. It would be a lot of work but Pythagoras would be a good field hand once he recovered from his wound:

"Och, man you should stay inside. That wound will open again if you're not careful…"

Carver knew he'd been lucky with the arrow in his chest. George Essler, the fiddle player, had once been a pharmacist and had been on hand to oversee the breaking off of the arrow shaft and supervising the men pushing the iron tipped point out through his back. It had been a near thing and Carver's fever had soared but, after several days close to death, had abated enough for the wolf skinner to sit up and talk.

"Do what the lady says Mr Carver! You're in the charge of a real human being now," called Henry as he packed his horse ready to leave.

"Where you goin' hoss? You not stayin' with the Schengenhorns?"

"No, I don't believe I will…", said Henry, pleased to be out of the clutches of the murderous Wutapiu woman – he had been forced to drag her off the corpses of White Rain and Sweet Water to stop her taking scalps.

"New York, Boston maybe…I may visit home and see if I like England again…", he said vaguely and walked over to Carver.

The men shook hands in silence; each shrouded with their own culture of how men should behave.

"Safe trails, hoss," croaked the wolf skinner as Henry walked back to his horse.

"Thank you, my friend…" said Henry turning round, "…until someone shoots us both out of the saddle!"

"Not in this life, Henry, not in this life."

With that the Englishman mounted up, tipped his hat to Sadie and headed north.

---- o o o ----

See the Dark, heartsick and weary, eventually led the small defeated band of warriors to Yellow Bear's camp in the mountain forests. Hopefully they could stay here a while to rest without being caught by the whites – who would soon be in pursuit. He had been strict about covering their tracks and had sent out two riders with a few of the head of stolen horses to lay false trails to the west.

Dark was overcome by the losses – his own White Rain and Sweet Water – he hadn't seen them fall and had no idea how they met their deaths – he'd been in charge of rounding up the stock in the pasture. By the time he'd met up with Bad Elk, the Suhtai leader was in a bad way from his bullet wound and unable to speak. Two days into the journey home, despite being on a travois and cared for by Crow Dress Woman, Bad Elk had died.

The encampment was subdued and cast into gloom. His aunt, Burnt Hair had hacked off her long locks and slashed her calves and arms, shrieking in mourning for her husband while the parents of the dead Forked Lightning Women wailed for their daughters; there would be no grandchildren now, no-one to keep the tribe strong and vital.

See the Dark went off into the treeline and puked. Raw and bitter failure seeped through his bones and his gut. Most looked to him now to lead the Suhtai – the Arapaho had decided that they were plagued by bad medicine and had promptly ridden off – what was *he* expected to do? He still thought of himself as a sunny youth, riding and raiding on his own trail with Viajero, courting and pretending to settle with White Rain, though she never seemed convinced and just leading the perfect life of warrior and hunter. But ...*this*?

Yellow Bear had followed the sound of his retching to find him and sat down on the log beside the young stone-eyed warrior. He knew what the boy was feeling:

"Little brother, right now some Iron Sky has slipped onto your shoulders. It is a terrible burden but won't last for ever…"

"Just *some* of it? It feels like all of it to me…"

Yellow Bear patted the young man on the shoulder:

"The Cheyenne - us Suhtai – need to survive. Remember our great times of hunger or attacks by the Pawnees? Then the Iron Sky fell heavily as well, but your uncle, your father and others brought us back from the edge of death. Those men are gone now but others must ride into the battle line in their place – that is *your* way forward. Think on it awhile, then let us know what you wish to happen."

See the Dark, with his warrior's judgement, knew that the Suhtai needed allies around them to live again. He would tell them tomorrow - they would head north and join up with their cousins near the Powder River country.

It now dawned on him that he was a man alone – the Iron Sky had exposed his weakness and vanity but worse, it had crushed his heart.

In the growing twilight and under a blaze of silver stars, Dark wept for the loss of his family, his people and his country.

---- 0 0 0 ----

FADING TRAILS...

ONE.

Extract from 'The Cumberland Gazette' dated January 6th 1919.

Webb and Bowman, Auction House of Carlisle announce a house clearance sale on behalf of the estate of Captain JW Armstrong, killed at Passchendaele in July 1917.

Capt. Armstrong, son of the late Henry L Armstrong of the Bewcastle area, had retained many of his father's historical artefacts from his extensive travels in America in the last century.

Important items are:

A Model 1855 Sharps carbine with possible Indian native markings on the woodwork. Small silver plates alongside each hieroglyph (probably added by Mr HL Armstrong himself) perhaps indicating the author of each mark. The weapon is clean, unloaded and has probably not been fired **(Reserve price: 70 guineas)**

...a leather-bound journal or sketchbook kept by HL Armstrong himself containing original drawings of Red Indians, maps and musings on frontier life **(no Reserve price – offers accepted)**

---- o o o ----

TWO.

Translation of a State Police (*Policia Estatal*) Report – Bavispe, Sonora dated 3 May 1924.

From: *Comandante* Javier Luis Reyes

Interrogation of suspect involved in a raid on a Bavispe farm, 30 April 1924.

… the raiders struck the Hernandez farm at dawn on the stated day. Witnesses claim four male riders ran off stock, abducted two teenage girls and escaped to the mountains. One rider (the suspect) was hit by a shovel thrown at him and fell from his horse…

Suspect is of average height, skinny build, long black hair; dressed in loincloth and moccasins. He appears to be around thirty years old, speaks Spanish and confirms he is an Apache…he will not disclose the location of their camp though I have dispatched a patrol of locals to track the escapees…

…he will not disclose his name …

…however, he spoke animatedly about the necklet he is wearing – leather thong with small silver amulets, blue lapis lazuli stones and an eagle's feather. He says it was made by his grandfather's mother, who was Lakota (Sioux)…

…His grandfather's father was also an Apache warrior with a Spanish name. He is not on our records of native names either here or at the San Carlos Reservation… his name was Viajero…

---- 0 0 0 ----

THREE.

Extract from a charred war diary (no name but, from other entries, assessed likely from a Corporal in 7th US Marine Division) found in a tin trunk after a house fire at Crow Agency, Montana in 1986.

Peleliu Island, Palau archipelago, Western Pacific – unknown day, April 1947.

…never thought I'd go back to that hell hole – me and the boys were lucky to get off it back in '44. Returned this time to escort a Jap admiral into the jungle to tell some dumb holdouts there that the war had been over for two and a half years!...

…out of one cave – had probably heard us squawking on the megaphone that we were coming – stepped a Lieutenant and 33 Nip soldiers – Jesus!...

Escorted them back down to the beach where the admiral told them about the war, the big bomb and so on. The officer, Yamaguchi I think his name was – bowed and handed us a bamboo box of personal effects of our buddies who they'd killed near their positions…I was near to tears …

…wristwatches, dogtags, St Christopher medal and such – all claimed by our own Chaplain to be sent back to families. One thing that no-one claimed, so I asked if I could have it – yes said the Chaplain.

It's a strange thing but I think it belonged to an Indian – perhaps why I like it – a black obsidian globe, size of a golf ball maybe, with a deer etched on one side. Could be sacred so I buried it at…*(The diary contained no more entries)*

---- o o o ----

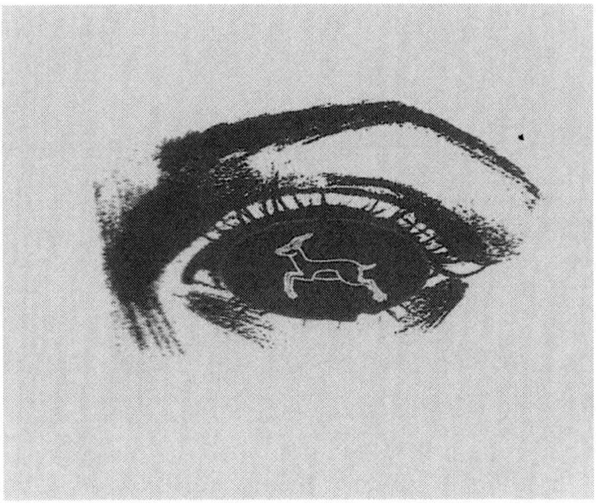

Printed in Great Britain
by Amazon